Unbecoming

Unbecoming

A MEMOIR OF DISOBEDIENCE

ANURADHA BHAGWATI

ATRIA BOOKS

NEW YORK   LONDON   TORONTO   SYDNEY   NEW DELHI

ATRIA
BOOKS

An Imprint of Simon & Schuster, Inc.
1230 Avenue of the Americas
New York, NY 10020

First Atria Books hardcover edition March 2019

ATRIA BOOKS and colophon are trademarks of Simon & Schuster, Inc.

For information about special discounts for bulk purchases, please contact Simon & Schuster Special Sales at 1-866-506-1949 or business@simonandschuster.com.

The Simon & Schuster Speakers Bureau can bring authors to your live event. For more information or to book an event, contact the Simon & Schuster Speakers Bureau at 1-866-248-3049 or visit our website at www.simonspeakers.com.

Interior design by Kyoko Watanabe

Manufactured in the United States of America

10   9   8   7   6   5   4   3   2   1

Library of Congress Cataloging-in-Publication Data
Names: Bhagwati, Anuradha Kristina, 1975– author.
Title: Unbecoming : a memoir of disobedience / Anuradha Kristina Bhagwati.
Description: First Atria Books hardcover edition. | New York : Atria Books, [2019] | Includes bibliographical references and index.
Identifiers: LCCN 2018034263 (print) | LCCN 2018050734 (ebook) | ISBN 9781501162565 (ebook) | ISBN 9781501162541 (hard cover : alk. paper)
Subjects: LCSH: Bhagwati, Anuradha Kristina, 1975– | United States. Marine Corps—Officers—Biography. | United States. Marine Corps—Women—Biography. | United States. Marine Corps—Minorities—Biography. | Women marines—Biography. | East Indian American women—Biography. | Bisexual women—United States—Biography. | Women political activists—United States—Biography. | Women and the military—United States.
Classification: LCC VE25.B47 (ebook) | LCC VE25.B47 A3 2019 (print) | DDC 359.9/6092 [B] —dc23
LC record available at https://lccn.loc.gov/2018034263

ISBN 978-1-5011-6254-1
ISBN 978-1-5011-6256-5 (ebook)

Author's Note

This is a memoir based on my experience as a former officer in the United States Marine Corps and subsequent advocacy. Certain names have been changed. Certain quotes have been reconstructed from memory, to the best of my ability.

For my mother and father

I hate myself for loving you.

—*Joan Jett and the Blackhearts*

Contents

Unbecoming

Introduction

> Your parents need the crap kicked out of them for
> raising such a disrespectful little terd.

A disgruntled Army veteran sent me the tweet on August 10, 2015, while I debated a retired three-star general on Fox News. It was the most colorful response I had ever received from a brother-in-arms. The general and I had been discussing how much to open combat roles to women. My take? All the way.

My fellow veterans had a habit of throwing the worst insults at me in order to defend the military's sacred status quo. In part, the troll was right. General William "Jerry" Boykin was a warfighter several times over (I most certainly was not). I had offended all sense of military decorum by talking back to an officer several rungs up the chain of command, without any hint of shame.

In the heat of the segment, Boykin said, with more than a little flourish, "You cannot violate the laws of nature without expecting some consequences . . . The people that advocate for [women in combat] have never lived out of a rucksack in a combat situation."

I hit him hard. How else were you supposed to hit a general? "I think the general is just wrong. Thirteen years of warfare have proven that women can live out of rucksacks in completely hor-

1

rendous conditions in combat alongside men . . . They have fought and died in combat, in fact. And we should remember that."

Of course, my words out of someone else's mouth might have been less shocking. I was a woman. With brown skin and a name that certainly did not hail from the Bible. Boykin himself was not your average general, having made a hard-core turn to evangelical Christianity after retiring his uniform. He was now the executive vice president of the Family Research Council, an organization the Southern Poverty Law Center classified as a hate group. All of this was supposed to bolster his assertion that women had no place in the infantry.

Boykin's military background and his Christian creds made him a beloved Fox guest, the kind who inspired nods and Amens all across America. His voice had the deep, weathered bellow of someone who had made a lot of people run for their lives. (Truth be told, the junior officer within me wanted to *Sir* him up and down, even while I ripped apart his arguments.)

Where did that leave me? On Fox News, I was a Brown female target with a name no one could pronounce and loyalties no one trusted. A former Marine, I was possibly the only activist around who would speak to the conservative masses about what the military needed to do for women in uniform. For Americans who saluted the flag no matter what the state of the union, it meant that my words often amounted to heresy.

Being an ex-Marine gave me some cover when talking about things like sexual violence in the military, or, in this case, integrating women into combat arms jobs. It meant that my trolls had refrained thus far from sending me rape and death threats, the kind usually sent to my civilian women counterparts when they spoke their minds. Still, what I did receive was unnerving, and sometimes terrifying. Women were not supposed to say what I'd been saying for years now. It was unruly. It was unbecoming.

A former Army Ranger, Boykin had recited a series of not-so-relevant talking points from the nineties about women in combat, including the propensity of uniformed men to lose their marbles at the sight of a nubile woman. All his claims had been debunked this week by the first two women who had graduated from Ranger School, the Army's grueling combat leadership course.

Taking on an evangelical Christian general and ex-Ranger who'd served as an Army infantryman more years than I'd breathed oxygen took gumption. A year earlier, the organization I led had joined forces with four uniformed women and sued the Pentagon so all jobs in the military would be open to women. And it worked. The floodgates opened, as service women who wanted to see what they were made of entered all-male schools and assignments, and the defenders of the fiercest old boys' club in America dug in like their lives depended on it.

The military's culture wars had been brewing for decades. Hundreds of thousands of women had served in Iraq and Afghanistan. And back at home, we were ensuring the military did right by them. It meant confronting some of the nation's most precious myths about men in uniform. It meant exposing truths about sexual harassment and sexual assault, and the daily humiliations women had to suffer through in order to wear the uniform. I'd seen it all firsthand. And there was still no end in sight.

I knew the military was better off when women succeeded, and no decorated Army general was going to convince me otherwise. The days when no one was listening were over. We had organized and spoken out years before #MeToo made headlines. And we had convinced an entire nation that service women were worth caring about.

These changes didn't happen by chance, nor did they happen overnight.

As for me, it took joining the Marines to find my voice. Once I realized I could trust it, there was no turning back.

PART I

CHAPTER 1

Home Fires

Anyone watching closely would have understood. I joined the Marines because of them.

I had always been my parents' little girl. Their only child, for some reason. I was shy in front of people, and terrified of being in groups. I listened to Mom and Dad completely. Because they had a lot to say, I did a lot of listening.

Mom met Dad in Boston when she was in graduate school at Harvard and he was teaching at MIT. They were both economists. This all meant nothing to me except that they were always going to the office or on their way to conferences. I remember flashes. Mom wore saris and a red powdered bindi on her forehead, and Dad made me a mug of hot chocolate with Hershey's cocoa powder and milk for breakfast. Sometimes he and I sat together before sunrise in the quiet house while I sipped my cocoa through a plastic straw and he listened to the morning news on a tiny black-and-white television set.

I remember snow blanketing our neighborhood in Lexington, Massachusetts, for months, and Dad, in his black woolen overcoat, thick black-rimmed glasses, and Russian fur cap, trying to push our car up the hill to our house. Dad was dark brown with wild bushy eyebrows and a thick head of black hair that he matted down with gel and a wooden horsehair brush. His eyes danced when he spoke, and laughter always preceded his punch lines.

Mom was just a shade more olive than white, with thin arms like a cartoon princess. Her hair was black and wavy, and tied back into a bun with a long piece of black yarn and a dozen black bobby pins. She had a straight nose. Dad had a round nose. Everyone said Mom was beautiful. Everyone said I looked like Dad.

I was born in Boston in 1975 when the city was mostly white. Though Black families existed in small numbers, Asians were practically invisible. A few months earlier, a federal judge had ordered the integration of Boston's public schools. White parents organized a boycott. There were riots and attacks on Black children. It could have been the Deep South.

For Mom and Dad, there was simply India, and there was here, where Mom was re-creating her life from scratch with a focus that allowed for no distractions. They were working to achieve the American dream. They were protected from the worst white animosity by the bubble of the ivory tower and the enclave of intellectuals who were moving to the suburbs outside Boston.

In the fifties, Dad was taken in by a cadre of Jewish mentors at MIT, men like Paul Samuelson and Robert Solow, who would win Nobel Prizes and rewrite how economics was understood in the Western world. In 1968, Dad's professors gave him early tenure, and he and Mom moved from a cramped apartment to their first house in Lexington.

I was about three when Dad was driving us one day along winding suburban roads. Being economists, Mom and Dad could tell you where everything in the world came from, like cars and refrigerators and crayons. If you were sensible, you drove only Japanese or German cars, because they were better made. This was why we had a Toyota.

I was in the back, strapped behind a seat belt, reading. Mom was in the passenger seat. Dad had stopped driving. Maybe it was a red light. Maybe he was lost. A car sped up from behind us and screeched to a stop alongside us. A man was making big movements with his arms. Dad rolled down his window.

The man's face looked like boiling water. He was yelling at Dad. I didn't understand what his words meant but they scared me. I was too young to know much, but I knew that this man felt like he was better than Dad, and this meant we were different. I looked away from the man's face, which was red and white at the same time, because he reminded me of monsters in my picture books.

Dad didn't say anything. Something uncomfortable was moving in my belly, like a stomachache when I was sick. The man suddenly drove away. Dad and Mom were still quiet. Then they began whispering in Gujarati. I felt something new rising up inside me. I felt shame. I wanted to be as powerful as the light-skinned monster man. And I did not want to be like Dad.

· · ·

My father was constantly being told he was brilliant, and he believed it. When we walked through airports on trips to India, random men would stop before him and bow. Dad loved these moments. Mom hated them. But for all of Dad's fame, he never seemed settled.

It is a testament to my family's strange narcissism that I knew what a Nobel Prize was when I was a toddler. My parents referred to it as "The Nobel," and the consensus was that Dad had been robbed. Every September I witnessed my parents' tortured theater as they tossed the names of potential winners around the dinner table.

Each year when Dad was passed over for one of his colleagues, I would ask him gingerly how he was. He delivered the only line that ever made him feel better.

"Oh, I'm fine. Even Gandhi-ji didn't win a Nobel."

· · ·

I was five years old when Mom was offered tenure at Columbia University. Dad quit his job at MIT to support Mom's career, and we moved to New York City. The girls and boys in my new school were mostly white and Jewish. I'd been to many synagogues in the city but couldn't recall ever visiting a Hindu temple.

"Daddy, are we Jewish?" I asked when I was six. We were not. I would never have a bat mitzvah. It was a terrible disappointment.

Lunchtime at school was torture. In the early morning hours, my father made sandwiches for me with great care, wrapped them up in paper bags like my friends' parents did with theirs, and dropped me off at school. His sandwiches became one more reason I kept my guard up in the company of white kids. Their lunches held power over mine, even though their tuna fish was bland and mealy and their bread was white and crustless. My brown paper bag was flooded with Indian ingredients conquerors had traveled the oceans to get their hands on: finely cut vegetables flavored with cumin, coriander, and turmeric; shrimp salad sandwiches on whole wheat bread; and chicken sautéed in spicy tomatoes, mustard seeds, and onions. My lunch smelled different. It smelled, period. It made me want to hide.

At the dinner table, under the watchful gaze of Dan Rather and Tom Brokaw, we ate dal, subzi, raita, and rice that my mother had made from scratch after a full day at the office. Mom and Dad ate with their hands, while I clutched my fork and fumed, trying to reconcile their savage eating methods with the lessons I was being taught at school about the proper use of utensils and keeping elbows off the table. I didn't know that most Brown people around the world ate food with their hands. It wouldn't have mattered. None of those people had any leverage over my childhood.

One afternoon I was playing at the sandbox in our classroom. Joel Stein approached me. He was shorter than most of the other boys, and chubby, with wispy blond hair. He started talking to me about Gandhi.

Joel faked an Indian accent, in the confident way white folks fake Indian accents, not knowing they are widely missing the mark. He started prancing around the table as though he were wearing Gandhi's white dhoti and tripping over himself. Shy and introspective, I watched his performance. I had no witty comeback. I was too

young to summon outrage, though even then I wanted to tell Joel
that we called him Gandhi-ji as a sign of respect. I stayed quiet. It
was not in my nature to confront someone who was picking on me.
I remember the sting of humiliation. If India's national hero was the
object of ridicule, what chance did the rest of us have?

• • •

My parents made it clear to me that my grades mattered more
than anything else in the world. And so I studied, all the time. The
grown-ups in my life weren't just adults, they were elders. In Indian
culture, elders were practically demigods. Kids didn't just bow to their
grandparents, they touched their feet in respect. One didn't say no
to parents, aunties, or uncles. And every adult was called Uncle or
Auntie, regardless of their actual connection to you.

Mom and Dad had no rulebook for raising an Indian kid in the
States. Sex ed and the subversive nature of pop culture were not
things Indian parents had to contend with in the motherland. When
I came home at age nine singing Madonna's latest album and asking,
Daddy, what's a virgin? my father was stunned. Couples didn't even
kiss in Bollywood movies. (Dad rapidly deflected, telling me it meant
a person hadn't yet been married. I lost interest.)

As I approached preteen years, I was aware of the shifts happening
in the bodies around me. Training bras and boys' wandering eyes appeared suddenly, causing a disruption in the group order. This budding
sexuality was something I tried to ignore, but the buzz generated by
my light-skinned classmates let me know I could not just hide in my
homework. These kids outnumbered me and shaped my every move.

I went along with the charades my classmates played, but in my
gut I felt a separation that made me feel like a fraud. My classmates'
sexual and social preoccupations didn't correlate with the attention
and approval I would get back home. I lived in two worlds.

My Indian cultural indoctrination would be no match for the
influence of the prepubescent white girls in my life. At age eleven,
these girls were deep into gendered rituals that defined their changing

relationship to boys, before I was aware that gender was even a thing. For them, shaving legs and removing facial hair were vital to their survival. As I listened to them obsess about their transformations, self-preservation took root. The thought that I might be teased, or worse, forgotten by the other kids, became fuel for altering my skinny Brown body.

My hair was a problem. I used tweezers to yank out the soft black wisps on my upper lip and the tufts in front of my ears. The hair on my head was thick, curly, frizzy, and endless. Indian mothers were inexperienced and uninterested in the self-love birthed by the Black Power movement. Mom's solution for managing my lustrous hair was not to let my fro be free but instead to cut it all off.

No one in my world celebrated my mother's pragmatism, least of all me. An older Black girl—one of so few Black kids in our school that we might have banded together if we'd known any better—whom I looked up to approached me in the hall one day and declared, "You look like a boy."

I took this to mean that *boy* was the worst thing a girl could be called. I did everything I could not to cry.

I made my mother let me grow my hair out. But there was so damn much of it. I didn't understand why my hair didn't stay put like it did on the white girls at school. There wasn't a knot or tangle anywhere on their heads. Even the Black girls knew how to braid and barrette their hair. I was an outlier among all the kids, an ugly duckling who belonged nowhere and didn't understand why.

Still, I tried my damnedest. These white-girl rituals were expensive and time-consuming. I had to gather the right equipment: pink plastic razors, women's shaving cream, and cherry-flavored lip gloss. The careful, calculated entrapment of adolescent males was no easy task. It was pure orchestration, planning and counterplanning, like considering the best way to ambush one's enemy.

To tame my hair I tried bobby pins, elastic bands, plastic combs, and wooden brushes. Side parts and middle parts. I went through enough brands of shampoo and conditioner to make me a Procter & Gamble poster girl. But nothing would help me look like them.

In any case, my obsessive, unsupervised primping didn't seem to make a difference. I never got the attention the other girls got. White boys noticed white girls. This was the unspoken rule of things, but I figured it was my fault. My body would never be *that* kind of body, the one that got talked about by boys in hushed tones in the hallway, the one that provoked lust-filled glances from men on the street.

I learned about sex and love at the homes of my white girlfriends, where we watched movies like *Dirty Dancing* and played games like spin the bottle and truth or dare. Slumber parties were where I discovered important childhood rites of passage, where we assembled our sleeping bags in front of the television, bingeing on ice cream and watching late-night pornography on cable, where naked adult bodies engaged in acts of contortion and pounding that made no sense to me. I was in no place to ask questions. I kept my head down and ate my ice cream.

I was just the smart girl. But smartness had no currency in this world; it was only back home with Mom and Dad that it was both everything and never enough.

• • •

Every Indian family seemed to have a story about a handsy Indian uncle or neighbor. Stories about sexual violence were told in whispers, if they were told at all. Without any talks about birds and bees, I had no way of knowing the difference between sex, love, and violence. I had to find out on my own.

At thirteen, Bianca was one year older than me, and very thin, with budding curves around the hips. She wore shoes that adult women wore, with tapered toes and heels. Her jeans fit closely to her legs. I could spot Bianca in a crowd of kids by her bright-red lipstick. It drew out the green in her eyes and the dark brown in her hair. Bianca was some kind of Italian goddess, and I would never look like her.

Bianca was crying this morning, and our teachers had surrounded her. Mascara was dripping down both of her cheeks. She had a complexion that was beyond white. It was the kind of porcelain I saw in museums, where security guards warned us not to touch anything. A face like Bianca's inspired great art, and grave concern.

The news reached us like the telephone game, from one child's seat to the next. On her way to school, a strange man attacked Bianca, touched her in some harmful way. Bianca was still crying audibly, surrounded by a ring of adults.

I wondered who this man was. I imagined him as handsome. Even then, I recognized what jealousy felt like: a narrowing of my chest and heat behind the eyes.

• • •

Mom got a PhD in economics in the 1950s from Harvard, on full scholarship. The saris Mom wore to work in Cambridge were delicate and elegant, like her. She carried them in a single leather suitcase on a ship from India to the States. My favorites had flowers and plants, tiny elephants, and peacocks. They reminded me of the stone sculptures in our home, where the gods were animals.

In New York City, at her new job as a professor at Columbia, she was going through a wardrobe change. I accompanied her to department stores like Macy's and Bloomingdale's, where she tried on all the latest pantsuits by designers from Italy, because they were the best. Mom's red bindi powder remained unused now on her bedroom shelf. The elephants and peacocks came out of the closet only on special occasions.

There was that day when, early on in her tenure, Mom stopped by a colleague's office. He was a senior faculty member in the political science department, a large white man with a big reputation. He stood up to greet her. Then he unzipped his pants. She flew out of there before he could go any further. Mom told Dad immediately, and then reported the man to the dean, who said, "That's the way he is." Nothing was done. She wouldn't speak about it in public till she retired forty years later, after the guy was dead.

• • •

I was a quiet, good girl. Sex was forbidden to me. It surfaced in hidden places, where adults didn't roam.

When I was five, my camp counselor sat me on his lap on the train back from swimming practice. The others were doing kid things. Singing songs. Picking their noses. Zack embraced me in his sun-tanned arms and planted a warm kiss on my lips. Whatever line he had crossed with me was blurred by my sense that I was wanted. I adored him.

Three years later, my friend Sophie and I were hiding under a bed in my parents' apartment, with jigsaw puzzles, cards, and board games. Sophie told me to stay quiet and take off my clothes. I did. She got close, touching me in places I didn't know could be touched. I was shy, and willing. She was gentle, and very focused, as if she were following a script. Something was exciting me, and hiding from my parents and whispering was helping that. I didn't say much. She was in charge.

I was safe with Sophie, but something about her was unsettled. Mom and Dad spoke about Sophie seeing a therapist, which was apparently a serious thing. She sometimes picked her eyebrows clean off her forehead. Unlike Mom and Dad, I looked at Sophie's face and saw a face just as it was supposed to be.

I was accustomed to the rumblings at her enormous Park Avenue home, the raised voices, her mother's anxiety, her stepfather's scoldings. Sophie's anger with them was quick to burn. I could not yet relate to this anger, though when she cried afterward and refused to eat, I wondered what would make a child so sad.

• • •

For a teenager in New York City, taking the subway from home to high school and back was a pride-building rite of passage. Long gone were the days when my mother followed me like a private investigator, across the avenue and half a block behind, to make sure I looked both ways before crossing the street.

I spent most of my hours drowning in homework and a rotating schedule of extracurricular activities that would get me into the Ivy League. I went to Stuyvesant High School, a prestigious math and science public school, so Mom and Dad didn't pay a dime. It was okay to be smart now. Even the mean girls got good grades. I was surrounded by kids from poor, working-, and middle-class immigrant families whose hell-bent focus on hard work and getting into college was familiar. Asian kids made up the majority of the student population, and whiteness held less sway over me now—I sought refuge in my community of multicultural nerds.

One particular morning there was too little room on the train to open a book. So I shoved in and made my way to the pole. On its way down to the financial district, the train was crammed with brokers and briefcases and black-and-white newspapers held up and folded just so to maximize readability and space. There was no moving until doors opened and people forced themselves out, elbows, hips, and shoulders violently carving a path to the platform.

In this crowded subway car, where a person could barely breathe, someone was touching me before I even realized that I was being touched. His hand was up my skirt and his fingers were roaming on the surface of my panties, pressing and rubbing into me.

I looked up suddenly, wild-eyed. I only saw heads looking beyond or down into a sea of newspapers. *Did I imagine it?* I must have.

And as I settled back into the rumbling of the train, it began again, this humiliation I could not verify through eye contact, this pushing, searching, probing over and into the fabric of my underwear. I searched the crowd again, silently, and it stopped again. Still, I found no one to validate my experience. No witnesses to this scene, not even the guilty party.

I imagined I must be insane. My senses had heightened and my voice had disappeared, a combination that was infuriating in its biological design, making me feel useless. Any trust I had in myself eroded rapidly, like the safety in my childhood, like the certainty that I could succeed at anything by trying hard enough.

It continued like this, for minutes that seemed like hours, till the train came to a stop and the doors opened. Faceless, nameless bodies poured out and others rushed in. I stood at the pole, frozen and silent.

I told no one about this moment. I don't know why. What would

I have said? And to whom? I packed this morning away in the darkest corner of my memory and didn't think about it for twenty-five years.

. . .

As high school continued, I became increasingly aware of my ugliness. When curves arrived officially one summer, my father called me *fat* and *disgusting*.

I can't even look at you, he said, storming out of the bedroom and far away from me. I was used to this. Dad had always hated my curly Indian hair and grimaced when he saw me wearing it loose around my shoulders. It didn't matter that his hair was like mine. Or that he was far from thin. In fact, the only one who was thin and would always stay that way was my mother, who avoided things like butter and desserts and made sure you knew about it, too. My father's addiction to fried food and pastrami had already given him one heart attack. But none of this mattered. I was the one out of control.

I stood looking in the mirror, studying the rolls on my belly. The only thing worse than his cruelty was my self-hatred. Too ashamed to look into my own eyes, I vowed never to be fat again.

I disappointed my father in other ways because I loved sports, and by high school had become obsessed with basketball. I captained my team several years in a row, but this meant nothing to my folks. Dad may have disapproved of my body, but exercise was beneath him and organized sports were a waste of time. My straight As were irrelevant. Dad was fed up with the number of hours I spent training and became exasperated as I watched Patrick Ewing and the Knicks run back and forth on TV. Dad would storm into the kitchen, stomping his feet, gesticulating at the enormous men on the television set, turning it off while yelling my name. I would just turn it back on after he left.

I rarely went to school without a Georgetown Hoyas baseball hat, the rim curved just so, tugged down over my forehead and ponytail. I began to wear black, gray, and navy blue. My pants became baggy. I wanted to hide.

There was also the matter of my period, a monstrous thing filled with pain, hiding, and more silence. For as long as I can remember, that time of the month was excruciating. I hid in library corners, withdrew to bathroom stalls and private rooms, clutched my knees to my chest, and writhed in pain. My muscles wrapped around my intestines and squeezed until liquid gushed from every orifice in my body.

The toilet was my refuge. Urine-stained rims and dark brown halos below did not deter me from sprawling on bathroom floors. I emptied out my guts from both ends, as if to exorcise some demon possessing my body. When the pain turned from hot and searing to sharp and metallic, I vomited again and again. Sometimes too late to make it to a toilet, I wrapped my mouth around the nearest available bottle, filling it with stomach bile out in the open. I threw up so much that in the end, there was nothing left but empty heaving.

Through this private physical upheaval, I cultivated a long-suffering patience. I became an expert at masking pain. I thought this was my lot in life. And so I told no one. No other woman revealed any personal stories about pain to me. My mother had done a brief but shocking tampon demonstration for me when I was twelve, but aside from that—I was mortified to learn that she had private parts, more than anything—she had shared little with me about life outside of her academic obsessions.

As far as I knew, I was the only girl on earth who felt like I was being drawn and quartered from the inside out every month. No one told me it would be okay. For all I knew, nothing was okay in this world.

• • •

I was sixteen when I met Sam. She was point guard to my power forward. She was calm and moved like water, paving endless routes to the hoop without seeming to try. She didn't know how good she was.

She had shy eyes, except for the occasional glint of mischief that grew from a political sensibility about what was right and wrong with the world. She didn't like her whiteness. She believed white folks had irreparably harmed the world. At only fifteen, she took responsibility for that harm, even if she didn't cause it, even if it hurt.

I had my head lost in books, assignments, and expectations about my future. And then, suddenly, my world was Sam. She was everything I thought I was not—cool in the face of hysteria, unfazed by the pressures of striving for academic perfection. She rejected the systems that made book-smart people powerful. She preferred poets and writers who shaped minds and created revolutions off the syllabus. There was a vibrant world beyond school in which Sam seemed alive, a world of protest and revolution. I didn't know that world but I wanted in.

Sam told me I thought too much. She was present, and real. She took me to dives in the East Village that became places of refuge from home—holes in the ground with heaping pots of Middle Eastern lentils and hot pita bread, giant black bean burritos with fresh salsa, natural soft drinks in flavors I'd never imagined, like ginger beer.

That winter was my wonderland. Basketball was where I felt alive. I spent any feelings of inadequacy and rage on the court. One evening after practice, Sam and I walked with heavy book bags to one of her havens. Our faces were red, hair slightly matted from sweat, the backs of our chairs overflowing with scarves and hoods. As we ate, she grew quiet. Then she looked up from her plate and told me.

"I'm falling for you."

I didn't know what this meant. I shifted in my seat. I avoided eye contact. I chewed excessively.

I knew what this meant. Sam was my best friend. And Sam loved me. Did I love Sam? What would it mean to love her?

I don't remember how it happened. One week we were giggling, following some rich old lady in a mink coat down the street, yelling at her that she shouldn't wear fur. The next week she was in my arms, wrapped up on a sofa, and everything was quiet and still and warm, and I was in her hair, and all I could smell in my dreams was her.

Somehow I knew that what I felt was forbidden. No one else knew about us. But my mother was suspicious.

"Sam is a troubled teenager." And then, "Why are you spending so much time together?"

When Sam was over on weekends, my mother hovered and glared at us like we would burst into flames. Her anxiety turned into paranoia and then hatred.

On a mandatory family trip to Mexico, I pouted. I was silent and distracted. I wandered away for hours at a time to be alone. This infuriated my parents.

One night my mother stormed into our hotel room, sobbing, waving her arms around like some rabid beast. She declared that she had read my diary.

"You've written about her . . . her *hair*!"

She cornered me into admitting the truth.

I did. And then I wished I were dead.

The rest was a blur of tears and silence interrupted by fits of my mother screaming in my direction. I don't know how we got to the airport. On the flight back to New York City, my mother told me of the shame I would wreak upon her family in India.

"Two women kissing. It's dis-*gust*-ing." And then, before I'd fully digested all of this, she said, "If you do not end this now, I will kill myself."

She looked away wretchedly, and that was that.

I sat next to my father on the plane, crying, while my mother sat in a seat across the aisle, in some desperate, wild-eyed fugue state.

There was no question of who held the authority here. My mother had the only and final word. There were no opposing points of view to be had. No question of my mother's intentions, or her ability to follow through with this threat. Her ultimatum came from deep beyond her own language, as if brought forth by our ancestors. There was no question of my responsibility. My dharma.

My father was strangely gentle with me. He never raised his voice. He did not disapprove. He did not remind me of my unbearable shame.

Back home in the city I left my suitcase at the apartment and called Sam from the phone booth on my parents' college campus.

"I can't see you anymore. My mother found out."

Sam accepted this news, too quickly, too quietly.

At school that week, Sam avoided me, but I found her during lunch hour, pulled her into an empty classroom, and explained how much I still wanted to be with her.

She was detached and cold. I was hysterical. I crumpled up a piece of paper from my notebook and threw it at her. It was all I could do to connect to her, this pathetic act of violence. I hated her for being like this, for pretending I didn't exist. God, I loved her.

The next winter, my senior year and her junior, Sam didn't show up to our first practice. I was devastated. I found her in the hallway that week and asked why she wasn't playing ball with us this year. She said nothing. I was desperate for an answer.

"Is it because of me?"

"Yes."

I had lost her. Some part of me shut down then and never woke up again.

• • •

Silence over things that mattered most had held my family together for years. I had my secrets, and I discovered my parents also had theirs.

The sense that my mother was carrying some larger-than-life pain had weighed on me since as long as I'd been conscious. She said nothing in my childhood to explain the reason for her sadness. I assumed, because I was never told otherwise, that it was my fault.

My mother was capable of moments of great joy, but they were often interrupted by longer moments of melancholy. Dad was in his own intellectual world, oblivious to the full impact of her moods. Mom handled every challenge in her life by throwing herself into her work, obsessively. When they were together, my parents spoke for hours about international relations, economic theories, and famous thinkers, but no one ever explained why that's all they talked about. When I walked into their conversations, I became their audience. Who could blame them? They lectured for a living. They had no off switch.

My mother's sadness was my sadness. Her long, frequent moments of staring out into space became my responsibility. Her pain seemed to be provoked by me and my inability to do things right. Her tears came often, and hard, hitting me like giant waves and taking the ground from beneath my feet.

I was about sixteen when she told me she wanted to talk over coffee. I remember how strange this felt. My mother and I did not "have coffee." We had no mother-daughter dates, or heart-to-heart talks like I saw on television and imagined my high school friends having. The space between us was uncomfortable and vast.

In a coffee shop in the neighborhood, we sat on stools before large windows. Mom's revelations had no warm-up phase, no adjustment time.

"Dad and I thought it was time you knew," she said. "I was married to another man. In India."

I do not remember most details from this day. Whether Mom sipped coffee while she told her story. If she looked at me while she spoke. I don't remember what we wore, or the season, or the year. I just remember a feeling of falling.

As I sat there trying not to listen, my mind created ways to escape Mom's confession. I thought, *Oh god, is Dad not my father? Please tell me I was adopted. These cannot be my parents.* It would have explained everything. But I was not adopted. And in fact, Dad was my father. The narrative came at me like floodwater.

"He slept with prostitutes. He gave me a venereal disease. I couldn't have a child for years." I remember how clinical her words sounded.

And then.

"He seduced me."

What the hell did she mean, *seduced*? I knew something wasn't right, and I wasn't sure how, but I knew this like I'd always seemed to know about Mom. There was a moment when I was conscious and present, and everything seemed clear. I'm not even sure how I knew this word.

"Mom. Did he rape you?"

She looked away and paused. Mom was no longer lecturing.

"Yes."*

I was furious, mostly with my grandfather, who made sure that my mother married the man who "seduced" her. Indian custom wouldn't have it any other way. Consent was not a factor. Sex before marriage—consensual or not—was like heresy, and choices were irrelevant for women. But Mom was resourceful. She found a way out of her marriage by converting from Hinduism to Christianity, a dramatic move that circumvented Hindu law and left her husband powerless to prevent a divorce. Still, she felt that she'd brought shame upon her family and disappointed her father by abandoning Hinduism for her freedom. Even after all of this, she worshipped her father.

Mom's revelation would be the beginning of a lifelong dance between us. She was stuck in another time and place, with rules and language that did not apply to my present. For decades, I wrestled with her story. A few years after our talk, I had the audacity to ask her again, as if I hadn't heard it the first time, "Mom, did he rape you?" And she told me, "No."

I felt crazy. A teenage girl does not invent such horrors about her mother's past and then rack her brain from that day on to try to understand how such a thing could happen. Why would my mother, this pillar of precision and discipline, change her story?

Decades later, my mother still had an impeccable memory for details from her past, but did not remember that we ever had that coffee. *In what coffee shop?* she asked me. How is it possible for her to forget a day that I will never forget?

And just when I thought perhaps I'd gotten it all wrong, she slipped again.

Even if you don't want sex, it happens. You get used to it. Everyone warned me he was a horrible man.

---

* Even decades after Mom's abuse, marital rape not only continues in India but is widely condoned by the society and government. In 2017, despite marital rape affecting 40 percent of marriages, the parliament voted not to criminalize it.

It would take a long time for me to understand that trauma and memory are like that. Mom insists she wasn't assaulted. She was slowly, methodically lured into a relationship by a calculating man. In my mind, he was a predator. I believe that my mother was abused more than she does. The details of how this man hurt my mother are not as important as the fact that she continues to hurt because of him now.

I didn't tell anyone about Mom's past. I could have used a sounding board, but I could think of no one to confide in without heaping more shame upon my family. The thought of bringing harm to her and my ancestors caused visceral pain.

Now that I knew about her first husband, Mom spent years either pushing me away with dramatic retellings of the same painful memories—*You have no idea what I went through*, she would tell me ad nauseam as I listened dutifully, without any choice—or detaching and dissociating, like the disciplined intellectual she wanted to be.

Lost in her memories, she couldn't stop herself from reminding me, "When I was your age, I was nothing. I was nobody."

"Mom, you were not nothing!" She didn't believe me.

As her anxiety and sadness spiraled out of control, she and Dad refused to recognize the lingering impact of her trauma. The worst was this: ever the economists, Mom and Dad saw the time Mom could otherwise have spent building her career as the opportunity cost of her marrying a scumbag. I was infuriated by their pragmatism. All I wanted to know was if any of her academic success mattered if she was still this torn up inside. Dad sidestepped these questions with typical cruelty: *If only you would spend more time with your mother, she wouldn't be so anxious.*

Mom was terrified of me making some horrible "mistake" that would echo her own experience. She saw red flags in every option I had, for love, for life. So she and Dad dug in hard. And that meant I could not breathe. I suppose they thought that my knowing about her past would be the end of the story. But they did not account for how much work would be necessary for me to trust or let them in again.

Around this time I became aware that I could not allow them to touch me physically. I hated the feeling of my father's lips on my cheeks. Mom's arms around my rib cage felt like she was squeezing the life out of me. They left me feeling violated. I avoided them, locking myself in my room, storming by them when necessary, and rarely looking them in the eyes. I was done being the source of their comfort and the solution to whatever mistakes Mom thought she had made in her life.

If Mom had not been my mother, I would have been her ally. I would have been her advocate, and the one who raged on her behalf. But I was her daughter. When my mother got upset now, when she spaced out and drifted off, when something I did made her weep, my father mercilessly reminded me of the sacrifices my mother had made, like I was supposed to suffer for an eternity. I was suffocating. It was only a matter of time before I'd leave home and never look back.

CHAPTER 2

Are You a Girl with a Star-Spangled Heart?*

I was eleven years old when Swati took me to see *Top Gun*. At fifteen, Swati would have donated a kidney for a minute alone with Tom Cruise. I'd been following her around since I was born, taking mental notes on proper Desi girl protocol the whole time. My dad had taught her dad economics. Her mother was a psychiatrist. They were more traditional than my parents. They spoke Hindi at home. They celebrated Diwali. Before major events, they blessed the gods. They were strict with Swati and her little sister, Smita. Boys were outlawed. So were school dances. Mom and Dad figured that nothing would happen to me under Auntie and Uncle's close watch. Years later, even after we moved to New York City, Mom and Dad sent me to spend vacations with Swati and Smita so I would have a connection to my roots and a bond with other Indian kids.

We snuck away that afternoon from Swati's parents. I didn't yet know there were reasons to be sneaking around. Telling Uncle and Auntie that we were seeing some mild-mannered comedy instead of

---

* A slogan from a World War II recruiting poster.

a sex-filled military blockbuster felt like a horrible lie. The guilt and fear ate me up all the way to the theater.

Like many Generation Xers, my introduction to military culture came in a dark, air-conditioned theater, chomping on buttered popcorn and guzzling Coke while watching a twentysomething Tom Cruise and a chorus of drunken sailors shamelessly serenade Kelly McGillis.

You never close your eyes anymore when I kiss your lips.
And there's no tenderness like before in your fingertips.

I didn't know any of the tools men used to hook women, nor did I know hooking by either side was necessary. In my mind, couples simply existed. Like Swati's parents, or mine, paired off for decades in arranged or family-approved marriages that seemed both inevitable and unbreakable. This stunt, with dozens of boozed-up, muscled, virile men surrounding a stunned woman in a cramped bar with no way out came not long before Anita Hill testified about her former boss's sexual shenanigans to the nation. After dancing in his briefs in *Risky Business*, Tom was the hottest a guy could be in Hollywood. Harassing the older, wiser flight instructor in public, even following her into the ladies' room and cornering her against the counter, didn't work at first. But in the end, she softened. The guy got the girl, the boys won the war, and all was well in the US of A.

"Maverick" and his cut-up band of ass-slapping fighter pilots ushered a whole new generation of hungry young men into the US military. Even my preteen self recognized the recruiting power of Mav and his topless buddies playing beach volleyball in slow motion. But guys with rippling abs, joysticks, and big guns were never really my thing. (My crush was Mav's sidekick "Goose," who was married and wore his shirt playing volleyball. At eleven, I was clearly missing the point.) Kelly McGillis, the female lead, had brains and beauty, but she wasn't a fighter pilot. In the big picture, she was just Mav's girlfriend. Even back then, I wanted role models and company deeper than eye candy.

• • •

Ten years later, I was an undergrad at Yale University and struggling hard. I wish I could say that I loved college. Instead, I was resentful, and sometimes downright bitter. I can't tell you the details of what I studied, or the great conversations I had with my peers, because my primary feeling during that time was alienation. My classmates were smart, some of them geniuses. But what I remember most is how little I could relate to them, and that many were in pain, but no one talked about how or why.

I realized suddenly how sheltered I'd been. I'd never been interested in alcohol, and now it was everywhere. It was a rite of passage for the kids around me. My first party with beer kegs in the dorm and I couldn't stand the sight of my peers, half conscious and drooling. I left within minutes. This made me a prude and a loser. And because of that, a loner. I envied the ease with which other kids socialized, studied, and drank. But the truth was, the whole scene scared me. The boys who drank around me became larger than their bodies, aggressive and stupid. The girls became silly and powerless.

Awful things happened at night on the weekends that I'd find out about in the morning in the hallway bathrooms we shared. In my first semester, one kid who'd been drinking down the hall from me was hauled away in an ambulance after blacking out. No one blinked. A few days later, a girl I knew had been raped by an athlete three times her size, and when I asked her, horrified, if she needed any help, she simply shrugged her shoulders and explained, "He was too big and too drunk for me to push him off. Don't worry, it's okay."

But I worried. I felt like something was wrong with me. And I was also still trying to figure out who I was and how I belonged. One morning I found my freshman roommate deep in discussion with another woman from across the hall. They were talking about a student who'd cut her hair short.

"It means she's a *les*bian," she said, with attitude. I raised an eyebrow. What were they talking about?

"No it doesn't," I blurted.

They seemed surprised I had a point of view.

"Well, how would *you* know?"

"Because I just do." This did not satisfy them.

"Because . . ." I'd never used this word. It felt odd coming out of my mouth. But it felt right to say it. "I'm bisexual."

My roommate became completely silent. And then she stormed out of the suite. I didn't see her for weeks. The college dean called me in to tell me she had requested a transfer to another room but that he'd refused to give it to her. I felt the hurt surge inside me. I may have been in shock over this, but I was now accustomed to suppressing painful experiences and driving on. Besides, I had other pressures to contend with.

My parents had regaled me with myths about universities like Yale since I was a child. There was no debate or discussion over what I'd be doing in college. When they took me aside a few months before my freshman year to tell me they would no longer allow me to play basketball, my heart sank. I'd received a tempting offer to join the team at another liberal arts college, a pipe dream for an Indian girl like me, but I barely considered it. It wasn't an option I would have been allowed to consider. I wonder, even if I had known how to say yes, if they'd already made me too miserable to enjoy it.

At Yale, Mom and Dad approved all my classes before registration— each professor's reputation was considered and CV reviewed.

"Ah yes, he's quite famous," Dad would say. Mother concurred. If the professor was unknown to them, red flags were raised and other courses were suggested.

They furiously reviewed my grades at the end of each semester. I managed mostly As, but this was not enough. My interest in early Christianity and Buddhism threw them for a loop. When I announced that I wanted to major in religious studies, Dad got me on the phone while Mom listened in the background.

"Re-*lig*-ious studies? No. That's absurd. Why would you want to do *that?*" Over the years, this question would start to make me doubt that I ever wanted to do anything.

"Because it's interesting?"

"It's not something one studies in college," he responded, as if it were obvious. Mother grunted approval.

"But why not?" I didn't understand. Was this an economist thing? Or an Indian thing?

"Because it's something one studies in graduate school."

I have no idea where these rules came from. Dad had strict opinions about scholarship and Mom agreed, usually with vigorous head nods. By the end of my first semester, I was deeply depressed and no longer wanted to be there.

The only way out was rebellion. Ben was a skateboarder, a smoker, and a townie who worked behind the counter at Ashley's Ice Cream in New Haven. By my second semester, he and I were dating. Ben was sweet and handsome, tall and muscular, older than me by several years, and Black. He had far more interest in weed and alcohol than in higher education, and we didn't have a thing in common. I remember how his eyes glazed over when he was high, which was often. On some level, I must have known he was an addict. Still, he was a lot less threatening to me than the kids back in the dorms. I took comfort in the fact that the little I had with him was better than whatever I had with most of my classmates.

My parents didn't know about Ben's substance abuse issues, but what they did know was enough to make them nuts. They had been steeped in racist, classist immigrant lore, an Indian caste-based worldview that supported institutional racism in America. You were born into your caste, and you generally stayed there. Karma could be cruel that way. I did not understand them. What I did understand was that they did not send me to the Ivy League so I could waste my time with Ben.

During sophomore year, a friend of mine, an opera singer who was equally disillusioned with her college experience, had organized a surprise birthday party for me. Ben took me for coffee while a bunch of kids from my dorm and my parents, who'd driven in from New York, hid in my cramped suite with cake and candles. At the appointed time, Ben walked through the door, with me piggybacked on top of him, laughing and clutching his collarbones, to a chorus of singing. I saw my parents sitting in the corner under a storm cloud of judgment, and I knew nothing good was going to happen.

When the others left, I got an earful. My father was standing over me with his furious eyebrows and thick glasses. I hid my face in my hands, trying to block him out.

"And what on earth are you trying to do to your mother by spending time with this man? He's uneducated! He's beneath you! He's, he's . . ." My father, who was never tongue-tied, was desperately searching for words.

"He's a go-*rill*-a!"

My dad's Neanderthal reaction ensured I stayed with Ben for another two years before boredom got the best of me.

I was miserable, and my rage toward them was nearing a tipping point. The threat of my dropping out of Yale made them back off, temporarily. Their vision of my future was simple: college, grad school, marriage, kids. I was straying desperately from that path, and the shame that would bring hovered over all of us. Terrified, they agreed to let me take a semester off.

During those few months away from Yale, my parents forced me to see a shrink—my mother's, as it turns out, although for what reason she was seeing him, I'm not entirely sure. They were convinced my sadness was abnormal. He was a tiny, odd little man with many interests. He was a former Catholic priest, a gynecologist, and a psychiatrist. I was horrified by the whole scene.

The shrink prescribed me Zoloft, an antidepressant. A few weeks in, I felt numb, and no less alienated from the life I did not want to be leading. I tossed the pills out and never took them again.

I'd given plenty of thought to transferring schools, but had the instinct that if I didn't graduate with a degree from Yale—if I transferred to some small, lesser-known liberal arts college—I would hate myself even more than I hated myself now, and my family would never let me forget it. Fear of that dishonor was greater incentive than anything else I knew in the world. I already felt like I'd failed my parents. My joy was tied up with theirs, and it was often hard to tell where theirs ended and mine began.

I returned to Yale after my semester off and survived, in part thanks to joining the rugby club, where I met a group of ferocious and tender women around whom I was completely shy and intimidated (some of them were all-American athletes and twice my size), but who accepted me despite my awkwardness.

I finished Yale with my head bowed low to the ground, majoring in English—oddly on my parents' approved list of undergraduate fields—and graduating with honors. But I was depleted and uncertain.

• • •

After college, I wandered around Latin America, climbing mountains, trudging through a hot jungle with a machete, and studying Spanish. My parents had footed the bill, despite enormous resistance that I was wasting my time. I had notions of following guerrillas into the jungle and writing about Latin America's oldest power struggles. But my folks were having none of it. Under pressure from my father, I ended up applying to graduate school, even though I had no desire or reason to go.

Graduate school for a girl like me was inevitable. I could have gotten in anywhere, but my father decided, with a sense of urgency, that it was in my best interest to enroll at Columbia, the university where he and my mother were professors. I did not know how to say no to him.

I ended up back in New York City, enrolled in a double-degree journalism and international affairs program. I shared an apartment with Swati, who had thus far survived her parents' expectations and was now working as a health care consultant. Aside from the comfort of being around Swati and her enormous cat, Oliver, I was just going through the motions.

Against all common sense, I had enrolled in my father's class at

Columbia, a popular seminar on international trade. If he was such a big shot, I figured I'd get a glimpse of him in action. It was a giant, sloping classroom, and I sat somewhere near the back. I avoided eye contact with him, instead watching students from around the world hanging onto his every word. *God, he tells those jokes in public, too*, I remember thinking. I tried desperately to hide in my seat. I wanted nothing to do with him. Yet there I was.

I lasted only one semester. I remember the afternoon I walked into Swati's bedroom, crumbled into her lap, and wept uncontrollably. I couldn't do this anymore, going along with my parents' plans and feeling so broken inside. It felt like I was dying. She held me and stroked my hair, asked me softly what would help and what I wanted to do. I didn't know. I went where they told me. Choice was an abstract concept. Free will was something my white friends talked about in European philosophy classes and then expressed shamelessly in their own lives. In my world it was equivalent to disrespect for one's elders, a kind of Indian upheaval.

I did not know what it would feel like to stand tall, to trust my own feet, follow my own instincts, and breathe fully. I was too sad to dream. I wanted out of this cycle, only I didn't know where to begin. When I quit school suddenly, my folks were shocked and confused, as if after twenty-three years of watching me struggle to be like them, they hadn't seen it coming.

They loomed, calling constantly, asking what I was going to do next. *What are your plans?* I had none. Everything I wanted to do had been forbidden since long before I could remember.

• • •

G.I. Jane was supposed to be a distraction over the Thanksgiving holiday, not a call to duty. I'd taken Smita, Swati's little sister. We walked out of the theater onto a dark New York City sidewalk, jacked on adrenaline, hearts pumping. Demi Moore starred as Lieutenant Jordan O'Neill. Buzz-cutting her hair live on camera, clenched jaw and eyes on fire, ready to consume the whole world, O'Neill became my symbol of one woman bucking the system and thriving in spite of it. The one-armed push-ups didn't hurt, either.

Then a pre-Aragorn unknown, Viggo Mortensen played the part of Master Chief John James Urgayle, O'Neill's sexist, skull-crushing Navy SEAL instructor. Maverick and Iceman were no match for the Master Chief. I was wrapped up in his sadism and authority like a puppy starved for love.

I'd spent most hours in childhood and adolescence dutifully engaged in my studies. But after years of earning As that had no connection to a deeper sense of purpose, I realized that what I really wanted was some kind of physical and mental reckoning. Taming my body was a form of control that I didn't have in any other part of my life. Along with this, it became clear to me that being smarter than the boys wasn't enough for me. I wanted to beat them at everything else, too. And maybe, if I was honest, kick their asses a little.

G.I. Jane pushed feminist boundaries but took grand liberties with the truth—there were no women in the Navy SEALs,* and there was no desire at the Pentagon to change that—but I didn't know the facts then and wouldn't have cared. I was riveted.

In the film there's a well-known simulated hostage scene during Survival Evasion Resistance and Escape (SERE) training in which Viggo beats the crap out of Demi in front of the male trainees. Pinned down with her hands cuffed behind her, Demi seethes with fake blood spurting out of her mouth as Viggo cuts off her belt and prepares to tear off her trousers. Spent and humiliated, she finds a second wind, boots him in the nuts, head butts him hard, and kicks him to the ground.

He recovers, knocks her out, and gloats, while she gets back to her feet, spitting up blood, barely standing, proclaiming, "Suck. My. Dick."

---

* SEALs (Sea, Air, and Land forces) are the Navy's elite special operations warfare teams. SEAL training is known to be among the toughest in the US military.

Her team goes wild. She has become one of them while also rising above them. It still gives me chills.

I wanted that. Even more, I needed that. It felt strangely like lust. And I wasn't sure if I could see a line between lust and pain. No part of me cared to know why I was drawn to a culture in which degradation and humiliation were entwined with belonging. I needed to fight in order to prove myself, even if I wasn't sure whom I was fighting or what I was trying to prove.

Demi's transformation stayed with me. The following spring, I rode my bike down Broadway at 4:45 a.m. each morning. The lanes were entirely deserted except for the occasional delivery truck dropping off inventory at grocery stores. I entered Central Park and cut across the narrow lane alongside Sheep Meadow. I saw no one. Unlit, quiet New York City parks echoed generations of rape warnings, and looking over my shoulder was something I'd learned when I was a child.

I was meeting a group of middle-aged men and women, all white, mostly lawyers and bankers, New York's overworked, overstressed upper crust. I was unique among them, twenty-four and Brown, wide-eyed, a recent graduate school dropout, searching for meaning anywhere I could find it.

I locked my bike and made my way to a dimly lit cement patch, where a couple of bodies were hovering, yawning, and stretching under the black sky. Jack and his assistant came out of the shadows of Central Park's elm trees. Jack was a short, wiry man with hamstrings that popped and a tight, muscular chest. The sleeves of his T-shirt closely encircled biceps and triceps honed through a lifetime of lifting, pulling, and pushing large, unwieldy objects—bodies, boats, weapons, equipment—from one place to another over and through every conceivable natural and man-made element. Jack's voice was mean, firm, and strangely resonant. He was my first real-life Navy SEAL, and I was transfixed.

I was too naive to know the special brand of theater Jack was performing as he barked at us to get on the ground and push. I ate up every order, and I couldn't get enough.

Confined to small spaces on cramped boats and submarines, the SEALS had perfected infinite variations on heart-pounding, lung-bursting calisthenics. Something cosmic was playing out here in the thousandth push-up and five hundredth mountain climber, this dance with mortality and the will to ignore one's own screaming body. Jack was teaching us to embrace fear and accept misery. The body was merely a vehicle for the mind to experience something beyond physical limitation, and I pushed past it, with something that felt like faith, with Jack hollering an evangelism that conveyed absolute certainty in the soundtrack over my head.

My back flush against the concrete, hair beyond any hope of staying in my ponytail, grit digging into my palms and forearms, I summoned another hundred flutter kicks, hollering my count back to Jack's cadence, watching the city transform from starless black to dawn. I felt both numb and exhilarated. Penetrating muscular soreness and physical exhaustion would define my next few weeks. And because there was no feeling in the world like this, even this was not enough. I wanted more.

· · ·

Two months later, I arrived at a Navy recruiting station on Harlem's main business strip, where Dr. Martin Luther King Jr. Boulevard intersects with Malcolm X Boulevard. The walls were plastered with rah-rah posters depicting big boats and deadly planes, aircraft carriers, submarines, and camouflaged men carving through surf on Zodiacs. Every branch of service had been branded by billion-dollar advertising companies in fancy boardrooms, encapsulating the unfulfilled longing of American adolescents, down to each unique cultural or demographic footnote, with the ruthless precision of the nation's best political operatives. They'd hedged their bets that we were all suckers for something, rejected or urged on by society or family in some primal way, wishing for something larger than life, or at least something more than the mundane existence we'd been living.

As I stared at the posters, I was greeted by a dirty blond, mustached sailor and my heart sank. This was no Jack. This was no Jane. The man was dough-faced, soft around the waist, and covered in white.

I sat down and immediately felt too comfortable. Like a travel agent, the Navy's poster boy regaled me with stories about seeing the world. I looked at him, bored to death.

"So, how do I become a SEAL?"

"Excuse me?" he said.

I blinked.

"You want to be a Navy SEAL?" The truth was served like a hammer on my head: "You can't."

"What do you mean I *can't*?"

"Women just . . . can't."

"Why?"

He didn't know why, and by the sound of it, if *anyone* knew, they hadn't given this guy any explanations. He told me patiently about the prohibition on women in combat. Women were banned from doing hundreds of jobs in the military: SEALS, Delta Force, infantry, armor, artillery. The list was endless.

Reality was quickly setting in. *G.I. Jane* was a myth created by Hollywood. These glorified photos of special operators on the walls, trying to sucker me in with promises of being my best and testing my limits—all of it was bullshit.

We stared at each other.

"Well, what *can* I do, then?"

He whipped out a clipboard and pounded through a long list of questions, assessing whether or not I would qualify for the Navy. I appeared to be a standout recruit, and the sailor was eager to move forward. But I couldn't get over the man's gut. His friendly style. The cushy posters on the wall. This place was more a promise of a honeymoon than the first phase of the rest of my life. I didn't want to get a tan on the deck of some cruise ship. I didn't want a European vacation. I wanted trials. I wanted to be tested. I wanted something extreme.

. . .

I walked into my first Marine Corps recruiting station in downtown Manhattan wearing formal slacks and a blazer and found myself in a staring match with a silent, grisly sergeant. No one offered a friendly greeting, and apparently chairs were not meant for visitors. One dude dressed in a finely pressed olive-and-khaki uniform with shiny black shoes was sitting on a couch off to my right, pretending he was busy with paperwork, but keeping most of his attention glued to my every move. I got the sense he had earned the right to sit on that couch, and I had not.

"Good morning," I said.

Four eyeballs drilled into mine like screwdrivers.

"Uh, I was interested in finding out more about the Marine Corps."

"Oh, *she* thinks she wants to be a Marine," said the man on the couch in no apparent direction. The other one snickered.

His remarks worked like a charm. Now I was curious. I didn't realize that the men there were steeped in two treasured Marine traditions—fucking with the new guy and insulting women.

A staff noncommissioned officer walked in and introduced himself. He was clearly the assigned adult on duty, and his presence softened the wolves, just slightly. As he stood before me, I took him in. Soft-eyed, Puerto Rican, classic good looks. His uniform was a thing of beauty. I was being Ma'am'd up and down. I'd barely made it south of the Mason-Dixon line, and that was to go to Disney World. I was no more a Ma'am than his colleagues were gentlemen.

He asked how he could help me. I told him I was interested in joining the Marines. The man on the couch coughed loudly. The staff sergeant's eyes grew wide for a moment, but he quickly masked it. I guess they didn't see too many women around here.

He handed me a series of dog tags inscribed with Marine Corps "leadership traits." Initiative. Courage. Enthusiasm. These one-word values symbolizing the essence of the Corps reminded me of a cheap advertisement promising the fountain of youth. Maybe he sensed he'd already lost me, because he suddenly asked, "Wanna see a video from boot camp?"

"Sure."

The staff sergeant pressed play on the VCR. I heard grunts and thunderous yelling. On the television screen, I saw young people covered in mud, exhausted and on the verge of crying, gutting out some hell-like obstacle course in the shadow of drill instructors with terrifying grimaces and even more terrifying voices. I couldn't tell if the thick, slimy muck on their foreheads and cheeks was sweat, snot, dirt, or blood. I was hooked. Oh, how I was hooked.

"It's Parris Island. Interested?"

"Mm-hm. Yes. Definitely."

He grinned and sent me into a private room to take a preliminary aptitude test that consisted of basic English and math. A few minutes later, I gave him my exam and he was floored when he discovered I'd gotten all the answers right. Something shifted.

"You went to college?"

"Yes."

"Where?" The sergeant looked over at me from the couch, and then looked away quickly.

"Yale." No one coughed.

The head recruiter changed his tone now. I wasn't sure why.

"You know, you're qualified to be an officer."

"Oh, she wants to be an officer now," grunted the guy on the sofa.

"Ignore him." I did.

I was sent across the island to the Officer Selection Office near the World Trade Center, where Marine officer candidates were screened and groomed for ten weeks of harsh training in Quantico, Virginia. If the enlisted side of recruiting was scrappy, fierce, and irreverent, the officer side was built on pride and decorum. No one was playing, and the men made sure to let you know that casual activities like smiling were not encouraged. I had no idea whether or not this stiff-upper-lip approach rooted out the playboys and brats among the officer class.

In fact, I didn't know much about military rank or hierarchy at all. Class defined relationships in the military—initial rank was simply determined by whether or not one had a college degree, without any regard to why one guy had attended college and the next had not. There was a small class of folks who issued orders, and a large mass of folks who executed them, regardless of their opinions or talents. As an officer, I'd be doing the ordering, and I'd have to believe in what I was saying for folks to want to follow me. I didn't realize that this life might amount to something more than me pushing my mental and physical limits.

My model for officer behavior was Captain Irving, my officer selection officer. He had all the attentive qualities of the staff sergeant, but far more size. He had dark brown skin, was calm and intelligent, and was built like a linebacker, with enough meat in his lats, pecs, and quads to challenge the fabric of his uniform to an unfair fight.

Captain Irving seemed to think I would fly through Officer Candidate School, based solely on my fitness abilities. After working out with the ex-SEALs, my body could handle all sorts of physical torture. But I was skeptical. I was a solid amateur athlete, but I was no Olympian, and at 135 pounds, with legs like twigs, I was a lightweight. I was expecting to see thousands of real-life Joes and Janes once I was in the thick of it. Wouldn't everyone in the Corps be like them?

I imagined it was Captain Irving's bad karma getting an officer candidate like me. There was no end to my questions. About politics and war. American interventions in Vietnam and the Middle East. Shooting the enemy when the enemy was a child soldier, or an unarmed civilian. The poor man had probably never been grilled like this. And adding to a long list of insufficient answers, my captain could not quell my concern about the Marine Corps' oddest, most humiliating acts of gender segregation.

It was with great surprise that I learned that women in the Corps were not required to do pull-ups as their physical fitness requirement, but instead had to do something called a "flexed-arm hang." This bizarre upper-body task required a woman to hold on for dear life with her chin over a pull-up bar for seventy seconds. It wasn't a measure of much, except maybe how long I could tolerate a wounded ego.

Not being required to do pull-ups was insulting. Pull-ups were the Marine Corps' tried-and-true test of upper-body strength, practically its physical rite of passage into the brotherhood. Pull-ups were hard. I loved them for their physicality, and for the empowerment they symbolized—the feeling of lifting myself up and over whatever was holding me down.

I did only one flexed-arm hang, for official recruiting documentation. It left a sting and opened up a world of doubt in me about what I was doing here. Captain Irving calmly insisted that men and women were treated equally in the Corps, but I remained skeptical. In a desperate attempt to keep me engaged, he decided to put me on the phone with one of his colleagues, a female captain, so I could get the real scoop about women in the Marines. I got straight to the point.

"If women aren't supposed to do the same things as the men, how exactly do women fit in?"

"Well, that's just not true. I have to do everything the men do."

I was confused.

"Except the pull-ups, right? And what about the run time?" I ran fast for a woman. I ran fast for a man, too. I didn't understand why my score was rated differently than some dude's.

"The Corps is about a lot more than physical fitness tests." She went on about the amazing things she had done in uniform. She didn't care that there were two separate standards for men and women. Like all the Marines I'd met so far, she didn't ask questions. She was a true believer.

I eventually came to know the flexed-arm hang not as a test of strength but as a glaring symbol that separated women from the hardworking men who made up the real Marine Corps. It was a way to quietly integrate women into the Marines without actually letting us dream big. It was just one of many humiliations that bonded all women in the Corps.

The warnings were loud and clear before I ever signed my name on the dotted line. I would have been a fool to think that these unjustified acts of separating men and women would not define my next few years. But the part of me that wanted to get as far from my life as possible was much stronger than the part of me that believed in self-preservation.

In October 1999, I waved good-bye to my parents and drove south to Quantico.

CHAPTER 3

Becoming a Marine

Quantico, Virginia
October 1999

It was my first time on a military base. Trees in the Quantico woods had just begun to turn yellow, orange, and red. Several sets of rectangular barracks overlooked a barren cement parade deck, each brick building less warm and personable than the next. If I'd seen barbed wire fences, I might have confused this place with prison.

Marine Corps Officer Candidate School, like Marine Corps boot camp for enlisted recruits at Parris Island, South Carolina, was gender segregated. There were many things that made the Marines different from the Army, the Navy, the Air Force, and the Coast Guard:* the small size, the amphibious focus, the stubborn adherence to tradition. But gender segregation was the element that trumped them all.

Men would be trained by male drill instructors (DIs) in a separate area of the school, while women would be trained by females. My platoon was infinitely smaller than the male platoons. If the Marines

---

* Officially, the Coast Guard belongs to the Department of Homeland Security, while the Army, Navy, Air Force, and Marines belong to the Department of Defense.

were made up of "a few good men," few women at all joined the Corps. Only 6 percent of Marine officers were women, meaning that my miniature all-female platoon stood alongside four towering all-male platoons, each containing several dozen men.

The Marine Corps is the most physically demanding of all the service branches. Aside from pull-ups over push-ups, the Corps' physical fitness test requires the longest run, at three miles. And it's the branch that until recently restricted the majority of its job opportunities for women, with more than a little pride.

Officer Candidate School (OCS) was a ten-week hallucination. Mostly I remember the feeling of bewilderment, being tossed from insult to insult, and running from one end of a room to the other away from shrieking voices. I remember my body being physically thrashed and my mind slowly losing its grip on any reality I'd once known. I cannot tell you the first names of most of the women I served with. I cannot even tell you with whom I shared a bunk for the most transformative ten weeks of my life. My lapse in memory has little to do with me and everything to do with the Marines.

We learned each other's last names because there were no first names in the Corps. There was Sir, and Ma'am, and an explosion of ranks. The Marine Corps had no interest in sentimentality. Names didn't mean a thing here, unless your dad was a general or a senator, and even then, the drill instructors would try their best to whip the nepotism out of Junior without provoking the US government. The fact that we had names at all was merely to distinguish one body from the next. We had become a collection of blood types and social security numbers. I came to know myself as everyone there came to know me: Bhagwati.

The DI's job was to make Marines. Weeding out the unfit, undisciplined masses who didn't deserve to wear the Marine uniform was the highest calling. Drill instructors guarded the gates to the Corps. And they were not easily impressed.

My introduction to Sergeant Instructor Staff Sergeant Baughman, the DI whose mission was to break me, was like all our encounters: I was stunned into paralysis and she was profoundly annoyed.

On day one, my platoon was seated at the front right corner of an enormous indoor classroom. Sea bags we'd meticulously packed back home with dozens of required training items rested at our feet. I looked to both sides of me, eyeing the women I would be spending the next ten weeks of my life with.

Like me, dozens wore thick, brown-rimmed military-issue glasses. These ghastly things were called BCGs, or birth control glasses, because they guaranteed you'd never get laid. I saw an assortment of short haircuts, courtesy of home clippers and the nation's cheapest barbers. Bouncy ponytails and tight braids. Soft eyes and steel jaws. We were mostly white and a few shades of Brown. Only one of us was Black. Seated beside several hundred men, we were thirty-four women.

The waiting was making my stomach turn. And then, without warning, two dozen camouflaged Marines—our drill instructors—swooped into the hall like birds of prey, driving us to our feet with flapping arms and hollering at us to haul our bodies and bags outside into the open air.

There was not enough room to funnel ourselves outdoors at the speed the DIs desired, and the helpless clot that we formed at the exit drove them mad. I saw a blur of wide-rimmed hats tipped menacingly downward over enraged eyes; thick webbed green belts and garish gold buckles cinched tightly around impossibly narrow waists; sleeves rolled up in perfectly pressed white bands; veined forearms, bulging biceps, and chiseled triceps; shiny black boots practically blinding us; wide-open jaws spewing forth an infinite fountain of contempt.

I was eventually thrust out into the daylight by the force of the candidates behind me. I ran, tripped, and dragged myself across the pavement following and followed by dozens upon dozens of human bodies, toward god knows what, but herded forward by the maniacal chorus all around me.

I looked up suddenly, and saw her for the first time, in all her glorious redness. Staff Sergeant Brenda Baughman stood huge before me, roaring at me to empty the contents of my bags onto the parade deck. Like a fool, I hesitated. She sensed my hesitation and pounced, swallowing the last bit of personal space that buffered me from the Corps. I desperately overturned my bags and gouged out contents with my arms. I watched in horror as sports bras and underwear scattered on the deck and toiletries ricocheted across the concrete between hundreds of scrambling feet.

There was no time to be embarrassed. The sheer sight of this mess on the pavement—*her* pavement, I discovered—sent her into hysterics. She was in my face, her throat crimson and voice barking so deep inside me I thought my internal organs would blow. She wanted me to clean this *nasty mess* up, *now*, so I crawled on hands and knees, clumsily gathering toothpaste, tampons, and an assortment of socks and T-shirts, and stuffed them back as quickly as I could into my sea bag. But I wasn't quick enough, and Baughman let me know this with a deafening howl.

Somehow I made it into the barracks with all my belongings, Baughman spewing disgust in my direction the entire way. I grabbed one of the few racks and footlockers that were still available and stood at attention, one heel desperately seeking stability from the other, chest heaving, as Baughman, another staff sergeant named Reyes, and a tiny pugnacious staff sergeant with wire-rimmed glasses named Hernandez sauntered up and down the middle of the squad bay, glowering and looking for any excuse to snatch the eyeballs from our skulls. We had arrived at our new home. We were Charlie Company, First Platoon.

Within hours, Baughman had firmly entrenched herself in my brain matter, and the position of attention became my new normal. We stood for hours each week with our heels together and feet at a forty-five-degree angle. I showered and fell asleep with my feet at attention. It was the pose I would reorient my life around.

Baughman was a modern-day Cassandra. She declared during our first week that 50 percent of us would be gone by the time our company graduated. She wasn't warning us as much as telling us how proud she was of that fact. On day one, a handful of us, including me, were placed on her Got to Go list. She was rarely wrong with her predictions.

Another candidate from New York City—an attorney who had signed up to become a Marine Corps Judge Advocate—didn't last a week in our platoon. She had desperately long, wild, curly hair. She couldn't put it in a regulation bun to save her life.

Today was her day of judgment. She had Baughman on her right and Reyes on her left. The onslaught was deafening.

They'd been calling her "Horse Face" since day one because of her mane. Horse Face had responded to the charge of mismanaging her hair like a lawyer, as if the barracks were in fact a courtroom. She tried to argue her case before Baughman and Reyes, but this was not the time or place for a lengthy opening argument.

First Platoon held its breath. Standing at attention in front of our racks and foot lockers, we were witnessing the downfall of an officer candidate.

Horse Face was a vegetarian, and a picky one at that. She was refusing to eat the chow provided at meals, meaning her body was not going to get enough essential nutrients to survive training. This was unacceptable.

"What kind of a Marine is a vege-*tar*-ian?"

"So you can kill the enemy but you can't eat a freaking cow?"

"We're training killers, here, Horse Face, not puppy lovers!"

"Betcha the enemy could use a nasty lawyer!"

It was endless. Absurd. Priceless. Horse Face left the next day. We were one woman down.

DIs had a way of imprinting themselves upon a human being's deepest layers of consciousness—infiltrating dreams, altering language learned at birth, reprogramming basic bodily functions and priorities, desires and fears.

Brenda Baughman was a Marine Corps legend. She was a ferocious wave of dark orange hair tamed mercilessly into a Marine Corps regulation bun, and freckled skin the color of nectarines that burned beneath the sun.

Provoked, Baughman was human napalm. When she spoke, she bellowed, and her throat turned red-hot, expanding its circumference in all directions. Blue-green blood vessels punched through the skin on her neck, throbbing with each expression of disappointment. Grown men twice her size cowered before her. She was scared of nothing and no one.

It was Baughman's job to terrorize me. I was slow to learn, and walked around like a wounded animal. The DIs had concocted two names for me: Furby and Bag of Wheaties. Furby because my big brown eyes reminded them of those Gizmo look-alike dolls, and Bag of Wheaties because they had neither the patience nor the desire to acknowledge my actual name.

As my other platoon mates began to catch on to the rhythm of OCS, I faltered. I was often the last to get something done in the barracks, whether it was putting the hospital corners on my rack or laying out my gear for an inspection. It's possible I had no business being a Marine. I thought too much. I questioned almost everything. I didn't understand the meaning of age-old customs and courtesies, and like a toddler, I wanted to know *why* everything was the way it was. For Marines, thinking before acting was a liability. You were just supposed to do what you were told, and fast.

I realized how completely unprepared I was for OCS when we marched to the armory and I had no idea what the big deal was. Some of the other women had been foaming at the mouth to get their hands on an M16A2 service rifle. I had no appreciation for guns. I didn't know the difference between a sidearm and a howitzer. When I stepped forward to pick up my rifle, I hesitated. I didn't have a clue how to hold it. At 8.79 pounds with a loaded magazine—they were not yet loaded—it wasn't so much the size that flummoxed me as much as its overall presence. Like the newness of holding a squirming baby, I felt like it had far more power over me than I did over it.

Going forward, we orchestrated our entire lives around these rifles. Baughman spent days trying to get me to hold mine correctly, and then weeks getting me to respect it. We marched with our rifles, held them above our heads, and worked out with them. We slept with our rifles, the barrels wrapped tightly to our hips, the cold muzzle making contact with our elbows. We took them apart into infinite puzzle pieces and put them back together, till we could do it without thinking. We practiced drill with them, slamming them against our chests and clutching them just so for inspection.

Nothing spoke to the urgent matter of these rituals like the Rifleman's Creed. We delivered this ode to our new companions in unison, like true believers:

This is my rifle. There are many like it, but this one is mine. My rifle is my best friend. It is my life. I must master it as I must master my life. My rifle, without me, is useless. Without my rifle, I am useless . . .

When I first hollered the creed, I silently rolled my eyes. My perspective on guns had been shaped by a lifetime of liberal immersion. I'd grown up in the Rodney King era. Cops used too much force, especially against people of color. Hunters, with their funny outfits and Second Amendment ramblings, epitomized America's strange obsession with violence, and I was a Bambi-loving, socialist-leaning peacenik. The Columbine massacre had happened six months before I arrived at OCS. I believed in gun control and had no desire to fire a weapon. Yet here I was. And much to my disbelief, with Baughman's direction, I became as preoccupied with my rifle as she needed me to be.

One afternoon we were in an outdoor training area, deep in the Quantico woods. We had carefully stacked our rifles in balanced clusters while we got ready for the next period of instruction on offensive and defensive tactics. I volunteered to deliver platoon numbers to the company gunnery sergeant,* first ensuring someone made sure to watch my rifle. You never left your rifle unattended, unless it was locked up in an armory. Never.

I got some head nods from my platoon mates and took off to find the gunny. As I about-faced to return to them, I heard Baughman hollering my name through the woods. I sprinted back to my platoon area. The rifles were gone. My platoon had vanished. Baughman was standing there, holding a single M16A2 at arm's length.

"Bhagwati, what the freaking hell is this doing here?"

I peered a little closer. I knew that serial number like my social security number and blood type. These days I could recite assorted facts and figures without thinking twice.

I sputtered some explanation, appealing to her sense of reason, sure that she would understand. She did not.

"Get on the deck, now! Damn it, Bag of Wheaties, get down!"

My disbelief at this unfortunate turn of events and my slowness to drop to the ground were not helping my case. Baughman's boots began kicking up the earth like a mad bulldozer, showering me in dirt as I hit the deck.

Baughman shoved my rifle over my wrists. "Count off!"

Flat on my belly, I pushed up, down, and up again, pathetically hollering, "One, two, three, *one*! One, two, three, *two*!"

"*Louder!* Sound off, Bag of Wheaties, sound off!"

When I finally crawled to my feet, covered in grime and clutching the barrel of my rifle with two hands, Baughman ordered me to double-time it to the classroom. As I took a seat, snickers erupted from the men around us. Going forward, I would never fully trust the women in my platoon. And I would never leave my rifle alone again.

---

* A gunnery sergeant is a senior enlisted Marine at the rank of E-7, with about fifteen years of service, generally in charge of keeping logistics running smoothly in a unit and known to have the fewest fucks to give about anything.

I learned that there were two types of women at OCS: those who were in it for themselves, and those who had some interest in the group's welfare. Sometimes this "what's in it for me" attitude manifested in subtle ways, like keeping your distance from a woman who was considered weak, either physically or mentally. Though weakness was not, in fact, contagious, the powers that be often lumped women together, because there were so few of us. So it was considered reasonable to avoid other women who were struggling. No one was expecting warmth and hugs here, but, at times, women acted as though humanity itself were a liability. Many of these women were die-hard careerists who only looked out for themselves. They made me seriously doubt the military slogan "I've got your back."

Part of me sympathized with their instincts for self-preservation. If we didn't look out for ourselves, we faced the certainty of getting picked off and kicked out. Still, I could never support their methods. I preferred a collaborative model of coexisting with other women in this merciless environment. Thankfully, a few other women in my platoon were on the same page, including some who'd already spent years as enlisted Marines, like Stephens, a tiny sergeant with boundless energy and a cowgirl accent who never had a mean thing to say about anyone; and Hudson, who took charge never to save her own ass, but to finish the job and make sure none of us were making the platoon look bad. The only Black woman in our stressed-out band of misfits, Hudson was calm and confident, as experienced as Baughman or Reyes but never revealing the fact that she herself had been a drill instructor in order to maintain cohesion in our platoon.

While I struggled to fit in with my female counterparts and become worthy of the Corps, I was comforted by the fact that at least physically, I was in my element. In our first physical fitness test at OCS, we ran as a single company. I started my run with a pack of men and finished the end of my third mile with a solid sprint. As I began to walk it off, a male drill instructor appeared out of nowhere, accusing me of cheating, saying I didn't run the last mile. I objected, but he silenced me with one look. One did not have a two-way conversation with a DI.

"What's your goddang name, Candidate?"

"Candidate Bhagwati, Sergeant Instructor!"

"Get out of my face."

The next morning I was summoned to my platoon commander's office. Baughman gave me strict instructions not to fuck it up.

I stood at attention before the captain's desk while she pored over paperwork. We were not permitted to look an officer in the eye. With broad shoulders, square hips, and an average build, our platoon commander was nothing like the wiry, fiery Baughman.

"What was your run time yesterday, Candidate Bhagwati?" she asked me firmly. I muttered my time, calling her Ma'am.

"And what was your last run time back home?"

The times were different by a few seconds.

"You're dismissed, Candidate Bhagwati."

"Ay, Ma'am." I about-faced, poorly, and pivoted out the door as fast as I could. No one accused me of cheating on a run again.

In training evolutions where we were integrated with the men in our company, I felt free to run fast and push myself. I often noticed then that despite our DIs' tendency to call us *nasty females*, a handful of men were struggling as much as our weakest women. Unfortunately, not enough of our training was integrated.

My platoon's introduction to traditional Marine Corps physical training involved a dramatic safety orientation around the O-course (obstacle course), a series of towering hurdles made of splintered logs, wooden beams, steel poles, and thick, sinewy ropes, all of which had to be traversed within two minutes. It was the kind of upchuckworthy evolution that made me want to be a Marine.

The O-course started with a vertical jump and flip over a bar that was several feet off the ground. Before we gave it a go, our gunny placed a ramp beneath the bar. I looked beyond our O-course to where the male platoons were training. I didn't see any ramps.

I felt heat rush to my face. When I stepped up for my turn, I refused to use the ramp. The DIs didn't seem to care. But they certainly didn't encourage anyone else to avoid it. A few of my platoon mates followed my lead, but several didn't, even though I knew they didn't need that damn ramp.

As if the ramp wasn't enough of an insult, women also had three minutes to finish the O-course, an extra sixty-second cushion that no one seemed bothered by but me. However, much to my surprise, I sometimes found myself deliberately slowing down as I ran through the course. I knew that I could go faster, but I was cautious, knowing I could catch an extra breath between obstacles if I needed to. I had no incentive to do my best.

It seemed our DIs were not of one mind about double standards in the Corps. During group conditioning, the DIs led us to the pull-up bar. Only five women in our platoon aside from me could knock them out. Most women struggled to do even one or two, the pain visible in their faces. Baughman was aghast, storming up and down our platoon of sweaty green bodies. I was relieved to have one arena where she left me alone.

Back at the barracks that evening, Baughman gathered us together. Her tone was deadly. She said that to earn respect in the Corps, we had to train to do twenty pull-ups, just like the men. Some of the women looked confounded, but I felt a sense of hope. Baughman was the first Marine I met who demanded that women excel.

• • •

The longer I lasted at Officer Candidate School, the more I realized women were expected to behave differently from men in the Marine Corps, in ways that had no bearing on our ability to defend the nation, and in some cases, working entirely against it. Hair regulations were one of the best examples of the Marine Corps' gender dysfunction.

There was no shortage of male pride in the mandatory buzz cuts or "high and tights," sheer above the ears and shaped ever so gently into peach fuzz on the top of the skull—but they were forbidden to women.

One day, Peterson, who had blown her hip out in a previous class and come back ready to graduate or die trying, had cut the hair on her head dangerously close. She was crossing over into male territory and Baughman was not having any of it. We were not permitted to be like the guys. We got a theatrical lecture from Baughman on haircuts that day, and my platoon mate was forced to grow hers out another two inches.

I was convinced someone had deliberately designed hair regulations to make our lives a living hell. Long hair entailed unusual sacrifices. Hair could not *fly away* in strands, which meant loose hair had to be matted down with ounces of toxic goop that hardened over the skull like a helmet and caused irritating headaches. Ponytails were not allowed. In order to control long thin strands, wiry frizz, relentless curls, or other forms of unruliness, pins, bands, or other hair-taming devices were allowed but had to be completely invisible to the human eye once inserted. I had arrived at a place where the defense of the nation and *America's Next Top Model* intersected. Women's hair in the Corps was nothing short of a styling miracle, and though it sounded ludicrous, it was a very serious matter.

I hadn't thought twice about cutting my hair short. Much to my surprise, the majority of women in my platoon arrived at OCS with long hair, and willingly sacrificed the few hours of sleep we had each night to wake up an extra hour early to painstakingly primp, press, braid, mousse, gel, and pin their hair into Marine Corps–approved hairstyles. I would never understand why someone would choose to sacrifice sleep in this crazy place. (I empathized when news broke fifteen years later about the military's hair regulations discriminating against Black women—many hairstyles like cornrows and dreadlocks were banned by the military, even though this placed an unfair burden on Black women to adopt white hairstyles. Still, the whole fuss of women's hair regulations made me wonder why any of us were allowed to grow out our hair in the first place.)

One day, as we stood at attention before our racks, our DIs laid into us, proclaiming again that we were all a bunch of nasty females.

Our collective lack of femininity was making them hysterical. One of my platoon mates, Riley, a remarkable outlier who'd arrived at OCS with a PhD, had provoked this latest outrage. For a woman, she had a lot of hair on her arms and legs. We had all noticed, but what did we care? We were too busy surviving OCS.

Perhaps the DIs realized they couldn't single Riley out. We were all ordered to shave our legs at OCS from that day onward. This decision was well grounded in Marine Corps tradition. Beauty 101 lessons were part of the Corps' long history with regulating women's appearance. I found out later on that drill instructors subjected previous generations of women in the Marines to strict makeup lessons, including the proper application of lipstick. I was apparently living through an era of progress in the Corps.

• • •

Occasionally, someone or something would challenge my understanding of what mattered in this place, and what mattered most to me. Biel was a hyperintelligent candidate with flaming red hair like Baughman, but without any physical presence. She was bony and pale, with the posture of a jellyfish. To top it off, she had a high squeaky voice that was driving the DIs nuts.

Biel's voice was all wrong for the Corps. She could not possibly command troops sounding like a cat toy. Baughman and Reyes took arms against Biel's DNA and made it their mission to transform her wobbly soprano into a firm baritone. This morning, our platoon stood for ages, witnessing an attempt at a medical miracle.

"Get some goddang stinkin' *bass* in your voice, Biel!" Reyes bellowed.

They had her reciting everything from the four weapons-handling rules to the "Marines' Hymn" at the top of her mousey lungs. Biel belted out Marine Corps 101, trying to roar. She was no lion.

Despite her gelatinous slouching, Biel refused to flinch. Eventually, the DIs got tired of yelling, their vocal cords straining after weeks of shaming us into order. Three weeks later, Biel graduated OCS.

Biel's trial planted a question in my mind about what might

actually constitute presence, beyond the muscle mass, height, and deep voices of our male peers. My limited view—and the Marine Corps'—was based on patriarchal notions of toughness. This skinny, squeaking woman became an officer of Marines twice her size. Biel had verve, and she knew it.

I still wasn't so sure about myself.

. . .

I hardly received any mail while I was at OCS, but about halfway through I got a letter from my father. It was handwritten in almost indecipherable professor script with the black felt-tip pens that were his trademark tool over decades of writing near-perfect lectures from scratch. I was not expecting his letter. It was a confession. An apology.

I fear I am the reason you joined the Marines.

Emotions began to rumble through me. I was in no mood to dive into them, least of all here. And besides, something had already changed inside me. Dad's letter was too little, too late.

. . .

Despite our DI's best efforts to reform me, after several weeks at OCS I still hadn't picked up the rhythm of the place. I was one of the last two pariahs left on the Got to Go board. All the other rejects had quit or been kicked out of OCS. I was halfway between here and my former life, and the struggle was obvious to everyone around me. I spoke like some by-product of the ivory tower. Keeping up with all of these customs, without knowing why things were the way they were, was a commitment they wanted me to make on faith alone. I resisted, however subtly.

In the seventh week of training, we were all given an opportunity to drop on request. I gave it some serious thought, but I couldn't bring myself to quit. What would I have returned to? I could picture Mom and Dad, delirious with self-satisfaction, making my next plans for me. *Of course they didn't accept you. You don't belong there.* The scenario made Baughman and the Corps look like a benevolent escape plan.

One Sunday I attended church services on base with Jules, a candidate from Los Angeles with a knack for push-ups. Time with God was one of the few moments in which we were allowed to exist without DIs. I didn't believe in either God or religion, but I needed a break from the barracks, so I went.

Jules was Korean American and barely five feet tall. When First Platoon hiked through the woods, she ran the whole way to keep up, half of her body invisible beneath her enormous pack.

The military chaplain interspersed an otherwise typical sermon with anecdotes about the responsibilities of leadership. I didn't know what I was doing here. In church. In Quantico. In this camouflage uniform. I began crying, and then, realizing I was crying, I could barely stop.

Without saying anything, Jules reached for my hand and held it for the rest of the service. I looked over at her, my face wet with tears, and she nodded quietly. It was the only act of human connection I remember from those weeks. It was the most un-Marine-like thing anyone had ever done here.

A week before graduation, my status was still unclear. Baughman took me aside one morning on the parade deck while the company was practicing sword drill. I was the only one having trouble remembering basic moves.

"Bhagwati," she said, almost whispering. "Not everyone is meant to be a Marine. Do you understand?" She looked up at me, and it suddenly hit me that despite her demonic presence, she was shorter than I was. We made eye contact. I stopped breathing.

"Yes, Sergeant Instructor."

This new tack, gentle and deadly, got to me more than all Baughman's hysterics combined.

A few days later, I was called before the school commander, who would determine whether or not I was fit to be a Marine Corps officer. Lieutenant Colonel George Flynn was a Naval Academy graduate, and like most commanders of major Marine training facilities, an infantry officer. He sat at his desk like a monarch on his throne, flanked by two beefy young captains who commanded two of the all-male platoons. They glared at me as though I'd better not make an ass out of myself.

"Good morning, Sir. Candidate Bhagwati reporting as ordered, Sir."

I stood at attention, stiffly, till he told me to stand at ease. I separated my feet and placed one hand over the other on my lower back.

Flynn looked at me curiously, like he didn't know where to begin.

"Candidate Bhagwati. I'm trying to assess if you're Marine officer material. You haven't done much to prove to me that you deserve this honor."

He looked at me expectantly. I stayed quiet, my hands glued to my back.

"Just look at these grades. Do you even study?"

Flynn's question was rhetorical. I can't tell you if my mediocre grades were the result of the shell shock of being at OCS, or if I was unconsciously rebelling against the Corps. It may have been my way of saying *I am so much better than you, why should I even bother?* No amount of studying Marine manuals was going to make me ace those bizarre multiple-choice exams, where human experience and the entire history of the world were reduced to Marine sacrifices and victories on the battlefield. The Marine Corps wanted me to suspend all reason. It was causing some kind of short-circuit in my brain.

But none of that mattered now. The colonel was already shifting his tone and flipping through files.

"Candidate, when you were team leader at the Crucible and you were tasked with coming up with a plan, you let someone else on your team take charge."*

It was true. "Sir, that candidate had a good idea. This candidate didn't want to ignore her, Sir."

---

* The Crucible is a grueling team-building training exercise at the end of recruit training and OCS that takes place over several days, on very little food and sleep.

This response was Marine blasphemy. All folks seemed to say around here was that leading Marines was about asserting oneself, all the time. But I didn't care if someone else was stealing my thunder. Her idea *was* a good one. I didn't realize that the entire concept of joint leadership, something I would associate years later with women's willingness to work together and share rather than dictate and take credit, was not something the Corps appreciated.

Flynn seemed thrown by this. He looked at me silently. Something about my expression, which I hoped was still blank, must have triggered disdain in him, because he suddenly changed his tone.

"Your drill instructors say you're still having trouble adapting. And do you know why, Candidate?" He was speaking like Baughman now, accusing me.

I really wished I knew why.

"Because you're *lazy*, Candidate."

I was used to being insulted at Quantico. It was the price of being slow to adapt to Marine culture. But something deep inside me began to rumble. It was one thing to pick on me for not getting the Corps, its inane rituals, adherence to centuries-old traditions, and the psychotic earnestness with which Marines talked, walked, and did just about everything.

But *lazy?* Please. All I'd known since I was born was to work my ass off. And before I knew it, this one-way reaming session had turned into a two-way conversation. From somewhere beyond the Corps, I responded, with more than a little gall.

"No, Sir, this candidate is not lazy."

Flynn's eyes widened.

"Ex-*cuse* me?"

"This candidate"—I said, not skipping a beat—"is *not* lazy. Sir."

The pause this generated was infinitesimal. I felt the colonel's eyes boring into me as I stood still, steadily, with nothing to lose, eyes looking forward, over Flynn's head.

I was not backing down. I knew where I came from. And I knew who I was. I suspected whatever game Flynn was playing, he knew this, too. I'd finally found my voice.

"You're dismissed, Candidate."

I about-faced and got the hell out of there.

That day I volunteered to lead our platoon on its run through the woods, calling cadence while we ran far too slow for my comfort. I was desperately connecting colors of the rainbow to everything Marine, hollering as loud as I could. If these maniacs were going to kick me out of here, I was gonna go down fighting. My platoon hollered right back.

"Back in 1775 . . . my Marine Corps came alive! . . . First there was the color red . . . to show the world the blood we shed! . . . Then there was the color gold . . . to show the world that we are bold! . . . Then there was the color green . . . to show the world that we are mean! . . . Oorah . . . Gimme some!"

That evening, Staff Sergeant Baughman took me aside. She told me enthusiastically that Flynn was letting me stay. Baughman was no longer reprimanding me. She was proud.

On the verge of our commissioning, our DIs summoned us for a platoon photo. Marines didn't smile in official photos. If we bared our teeth it was only to bite your head off. Nonetheless, I stood in the back row, the only candidate with a grin on my face.

CHAPTER 4

Womanizing the Corps

Colonel John Allen was my introduction to the Marine Corps' living legends, men whose tactical greatness on the battlefield was superseded only by their flair for the theatrical.*

Allen commanded the school for the Marine Corps' newest lieutenants with the personality of a messiah summoning his troops to victory. He fancied himself a scholar-warrior and spoke to us about the realities of the Corps with a thundering voice that caused most of us to quiver. He recited Rudyard Kipling's "If—" as if our lives depended on poetry. I couldn't stand Kipling's racist colonial musings about my savage Brown ancestors. But none of that mattered here.

*If you can keep your head when all about you
Are losing theirs and blaming it on you,*

---

* Allen would one day become a four-star general commanding legions in Afghanistan. He retired early from the Marine Corps in 2012, after sending hundreds of emails to a Tampa socialite at the heart of the national security scandal involving CIA director David Petraeus and his biographer, Paula Broadwell. Later, Allen vouched for Hillary Clinton before the masses at the Democratic National Convention, and ultimately took the helm of the Brookings Institution.

If you can trust yourself when all men doubt you,
But make allowance for their doubting too . . .

Allen himself became Kipling, and his final words, *you'll be a Man, my son!*, landed with confusing resonance, making me wonder if either Allen or the creator of Mowgli, Baloo, and Bagheera had intended any inspiration for me or the other women in our company.

The Basic School (TBS), or The Big Suck as we quickly came to call it, was where officers spent six months learning the fundamentals of Marine Corps infantry, so in the event that any of us—attorneys, adjutants, artillery officers, etc.—were required to take over a provisional rifle platoon, we knew what to do. It was intensely physical, with agonizing hours that turned any natural rhythms we might have had left after OCS completely upside down for good.

We were now lieutenants. Enlisted Marines saluted us, and we were expected to act the part of officers, even if we knew little about what that meant. TBS was the first environment where male and female officers were fully integrated. One woman was mixed in with twelve men in each squad. We lived in the same barracks as the men, though I shared a room with three other women.

Gender integration was a rude awakening for everyone involved. I was told about a recent scandal at TBS in which a male instructor had had sexual relationships with female lieutenants. I didn't know the details, but the young captains who supervised us now were on their toes.

At TBS we learned to work as a unit while cultivating special contempt for one another. Each member of a squad of thirteen Marines had to regularly rate all the other members, causing the term "squad peer evaluations" to morph to "spear evaluations," or just "spearevals." We ranked one another ruthlessly, and the men in my squad often listed me toward the bottom. I got used to this after a while. I even expected it.

My big mouth was not helping. One day a guest instructor was sharing war stories from the Balkans. He'd been talking about joint operations with the other branches of service and must have said something about the Navy's submarine program, because when he finished his lecture and opened up the floor to questions, I stood up and projected my voice across three hundred bodies toward the front of the room, saying, "Lieutenant Bhagwati, Sir. I was wondering when submarines were going to be integrated with women."

My fellow lieutenants surrounded me with boos as I sat down, my head still held high. Those who remained silent fidgeted in their seats. The captain seemed surprised by the question, but didn't know the answer. (It would take another fifteen years to open submarines to women, after the usual political brouhaha about the cost of installing female bathrooms and the risk of close living quarters had quieted down.)

We learned to shoot in the icy Quantico winter. I took to it naturally, which surprised the crusty guys around me, hoping I'd drop more shots and wondering why I didn't. They didn't associate marksmanship with women. My staff platoon commander, a captain and the first infantry officer I would have as a boss, was terribly amused by my ability to shoot a target at five hundred yards without any previous experience.

When I was stationed on Okinawa a year later, I shot the range high among hundreds of Marines, some of whom had served for years, many in combat arms fields that demanded pointing big weapons at hopeless targets. When the range officer in charge announced my name as the best shooter, the sea of camouflage uniforms around me parted. Faces turned grim when they saw the name belonged to a woman. I'd really messed with their sense of order.

Shooting became a respite from the disillusionment I felt in my new world. Marksmanship had nothing to do with brawn. In fact, ego was a liability. To shoot well, you had to be in a state of relaxed concentration. You allowed the body to breathe and timed a slow and steady squeeze of the trigger with the pause after exhaling. Rushing, wanting, or trying too hard to hit black were recipes for failure. This was the domain of yogis and mystics. I dug everything about it.

My company learned to shoot in the elements, lying prone on

the snow-caked ground, our rib cages encased in load-bearing vests, freezing rain falling on our faces, air biting into our lips and turning our fingers into ice, so that at times I couldn't tell where my skin ended and the trigger housing group began. At OCS I'd spent weeks cradling my weapon at all hours of the day and night, learning to fear it and to fear losing it. But I didn't truly feel the rush of the Rifleman's Creed until I was at TBS, inserting live ammunition into cartridges, feeding rounds into my chamber, and shooting down range.

I may have been a crack shot with a rifle and pistol, but that's where my natural talent ended. I was absolutely out of my league when it came to other field skills, which made up the crux of our curriculum in the tick-infested woods at Quantico. We became intimate with every dip and dive in that thick, mad wilderness, and were expected to find our way out regardless of the visibility, the elements, or the time of day or night. Instructors spoke about the contours of the natural world with laserlike precision. Using a basic compass and a laminated map of the woods, we were expected to locate an infinite supply of tiny red ammunition cans, mounted on top of wooden stakes like mailboxes, each marked with a distinct yellow number, planted years ago in the soil, thick with rust.

Navigating three-dimensional terrain by looking at a two-dimensional map was supposed to be a teachable skill, but I was completely lost. A life spent traversing the urban wilderness prepared me for none of this. My idea of land navigation was knowing streets from avenues. My idea of wildlife was subway rats, pigeons, and roaches. Each hill and valley in the Quantico woods apparently had its own unique personality. How was I to know one peak from the next?

I tried desperately to keep up, leaning hard on the experienced Marines in my company to help me with skills like patrolling. I spent every free Saturday trekking through the woods, hunting down those insufferable bright red ammo cans from morning till sunset, until the blisters in my boots bled and I was thoroughly exhausted. Occasionally I got so lost I wouldn't make it back to the starting point on time, and I'd get exasperated looks from the officer in charge, which paled in comparison to my own frustration with myself.

According to the Corps, women (Women Marines, or WMs) were as bad at field skills as Black people (Dark Green Marines) were at swimming. Absurd stereotypes and specialized acronyms followed us everywhere. Failure was expected of us, and success was considered a rare achievement.

I remember walking into a squad member's room where my fellow lieutenants were hanging out. Someone had a Marine Corps poster lying out on a rack. One of my squad members, Jim, grinned at me and said, "You know what Crowley said would make this poster even better? If *she* weren't in it."

He pointed at the woman in the photo—a lone female Marine, in her female-only uniform, a round bucket cover,* skirt, and high heels, surrounded by half a dozen large, impressive-looking men in combat gear and sharp dress blues.

"What do you think of *that*, Bhagwati?"

"I think it's fucked up," I replied, turning red and walking out.

TBS was my first full introduction to men in the Corps. Some thought I was a spy, a backhanded way of referring to my allegedly big brain, and a stark reminder that not only did I not fit in here, I was probably working for the *other side.* "Blowing shit up," a phrase I was coming to know as key to a Marine's basic sense of his own identity, was not my primary obsession. And I asked questions unbecoming of a Marine, about culture, history, peoples.

No one appreciated my extra layer of interest. My spearevals reflected this. When the company was asked to pick adjectives to characterize me, I was rated as everything from "intellectual" to "sleepy." (The Marine-like traits we were all going for were things like reliable,

---

*A cover is a military hat. Men's barracks covers were broader and more angular than women's, and were widely considered to be superior. The women's bucket cover looked dumpy in comparison. It hardly seemed like something a real Marine would wear.

tough, and strong.) And while I was allegedly being assessed on my potential to lead Marines, I faced another layer of evaluation as a woman. As hard as I tried, it seemed impossible to shake this.

One afternoon, our company was cleaning weapons in the armory. We'd just finished a weeklong training exercise in the field and we were exhausted. Sleep was near, and the anticipation of hot showers and clean sheets was the only thing keeping us on our feet. Everything about being in the field was intimate. It wasn't just the shared experience of being taken to our physical or mental limits. It was the shared fluids.

It was going to a place beyond filth, beyond stink, where bodily discharge, environmental substances, and man-made chemicals combined to assault our flesh and senses. Putrefied sweat, vaginal fluid, and seminal emissions; caked blood and blisters on the verge of combusting; CLP;* Tabasco sauce and toxic runoff from everyone's favorite Meal Ready to Eat, the digit-size sausages known as the Four Fingers of Death; pound cake crumbs stuck like parasites on smeared green-brown camouflage paint; saliva, snot, earwax, and crusted eye goop oozing from the sockets—it was a merciless mess.

These forays into and out of the field provoked all sorts of spontaneous commentary from the prior enlisted grunts. It was a veritable slam poetry session. (One infantry boss I had years later referred to the vaginal discharge that was inevitable after days of not showering in the field as "grilled cheese." This phrase incited hysteria among the other infantry guys, who had never heard anything more hilarious in their entire lives.)

Jim was a prior staff sergeant and infantryman, older than most of us by about ten years, and therefore some kind of mentor to the rest of us sorry new lieutenants. I guess he figured the experience he'd gained in the Corps gave him a license for uncensored honesty. While we were scrubbing down weapons, he stopped to take a long, hard look at me.

---

* Cleaner, lubricant, preservative was the chemical substance we used to clean weapons. We kept it in tiny bottles in the buttstock of our rifles.

"Bhagwati, looking at you makes me never wanna have sex with a woman again."

This stung, as it was meant to, but I bore it, like most insults. I'm not sure what Marine coming out of the field was pinup material, but it seemed as though women's primary function here was considered to be the ability to turn men on. Mostly I was reminded that if I wasn't in the Corps to be someone's eye candy, I had uprooted the laws of nature and challenged men's purpose and sense of direction.

These reflections came freely and often, always unsolicited and unprovoked.

Officer dress regulations required collared shirts, trousers, and a generally conservative fashion sense. Knowing less about the relationship between the sexes than most women I served with, I took the regs at face value. The price of not playing the gender game, of not knowing there was a game in the first place, was steep.

My fellow women officers had clearly read some handbook I hadn't. Several women tested the limits of what constituted acceptable civilian attire. They avoided the mandatory collars. Their necklines plunged. Glutes and hips protruded through tight pants, and heels and makeup were all in. These variations on strict military regulations were clearly condoned, or overlooked. My male peers couldn't get enough of it. It was the most live stimulation anyone could get without leaving the base.

I was still processing the mixed messages. I was sitting in the barracks one evening in civilian winter attire—baggy pants, a warm turtleneck sweater, and comfortable clogs—waiting for liberty to sound. Some punk in my squad—he was one of dozens of small, bulldoggish Marines with a Napoleonic complex—looked at me and snickered.

"Bhagwati, your wardrobe reminds me of my grandmother's."

I shrank. Comebacks like "Your grandmother must be really hot" were nowhere in my toolkit back then. Not even a blip on the radar. I remember he was in charge of our squad during a night patrol. We were all lying prone for what seemed like hours, and I must have nodded off for a second, because all I remember was his shadow breathing into my face, "Bhagwati, wake the fuck up. If you weren't female I'd beat the shit out of you."

The only way I got this asshole to stop haranguing me was to outrun him in physical fitness evolutions. And I did. Often.

This was not what I signed up for, this place where women who didn't spend time working the guys into a sexual frenzy were looked down upon. I thought I'd be a part of an elite warrior society where the women who joined didn't give a shit about turning on some loser dudes by flirting or flashing skin. The Amazons, Joan of Arc, these icons of warrior society were mythical in this world. How my female peers couldn't see the role they played here blew my mind. It took several weeks before I realized things weren't as simple as that.

Tyler was one of my roommates, and a woman I might not have met were it not for the Corps. She was a real gem, an honest-to-god good person. Didn't judge or speak ill of others. She wasn't book smart in the least—I remember the men in the platoon making enormous fun of her for not being able to do basic math, while I seethed in anger in her defense—but she worked hard. She had a fantastic, enviable southern twang. She was petite and white, and unlike me, she dressed like a rock star during liberty. She quickly became one of the company's sex symbols. There wasn't a day that went by when she wasn't rejecting some idiot lieutenant's advances.

On Saturday evenings before heading out into town, she was obsessed with beauty rituals. One day she taught me the finer points of trimming the pubic region. I came to understand that her boyfriend back home preferred her like that during sex, which was the first time I'd given thought to the possibility of options down there, and the fact that someone else's grooming preferences might determine how much time I spent in the shower.

One night I heard sounds outside our barracks room but I didn't think much of it since we got so little sleep as it was. Outside our door, Lieutenant Hughes was trying hard to enter the room. He was an enormous man who had graduated from one of the big-football, big-fraternity colleges in Texas. It took a lot of booze to make a guy like Hughes drunk. He was shit-faced. He forced the door open and made his way into Tyler's bed. From the top bunk on the other side of the room, I shot up.

"Phoebe?"

There was a long pause. Was I imagining this?

"Phoebe?" This time, with more urgency.

"I got it, it's okay," she sighed.

It sure as hell didn't sound okay. Hughes was making sounds drunken morons make when they're trying to shove arms down trousers and roam hands over breasts. I listened harder, staring blindly in the dark toward her rack. Phoebe, one-third his size, was calmly talking to him, as if she were negotiating a hostage release. Her own.

Below me on the bottom bunk, my other roommate groaned and turned over. How was everyone not awake and alarmed? I sat through several long, hard minutes of back and forth, till Phoebe talked Hughes up and out of her bed, walked his hulking, drooping body out of the room, and locked the door.

I was bewildered. "You all right?"

"Yeah." She sounded tired. Resigned. Like she'd dealt with this kind of thing before.

No one mentioned the incident again. Except me. In the morning, I sat next to Napoleon in the large classroom, and when we were on break, I mentioned Hughes's frightening break-in.

"It was like he was going to rape her."

I didn't have a chance to finish my thought. Napoleon jumped down my throat with quick, agitated whispers, as though I'd crossed a major line.

"You need to shut your mouth. You could get Hughes into trouble."

Whatever flurry of nonsense he said to protect Hughes from facing any consequences for his actions, it made me pause. He was no ally. I looked around the room. Phoebe was sitting there stoically, looking like she'd moved on. She hadn't asked me for help. And my other roommates didn't care one way or another what had gone down in our room last night. I let it go.

My personal education about Marine culture happened in total isolation, and often in silence. I was learning fast now. Women appeared to have two choices in the aftermath of a sexual violation: either act like nothing was wrong and play along, like Phoebe, or suffer privately and keep quiet. If speaking out was actually an option, I hadn't seen anyone try it. Thus far, I'd been too busy just learning to get by.

Being a woman in the Marines was hazardous. Being sexually naive and emotionally sheltered like me was deadly. No one was going to save Phoebe, or me. The band of brothers didn't apply to us. And if sisterhood existed, I certainly hadn't seen any signs of it.

Baughman did not warn us about this. The tiny number of experienced women who might have been mentors or guides in some other universe were too mired in their own survival strategies in the Corps to lend a hand or offer words of wisdom to the next generation of GI Janes. Putting up and shutting up were being bred into us. Watching other women flail or fall by the wayside became a spectator sport.

It wasn't our fault. Sticking together would have been suicide here, as risky as lack of dispersion on a patrol through enemy territory. If there was not enough physical space between you and the next *female*, you would both be taken down. There was no refuge where you could seek solace in order to survive the next day. That was the stuff of sorority fiction and feminist mythology. In the Marine Corps, we had to adapt, assimilate, and move on, or suffer. And who the hell wanted to suffer? Most of us left that shit back home.

• • •

Things took a turn for the worse when, several months into training, I blew out my right knee running through the woods with a squad automatic weapon. I had to have surgery at Bethesda Naval Hospital and sat out several weeks of field training on crutches, making daily visits to the physical therapy clinic. Not being able to train with my company frustrated me to no end. I could no longer keep up physically, and the men grew resentful. I remember Hughes making fun of me as I stood on crutches, supervising my company's PFT, and thinking, *Motherfucker, you're lucky you're not in jail.*

In order to prove myself, I asked to be dropped to the next company and start my training over from scratch, but my commanding officer refused, insisting I'd done enough. I graduated The Basic School in the bottom third of my class, despite my best efforts to recover from surgery, absorb the curriculum, and fend off extreme scorn from fellow lieutenants. I was just relieved to get out of there.

Unfortunately, I'd been selected as a communications officer, something not remotely in the realm of my interests or natural skills. Technology was not my thing, and never would be. I had put intelligence officer at the top of my wish list, but any knack I had for analysis, languages, and observing human behavior was tossed out the window for the needs of the Corps. The thing I most wanted to do—human intelligence—was still off-limits to women, for no good reason I or anyone else could think of. My infantry captain had given up hope on my tactical skills long ago and once told me gruffly during an evaluation, "You're fairly intelligent." He had not meant this as a compliment. Perhaps denying me the intelligence field was his way of ensuring I stayed miserable.

The Marine Corps didn't believe in either comparative advantage or cultivating one's interests. At least, not for women like me. If the Corps had an HR philosophy, it would be "shut the hell up and do what you're told." But none of these occupational choices mattered much for me in the long run. Marine culture was the most galvanizing force in my life now.

*   *   *

Rites of passage in the Corps involved one of two things, violence or sex, and often both. Engaging in Marine rituals was high-risk, but alcohol was the fluid that lubricated the nerves. It either took the edge off or sharpened it, depending on what unresolved issues were eating at you most.

My first invitation to a strip club in Quantico came early on in my communications training. The clubs outside military bases were as plentiful as tattoo parlors, dive bars, and chain restaurants. Despite urging from my fellow lieutenants, I declined. I was not interested in paying people to take off their clothes. Married, single, monogamous, cheating, it didn't matter—my fellow lieutenants were all in.

The next morning I was overwhelmed with stories about lieutenants getting lap dances from the girls out in town, some very likely the girlfriends or wives of men we would soon be commanding in the fleet. I felt embarrassed and kept my head down.

A handful of women in my class joined the men on this field trip, a decision I didn't understand back then. These women weren't queer, as far as I could tell, although if they were, "don't ask, don't tell" would have made them anxious about tagging along. Whether and how uniformed women took part in these sexualized rituals was confusing. We worked our asses off for the rank we held, but moments like this reminded me that we only seemed to be separated from the young women writhing on the poles by the dollar bills in their thongs.

The roles service women chose—in my case, the proud protester—had lasting repercussions, so we had to be sure before acting. To be a woman who commanded men in an institution where men had asserted their physical and sexual dominance for so many generations was complex. "Leaning in" was irrelevant for us, and resisting seemed like a path to martyrdom. I was still discovering the rules of engagement in this world. It seemed time to test them.

Captain Hoffman was one of our main instructors at Communications School and a first-class egomaniac. He was obsessed with the infantry. He made up for the shame and indignity of his lesser status as a communications officer by telling stories about how much time he'd spent working with the grunts. His proximity to infantrymen was supposed to mean he had gained some kind of leg up on the rest of us POGs.[*]

The man had a squeaky, slippery voice that he tried to mask with the intensity of his storytelling. Today, Hoffman was going on as usual about some deployment with an infantry unit. He considered himself an entertainer, so he shifted gears with some levity. I had no idea what led Hoffman to this particular theme: "I mean, if he's on top of you, and if there's nothing you can do about it, then you might as well stop fighting and relax, right? I mean, why waste your energy?"

Oh *shit*. Did this guy just give us guidance about how to be raped? Quick glances were exchanged around the room. Or maybe it was just me, looking for affirmation. I was still fuming when his lesson finally came to an end. Against all laws of self-preservation, I approached Hoffman.

"Sir, can I talk to you about something for a minute?"

"Sure, Lieutenant Bhagwati."

He took me into a tech closet on one side of the room. There was no backing out of this now.

"Sir, that joke in class, about the woman being raped. It was really offensive."

There was a pause and a shift in his eyes, as if he were taken aback.

"I mean, don't you have a mother, or maybe a sister, Sir? Imagine if that happened to them."

Even in the shadows, I sensed him planning a response. He spoke slowly, methodically. Without the bravado he usually dressed his words in.

"Okay, Lieutenant Bhagwati. I get your point. Thanks for talking to me. Is that all?"

"Yes, Sir. Good afternoon, Sir."

---

[*] Persons Other than Grunts, the Marine Corps' primary term for losers.

My rape lecture made the officer rounds at school. It came up one day when I sat down with my supervisor, Captain Wolf, for a performance evaluation. After I'd spent a year in the Marines, he was the first officer I'd met whom I looked up to and who valued my contribution. Not surprisingly, for the first time in the Corps, I was doing well among my peers.

"Lieutenant Bhagwati, I see you as one of these officers who's going to be really good." He compared me to another captain at the school, a physical specimen and a woman whom every man and woman among us worshipped. In my mind she was Xena the Fucking Warrior Princess. I could barely contain the compliment, and I'm pretty sure I blushed. (Almost twenty years later, Captain Nethercot would be the first woman in history to command Officer Candidate School.)

"But the culture, it's going to challenge you. And it'll be up to you to pick your battles." I took this to mean that Hoffman was not the only knuckleheaded Marine who told casual rape jokes. But I already knew that. Wolf was trying to warn me before I got out into the fleet and commanded Marines on my own: success meant overlooking the Marine Corps' sexism.

I had no idea how to do that.

· · ·

The lieutenant who graduated at the top of our communications class was a woman. Robbins was a prior enlisted non-commissioned officer, and focused on her studies to the point of ruthlessness. I happily rooted for her, because she had outperformed all her male peers, causing more than a few guys to grumble.

Several months after graduation, I was in Okinawa, commanding a radio platoon. I ran into Robbins at the post office. I'd just experienced a public humiliation on the rifle range that was playing on repeat in my mind. A staff sergeant who was working the range had approached me before dozens of wide-eyed enlisted Marines.

"Ma'am, do you like to dance?"

I looked up from my rifle. "Excuse me, Staff Sergeant?"

"Do you like to dance, you know, salsa, merengue . . ." The guy gently swayed his hips. He was no Ricky Martin.

"Yeah, sure." The men around us, junior both in chevrons and years, grew silent. The staff sergeant was my age, maybe older, but I outranked him, and military law prohibited anything he thought he was going to get out of this exchange. Marines were staring at us expectantly. I tried to block them out, looking away, fidgeting with my manual, where I was recording all my shooting data.

"You wanna go dancing in the club this weekend?" The wind on the range seemed to suddenly die down.

It finally came to me, this word that a lifetime of submission had repressed deep down.

"Uh. No."

"You sure, Ma'am?"

"Yeah. I'm pretty sure, Staff Sergeant." I looked at him. I held his gaze. He eventually wandered off.

With my authority in question, I knew I had rejected his advances too mildly. The Marines around me were expecting more, and judging from their reactions, I had seriously disappointed them.

I told Robbins the story. She listened without any emotional response. I had forgotten how icy she could be.

"What should I have done?"

"Well, guys don't mess with me, because they know I won't put up with it."

I was rattled. Even subconsciously, I began to connect the dots. *Women who are targets deserve to be.* Robbins may have been a poster girl for the Corps, but she was no longer mine.

My bruised ego did the only thing bruised egos do when they want to fight back. I found some additional reason to harbor contempt for Robbins. Fueled as I was by a desire to find some additional flaws in a woman who didn't help other women, it came easily: Robbins had married an officer several rungs up the chain. In the military, fraternization was a criminal offense. It's why the staff sergeant shouldn't have hit on me, and why it was suspect that Robbins had married a senior officer.

The truth was, I didn't actually care about any of this. The Corps made a huge stink over sex and love between consenting adults, but didn't seem to flinch over nonconsensual incidents. I had barely scratched the surface of how hypocritical a world I was living in. And behind closed doors, I was already beginning to break the rules.

CHAPTER 5

Heart of Darkness

My own descent toward violence was slow, but not unpredictable. I was a kid who had heard *you're not good enough* one too many times, and was sensitive enough to believe it. I was not a natural-born Marine. I was a nerd, an Indian, and a woman. I questioned too much too often. But one thing was for sure. The voicelessness I'd felt throughout my childhood had stoked a world of rage inside me. It was only a matter of time till it came out.

As a Marine, I knew violence as something that, like my sexuality, was not yet fully realized.

On one unforgettable day when I was twenty and still at Yale, I had become the object of an explosive parental intervention. They had cornered me in their living room. Everyone was standing. My father was shouting, my mother looming supportively by his side. I had committed the most horrendous offense imaginable: I had gotten a B on my college report card. It was quite possibly the first B of my life, but what followed had been coming for a long time.

"You," Dad fumed, "are wasting your education."

What my father was trying to say was that I was not just wasting my education, I was wasting my life, and calling their lives into question. Trying my best at Yale despite a world of hurt was not the point. This failure of mine would have karmic cost. We were dealing with ancestors and family reputations. The disgrace had intergenerational, cross-Atlantic consequences. This was a matter of second-generation Desi diaspora shame.

It was a royal mismatch. I looked away to deflect Dad's vile pronouncements and Mom's ravings. I cowered and attempted to escape the living room. They followed, down the hallway to my bedroom, shouting the whole way.

There was really no way out of this, never living up to what I would have been had I just been born in India, where parents didn't have to deal with the embarrassment of ungrateful progeny, where daughters existed to obey and serve, and parents were worshipped, idolized, and always right.

I was in no place to stick up for myself. Dad's cruelty had many layers. He loved to pick on those who couldn't defend themselves. He attacked from the flank, taking down my friends.

The company you keep
Divorced parents
Lost children
Idiots
Degenerates

Insulting the young women who had befriended me over a lifetime of feeling alone was too much. I took his abuse, but I would not accept what he was doing to them. A lifetime of suppressed feelings rose up.

Stop it, stop
Stop saying that
Stop calling me fat
And ugly
I'm not stupid, just
Leave me alone

And with this flood of resistance, something else arrived. A moment without any foresight. A brief taste of freedom. My hand rose quickly, striking him across the arm. I wanted more, but I did not yet have the confidence to summon a solid jab to the jaw. It was enough for both of us. I froze, while he grew silent.

My mother inhaled the whole world, pronouncing, as if we didn't all know, "Oh my god, you hit your father."

Her dumbfounded voice and wide eyes made me sink my head to my chest in absolute despair. I sobbed inconsolably for hours on end, so that for days afterward my head hurt too much to move, or speak, or eat.

The feeling of being this small in the world would prepare me for the Marines like nothing else. I shut down, and for the first time, felt my potential for indifference. I didn't need to think or feel anymore. Emotional detachment felt powerful. Engaging again with my true feelings would require incentive. And that kind of reckoning would only happen after years of humiliation in uniform.

· · ·

As a radio platoon commander in Okinawa, I was in charge of fifty-odd Marines, most of whom were young men. The transition to management was a shocking one. I leaned heavily on the senior enlisted men in my platoon to show me the ropes while I learned to navigate what being an officer was all about. Most of my Marines were teenagers and men and women in their early twenties. I was twenty-six. We were all on the other side of the world from home. My first weekend as a commander, one of my lance corporals got caught drinking and driving out in town. I had the whole platoon at attention, reaming them all for his mistake. I was balancing absolute power and a multitude of relationships for the first time in my life.

Before and after work, I hit the gym hard, and ran along the roads in town like a zealot. I had healed my knee and had no intention of slowing down. I'd cut my three-mile run to under twenty minutes, provoking a "Damn, Ma'am" from the Marine who ran my shop, Gunny Cain, as I ran past him on our platoon PFT.

I had a lot to prove, and a lot of rage to work off. It seemed that most of the treatment I was subject to in the Corps was outside of my control. The one thing I could do was commit to getting stronger. It was my personal mission to become physically larger than life, to outgrow the skin-and-bones, Gandhi-esque frame I'd been cursed with by genetic default. Working harder than everyone else had only gotten me so far, because I was trapped inside this miniature body.

So I trained, relentlessly. I trained with men who were enormous and capable of superhuman feats, carrying three times their body weight, some double or triple my size. I would not let the Corps define how little I was, how little I could do, how little I could move, or pull, or push. I was hell-bent on proving them all wrong.

The more men wanted to hold me back, the more I wanted to fight. Most guys wanted women to train with women, like some auxiliary fitness club where saying sorry was required before you kicked someone's ass. This was no way to get stronger, to improve oneself, to be a better Marine.

I ate carefully, conscientiously. I ate large amounts of animal protein. I started taking creatine. I lived for the bench press and stacking on more and heavier plates as each month went by. The lat pull-down machine was making my back huge. In my tank tops and shorts, I got shameless stares from guys at the gym, thick with some combination of awe and lust. I ignored them, did more sets of pull-ups, and sauntered in and out with my sweat-soaked towel, hungry for the next workout.

Two years into the Corps, I returned home to visit my family. My mother took me shopping for new civilian clothes, because my back and arms no longer fit into my wardrobe. She was terribly distressed over this fact. I asked her if she knew what I did for a living, if she knew what a Marine actually *was*. She ignored me.

My father, who always had the last word, who relished dishing out phrases that damned women and girls like me to the deepest realms of low self-esteem, told me emphatically, "No man will ever marry you."

• • •

Most Marines found their inner warrior at boot camp or OCS. My switch should have been flipped in those first few weeks with Baughman, but I was on a delayed timeline. I faked my war face as I floundered through the Corps' aggression-building lessons. The natural-born killer within me was nowhere to be found. Like a dormant virus, violence found its way in me when it was good and ready. Two years into the Corps, I finally discovered my bloodlust.

While stationed on Okinawa—the *Rock*, where Allied forces and Japanese soldiers had slaughtered one another and civilians in the last and bloodiest battle of the Pacific War—I volunteered to attend the Marine Corps' close combat instructor training program. The system, which had been developed to deliver deadly hand-to-hand blows to the enemy, was being revamped by a legendary warfighter named George Bristol. The Corps was now cautiously integrating women into its instructor ranks.

Bristol, then a lieutenant colonel, had spent over thirty years practicing Eastern martial arts, making him a perfect fit for developing the Marine Corps Martial Arts Program (MCMAP). He was trying to update a close combat system known for its brutality. Gouging out eyes and disemboweling guts were beloved jarhead preoccupations. Marines needed to do all of these things to the enemy when necessary and still look dignified on the nightly news. And now revolutions and riots the world over were being televised 24-7. MCMAP was going to bring some Zen and civility to bone crushing.

The program had a belt system just like the traditional Eastern arts, and training was now required across all ranks for promotion. I earned my tan belt on a hard green field at Camp Hansen from a short, fiery lieutenant who made up for his lack of height with chunks of muscle and a contagious amount of energy. Throwing giants across the field without breaking a sweat, he looked like Mighty Mouse.

We started our daily regimen by "body hardening" with a partner, training each limb and major muscle group to withstand punches, kicks, and throws. For minutes, we'd pound forearm against forearm, fist against belly, and bootlace against inner and outer thigh, till the grimaces on our faces turned into a passive acceptance of our reality. We wore our bruises with pride.

Unlike professional gyms or dojos, we didn't use mats when we threw each other to the ground. We'd hip check bodies hard to the earth, tumbling again and again across the field as we learned the proper ways to roll and fall without causing too much permanent injury. The older Marines twisted their faces in pain or tried to mask it, poorly, as they hurled their beaten bodies down to the dirt with guys half their age. I couldn't get enough of this, so when the opportunity to become an instructor arose, I jumped at it.

In our green belt class of sixty-some-odd Marines, Sergeant Ortiz and I were the only women. Eternally reliable, Ortiz was the platoon sergeant of my radio platoon. It was a huge résumé builder for any Marine. At four eleven, she was not to be underestimated. Ortiz was a quiet, humble, and determined spitfire, organizing our ragtag group of junior Marines into an effective unit that was ready for deployment at a moment's notice. She was also a master of pull-ups, with veins bulging from her wrists and forearms.

Our green belt instructors were three of the Marine Corps' senior instructor trainers. They wore black belts marked with one or more red stripes, each signifying how much advanced training they'd received. Our group was led by a tough reconnaissance master sergeant and two staff sergeants—one six feet eight inches of solid muscle who was a larger version of Sly Stallone in both speech and size, the other a wide-chested African American karate sensei who somehow mustered equal amounts of ferocity and warmth. I was in heaven.

I returned to the barracks each day with bloody knuckles, torn palms, and purple legs. Ortiz and I were at the top of our game. Guys back in our battalion made comments that we'd changed their minds about what women could do. One guy, a lanky sergeant with a mouth too big for his own good, hinted that he'd be happy to serve with us in combat. I made him repeat it out loud, and privately rolled my eyes.

When we trained, I carefully partnered with guys who were larger than me, sometimes carrying Marines who outweighed me by eighty pounds up hills and across fields, fighting in mud, sand, and wet grass, and tossing them again and again to the ground. Their weight was one thing, but what was hardest was finding their center of gravity within all that body mass. They didn't fall as easily, and lifting them over my shoulders felt like carrying unwieldy tree trunks. Most of the guys treated my body as if it were any other, and I appreciated that. Some dudes hit me harder than necessary for learning purposes. We all had different points to prove. I took it willingly.

One morning I stepped up for a pugil stick battle with a Marine who had an upper-level belt in tae kwon do. Pugil sticks were quintessentially Marine. Using them simulated close combat with a rifle, with each end representing the bayonet and buttstock of an M16. But rifles and bayonets were deadly and graceful. Pugil sticks were heavily padded, clumsy, and enormous, like Q-tips for giants. We often looked like clowns in our headgear.

I was tired of waiting for a fight, so I swung at his head, hard. He had no patience for my enthusiasm, settling things quickly with a single uppercut to my jaw. I barely saw it coming. I sank to my knees, hearing my instructors' voices and watching various shades of green dance before my eyes. It was the first time I was knocked out. I could barely put words together, but I glowed on the inside with pride. I didn't care that I had lost. I was trying to prove that I wasn't afraid to fight.

A few days before graduating the course, we were practicing chin jabs in an indoor facility. I took a stance like Muhammad Ali, left foot forward, left hand protecting my skull, knees bent and relaxed. I swung my right elbow back and low, preparing to strike the heel of my hand an inch from my partner's jaw. I came up swiftly with the full force of my right hip behind me. Something popped. And just like that, I was on the ground.

Marines started running my way. An older recon guy was calmly hunched over me, hiking my trouser up over my knee. This was the same goddamned knee that had healed from surgery a year ago. My kneecap had flown out of the socket and settled back in. And as if the pain itself wasn't bad enough, the knee was swollen as wide as the largest part of my thigh and not much was keeping the patella in place.

Just that week I had volunteered to represent my battalion and go to Quantico for the Marine Corps' black belt course, where I would be training with Bristol himself. I had one working leg. I sat down with our head martial arts instructor, whom I'd come to idolize.

"You think I'll be okay, Master Sergeant?"

"Ma'am, you'll do better than some of the guys there," he said, smiling. "Just take care of that knee."

Back in my room with my new green instructor belt cinched around my trousers, a brace wrapped around my kneecap, ibuprofen and bags of ice at the ready, I tried to fast-forward my healing. The battalion commander had been briefed about my injury. To curb any doubts I might have had about the black belt course, he sent word that I was going to go stateside unless my femur was sticking out of my thigh.

It was settled, then. I was headed back to Quantico.

· · ·

In our first of six weeks of black belt training, my squad was deep in a three-hour evolution, a deceptive word that suggested the gentle drag of time. The twelve of us had been bear-crawling on our hands and feet for an eternity, sticking our asses high in the sky as we inched our way over a grassy landing zone.

I had long since stopped feeling my arms. It was a thing of beauty how much the body could do when it lost all sensation.

We were starting to resemble an accordion, with folks going too fast or too slow. Disorder was death to Marines, so someone's voice down the line had begun calling cadence to keep us moving forward in sync.

One . . . two . . . step! One . . . two . . . step!

I kept up, my head down, eyes blinking sweat onto the grass, determined to bear-crawl till hell froze over, never allowing a knee to hit the deck.

All of a sudden, a large pair of black boots appeared under my chin. I had no time to think. I was hauled into the air like a rag doll and tossed over a wide set of shoulders. I saw blue sky, tree line, and my squad's camouflaged rear ends still pointing toward the heavens and trudging along. In the confusion of being upside down and half delirious, I didn't see a face. I wondered what asshole instructor, what godforsaken beast of an infantryman with an ego too large for his own good had dared to fireman's carry me, my chest smushed into his back and my ass still facing the clouds.

The voice would give him away. It hinted at thunder but never broke. Always composing verse, George Bristol filled his sentences with carefully constructed pauses that lingered and haunted, that made you wonder if the next burst of words would take your head off. He was a midrange tenor, but his language operated in a place that was deeper and more deadly. His voice was as smooth as mercury. He would never need to raise it, this large, sadistic monster of a man. If he spoke any louder, ceilings would crack, grown men would shudder and crumble, and never get up again.

Lieutenant Colonel Bristol, who had birthed this close combat program from the darkest recesses of his imagination, had removed me from my squad as if he'd just orchestrated a high-stakes kidnapping. As if I was about to be sent to a very dark hole in the ground. I was now being paraded around the eleven men below me. Immersed in their own physical pain, they didn't even know that I was gone.

Bristol's nose was crooked from years of being smashed against fists, knees, floors, and walls. His white skin was roasted from years of patrolling beneath the sun. He was the size of Godzilla, each leg a mighty column leveling the ground beneath him. I was one-third his mass, making me the goddamned queen of underdogs.

Bristol was a master manipulator of human emotions. I was spellbound, and wary of letting him in. Rumor was he had delved deep into psychological warfare and special operations, and mastered the grisly stuff American moms and dads never knew about and congressional intelligence committees took to their graves. This made him legendary. A prior enlisted infantryman, he'd been in the Corps more years than I'd been alive, and spent several of those years manhandling America's enemies overseas.

We had circled my squad three times now, I his nonconsensual partner in a dance that had no clear mission. I was trying to breathe as his shoulder cut into my gut. Upside down, I saw my squad, still inching forward. Whatever he was up to, I couldn't stand that I was getting a break from my squad's collective agony. I had to earn my respect.

Bristol was lecturing me on nothing in particular, but then started talking about my role here, informing me that I was responsible for my roommate's poor performance. He was talking about Riley, the PhD from OCS who'd been responsible for our leg-shaving orders, and the only other woman in the black belt program. She had a temper like a maniac, and was just not cutting it physically. He wanted me to know that if she had a problem, it was my problem, too. This was no feminist motivation speech about women lifting one another up. He was insulting Riley and taunting me at the same time. This was all a game to him.

I thought, *Goddamn it, put me down, motherfucker.*

Eventually, he did. I yes Sir'd everything under the blazing sun and scurried back to my squad.

Bristol was eager to prove that I was different. It wasn't enough for me and my squad to know that I was a woman. He had to show us.

We were on the obstacle course early one morning. Bristol had been shadowing me that day. Officers did this often, calling it supervision, but sometimes I wondered. He was like a mosquito in my ear, whispering tales about each obstacle in the evolution, giving me tips that I didn't need on this course that I knew in my sleep, while I heaved and pulled myself along with my squad. At some point I thought I'd lost him, and I exhaled a bit under my flak jacket. Moving as a unit, we began to traverse the wooden hurdles. Suddenly Bristol was there.

He stopped our squad and approached me, casting a shadow over the course. He reached his enormous arm behind my head and grabbed my hair in one giant fist, pulling my skull back, slowly, as if to make sure my face would be seen. I saw the men in my squad as though I were seeing them for the first time. I do not know if the same was true for them.

I wasn't looking for protection. If he was going to use me as a prop, I wanted witnesses. Bristol could only execute this sort of thing in front of the guys. My guys. Humiliation of women had a particular flavor when executed before silent men.

"*This* is what they'll do if they get their hands on you. What are you going to do then, Lieutenant?" My face was frozen but my brain was operating on rapid fire now.

The smart-ass in me totally agreed.

Uh, I don't know—buzz my head, Sir, but the Corps won't let me.

The other side was goading him.

Say it, Sir, say what they'll really do to me. Or just fucking do it. Or are you scared I might cry? I was preparing for his next move, which I knew would happen without any warning. I was no hero in a Ridley Scott movie. *G.I. Jane* was a fairy tale. There were no comebacks with Bristol.

He eventually let go. Maybe it was the quiet stink in my eyes, or the steadiness in my presence. I had learned by now to hold and wait for him to shift gears. When he moved on, we went back to training as if nothing had happened.

I was a lightweight compared to the hulking guys in my course. They responded to me in different ways. The other officer in my squad, a major and a helicopter pilot who treated me like a daughter as much as a training partner, pissed me off to no end when we partnered up in ground fighting. A former competitive wrestler and a push-up champion, he just sat there beneath me, refusing to offer any resistance for me to practice my guard or mount techniques.

"Come on, fight me, Sir!" I hollered at him.

Another time, I was matched with a dude twice my weight, and after rolling around for a bit back and forth he just straddled me, sat down on my pelvis, and checked out. The guy was practically taking a cigarette break. I couldn't move out from under him to save my life, though I was making a hell of an effort to. Bristol walked by, unamused by my wriggling.

"You're not going to win like that, Lieutenant. Figure it out."

A few days later, I was summoned into a boxing ring to spar with one of our instructors, a beefy midwestern staff sergeant whose back and chest threatened to swallow my skinny Indian skeleton whole. I took a fighting stance, ready to pound on him and receive whatever punches he threw at my rib cage and gut. I summoned my adrenaline and braced for impact. Whatever I lacked in size and brawn I tried to make up in willpower and capacity to take a pounding. But he refused to meet me in the center of the ring, saying, "I need you to put on a flak jacket, Ma'am."

I paused. (Pausing was a luxury occasionally afforded to officers, a relative privilege that only sometimes made up for the fact of being female.) Something wasn't right here. The men in my squad who fought before me in the ring had not worn flak jackets. Why would I strap an extra sixteen pounds onto my chest and back to take on the Incredible Hulk when he already outweighed me by 125 pounds?

Pauses were risky when you were physically exhausted but not nearly done with whatever physical pain lay ahead. Pauses broke your momentum and messed with the chemicals that were short-circuiting your better instincts not to hit someone twice your size. I was spent from having my ass kicked for days on end, indoors, outdoors, and every which way by very large Marines, on one good leg no less. I was exhausted just trying to walk straight.

I was the only woman in this squad. And I'd experienced just enough to know the difference between safety and bullshit. The staff sergeant was a Muscle Milk–guzzling machine-gunner whose main education in life came from Marine Corps infantry. He was our lead instructor and an expert on tearing humans limb from limb. I couldn't possibly adopt a separate training uniform and be padded up like some princess.

The rest of my squad, a group of infantrymen, a reconnaissance Marine, and a massive former cook, grew still, sweating profusely, watching this drama unfold.

"Ma'am, it's standard safety gear for females."

"But I don't need any safety gear."

"Ma'am, it's—"

"Staff Sergeant, the guys don't have to wear this. So why should I have to wear it?"

"Ma'am." He paused, and summoned a poker face for me, the female officer, who, despite any natural laws he thought ruled the order of things between men and women, technically outranked him.

He said this cautiously.

"It's for your protection, so you don't get hurt." He blushed. *Oh lord.*

The idea that this burly staff sergeant and his cadre of tough guys had given enough thought to consider the safety of my breasts stunned me. It meant he'd actually considered that I had breasts. I quickly shook the thought from my head.

What female weakness was it this time? Was it breast cancer, or baby making? Or, god forbid, was it simply cosmetic, that they didn't want my boobs to suffer the indignity of bruising?

I didn't believe that the Corps gave a rat's ass about the health of my breasts or any infant's chances of successfully breast-feeding. They were *my* goddamned boobs, and little did they know that I did not consider myself either a milk production machine or a cautionary tale for oncologists. Being forced to wear breast protection gear, among a sea of hardened dudes with rock-solid chests, was like few other humiliations I'd endured in uniform.

Everyone was waiting. My squad knew I was feisty and strong-willed, but they didn't know how far I'd take this. Some of these guys tiptoed around me, these enormous, hulking men, treating me like a doll. *I* had to toughen *them* up. A few were blessed with common sense, and I respected them for it. My favorite instructor was a short, stocky infantryman, Sergeant Doyle, who wasn't afraid to kick me hard in the gut and send me flying across the room to get me to learn something. He didn't believe in coddling me.

This was not that Marine. But I was fed up and getting nowhere, and the embarrassment was slowly taking over any will I had to hold out. What was I going to do, complain to Bristol, who had likely orchestrated the whole thing in the first place? I slung the jacket over my precious chest and swung as hard as I could at that cocksucker.

· · ·

Bristol hazed the first woman who attempted the course a year ago, a physical specimen who was built thin and compact like me but could do more pull-ups than lots of guys. Several hours a day for six weeks, in the heat of summer, he'd subject her to extra drills, after everyone else had been dismissed from a full day of grueling training. Apparently, Bristol's infantry minions nervously watched him from the sidelines until they told him what he was doing was unfair, and even more, dangerous. I don't know if he was trying to prove women didn't belong here or simply knock her out of training with heat exhaustion or heart failure.

I was his second experiment, though in what I wasn't sure. Bristol's bottom line was that killing took a certain brutality that women did not possess. No amount of superior fitness, physical strength, or sociopathy would make women suitable for the art of killing. Remembering my rugby team from college, I thought Bristol had a lot to learn about women.

Pepper spray—oleoresin capsicum, or OC—was one of Bristol's favorite training tools, the kind that separated the boys from the men, the pussies from the warriors.

When our OC qualification day finally arrived, Sergeant Doyle calmly stood in front of me. I closed my eyes, as if that were going to help. An equal-opportunity distributor of pain, Doyle held the can of pepper spray three inches from my eyelids and pulled the trigger for what seemed like minutes, till my forehead and cheeks dripped with chemical ooze, my skin seemed to melt, and my eye sockets felt like they'd been filled with gasoline and set on fire.

Virtually blind, I swung at a series of targets with batons, elbows, knees, and fists, egged on by my instructors, and using whatever other senses I had to decipher what around me was real and what was not.

After I'd made it through the striking course, cursing whichever desperate Brown people had first surrendered their hot peppers to these sadistic white men, shaking my head furiously to try to purge the burn from my brain, Bristol came toward me, hovering.

I distinctly sensed glee in his voice when he told me, "It's like watching *Planet of the Apes*."

I took this to mean I was the fucking monkey.

The fire lasted for several hours, and no amount of rinsing our eyes with cold water eased the burn. A bunch of us from my squad were huddled together, commiserating, waiting and praying for the searing to stop. One recon Marine, his white face splotched with red marks and eyes still clamped shut, compared it to having his head dipped like French fries into a vat of boiling oil. Some guys were crying. Bristol stood above us, overlooking the chaos, satisfied.

I might have been Bristol's experiment, but he became the object of my curiosity. He must have known there was a way to get to me. It was only a matter of finding and pushing the right buttons, and no Marine had found mine thus far.

Bristol's war stories were private, but he revealed information if it served his purpose. He wanted me to believe that he and I shared many things in common. He let me know he was a cultured man, a reader, an aficionado of travel and philosophy.

He dug into my past. He sat me down in his office one afternoon and talked about his appreciation of my education, my cultural grooming. During his martial arts forays around the world, he'd spent time in northern India with an ancient society of wrestlers. Bristol made me his private audience. He knew I was listening closely, that he was building a bond, that intimacy between us could be created through a regular dose of intellectual banter, that his attention would make me vulnerable, and susceptible to the power of suggestion. I knew all this, even as I let him draw me in. As if I had a choice.

One day the whole sore-as-hell lot of us were sitting in an indoor auditorium, relieved to be resting our bodies. Bristol was standing on stage, sucking us in with tales of Mogadishu, one of many spots in the world where he had left his mark and probably thousands of shell casings. God knows what had been declassified by then, but he began to recite verse, which became clear to me was something he had written himself, about his exploits.

Kipling's "White Man's Burden" had found its way to Quantico, once again, only Bristol's burden was not just the weight of empire. He was talking about taking a human life. He was describing a nameless, voiceless Somali, a pair of dark eyes on an equally dark-skinned person, a man who was exchanging his last look with Bristol. I wonder if this man felt hatred in his last breaths, and if his contempt for Bristol was anything like mine. Had Bristol shot him then, in the skull? Or had he cradled him in his arms? Or did Bristol stand, detached, in the rubble and dust till the Somali man was dead?

This was Bristol being human, perhaps. But if he was expecting me to open my arms to his war story, he was going to have to wait a long time. I was tired of tough white men with weapons suddenly realizing their own humanity, or lack of it, at the expense of Brown and Black lives around the world. What right did he have to pen this poem about this man's body? He was a trained killer by choice. His confessions needed to go elsewhere.

While I judged him silently, he was still reciting. Slowly, familiar verses came to me.

And the seasons, they go round and round.
And the painted ponies go up and down.
We're captive on the carousel of time.

My eyes, which had barely recovered from the recent onslaught of pepper spray, were unblinking and wide. I had no idea if anyone else knew the man had just invoked the folk singer Joni Mitchell in a lesson plan on killing, without even skipping a beat. For all I knew, they thought the big bad boss was still talking about the desert. I loved Bristol for knowing these lyrics. I hated him for using them. He had no business quoting "The Circle Game" while teaching us to tear apart human flesh. I would have much preferred that he recited death metal.

I needed a moral rerouting, badly. I was repulsed by Bristol, and at the same time, I wanted desperately to be more like him. I wanted his approval. He was getting to me.

• • •

I wasn't at my best. I was still nursing my waterlogged knee, which was only getting worse with each training day. During lunch hour while the others chowed down, I headed to the rehab room at The Basic School, my old haunt, where a loyal Navy doc gave my knee electrical stimulation and an ice down, and then wrapped me back up for afternoon training. It was my second tour to this room in a year and a half, and some of the sailors remembered me.

My damn kneecap wobbled around in a pool of jelly, reminding me of my fallibility and pride with every movement I made. It reinforced my inferior size and strength, and boiled down the essence of this fight to how much will I had. Some of my squad members wondered why I would subject myself to this pain. At the end of each day, I could barely walk without going numb. I fell asleep on several tablets of Naproxyn and bags of ice melting in between my legs.

I had to prove I could make it on my own. Every time someone in my squad said to take it easy, I wanted to stab them. We had just done the O-course five times in a row. I was making up for my injury by muscling my way through almost completely with my upper body. On one occasion, surprising even myself, I had managed to climb a rope without using my legs. But this was no long-term strategy. Bristol came to my side and took a long, slow look at me while my face attempted to mask the misery of stabbing knee pain.

He said, in almost a whisper, "It's easy to be hard, but it's hard to be smart."

Perhaps he was alluding to his own battered skeleton and the wisdom that came from decades of retrospection. But probably not. I'm sure the motherfucker wanted me to quit. I wasn't going to give him the satisfaction.

· · ·

Two weeks later, these days had turned into long and restless nights. Bristol appeared and disappeared during training, without notice, without much input or insight. I saw him now in my sleep. I was armed in my nightmares, moving through thick Quantico woods with a bayonet, ready to gut anyone who got in my way. Bristol's eyes were on me, assessing all angles and steps, reinforcing my vulnerabilities without saying a word. There was no exit.

Bristol called me into his office one week, out of the blue.

"You're not cutting it. You're hesitating. Something's missing, Lieutenant." I was disappointing him. And yet he had me by the throat. I was lulled by his voice. Bristol had found it, finally, the son of a bitch, found a way to unnerve and destabilize me, to prove to me I would never be good enough to belong in his universe. Bristol was playing dad. *My* dad. I told him on the inside to go fuck himself. I'd rather take another blown leg than this psychodrama bullshit. And yet there was no way out of this chokehold but through.

Our final training evolution was something out of my dreamscape. We traversed a six-mile confidence course through the Quantico woods. I was half jogging, mostly limping, biting my tongue, muscling my way through and over each obstacle with limp legs, like a mermaid. We each had one simulated wooden rifle, carved extra long to account for the length of a bayonet. I clutched this stick, cursing my floating kneecap, shuffling along.

I was pissed off—at Bristol, at my knee, at the goddamned universe. As we turned the corner on the last obstacle, our instructors stood with cans of pepper spray at the ready, pulling the trigger, misting us as we shut our eyes and passed through the cloud. I opened my eyes and saw Bristol, looming and enormous, his giant hand outstretched in my direction, long fingers ushering me toward him. Furious, I forgot my pain. Legs suddenly pumping, I charged at him like I was going to knock his skull off the root of his neck. I was conscious of nothing.

Yes. Like that. Yes. Bristol was speaking, but I was somewhere else. Still a woman enraged, I left him behind me in the OC cloud. The adrenaline was wearing off. I limped uphill, facing my meathead staff sergeant, throwing a swing that had nothing left in it, and we both knew it.

"Harder than it looks, huh, Ma'am."

Oh, go fuck yourself, Staff Sergeant, I thought, half sinking to the ground. So much for storming the hill. Either way, it was over.

I walked downhill, slower than ever, and joined my squad. Whatever I did, whatever madness-induced overmedicated haze I was operating within, Bristol was impressed. His eyes were wide and clear. When he gathered our class together, the glorious, dirt-encrusted mess of us begging for rest, he improvised poetry, calling me the one-legged wonder. I had finally arrived.

Bristol promoted me at graduation to first lieutenant. Each member of my squad had purchased a new knife, a weapon that, thanks to my agility, I'd taken to naturally. I looped my black belt with a single red stripe around my camouflage trousers and tucked my switchblade away in my pocket, ready for use at a moment's notice. I was a new woman.

CHAPTER 6

A Few Good Men

The Marines I have seen around the world have the cleanest bodies, the filthiest minds, the highest morale, and the lowest morals of any group of animals I have ever seen. Thank God for the United States Marine Corps!

—ELEANOR ROOSEVELT

Bristol had distracted me and a hundred other Marines from the aftermath of 9/11. A month before his course, I watched the Twin Towers go down on a tiny television box in Okinawa—*crash, burn, crumble*—ad fucking nauseam. My hometown was burning, and, stuck on this useless coral rock eight thousand miles away, I could do nothing to help.

In December 2001, with my black belt cinched around my waist, I got back to Okinawa and returned to training, hard. I took my platoon through predawn drills, turning a bunch of radio operators into hard-core warriors. When we ran by the infantry barracks in the dark wearing flak jackets and carrying simulated bayonets, the grunts would stare at us. I was getting my Marines ready for something big.

As a GI in the Far East, I was at the intersection of foreign power plays and indigenous ways of living. Okinawa was not only the graveyard of one of the bloodiest battles of World War II. It was the birth-place of karate, a world-class scuba destination, and a region famous for its healthy lifestyle and diet, with elders who defied aging, living active lives into their nineties and beyond.

Okinawa was also the site of major protests by locals, who were fed up and furious with the presence of American GIs after a handful had raped and murdered Okinawan women. Occupying someone else's land with big guns, bigger jets, and no sense of history was never a pretty picture. Indeed, across the Far East, GIs roamed with little to no supervision, free to discover the nature and limitations of their manhood. I had no idea how deeply immersed in this world I would be until my battalion deployed to Thailand for three months.

We were in Pattaya, Thailand, as part of an annual joint exercise meant to bolster relations between the United States and our Asian allies. I spent my working hours there with a handful of junior of-ficers and senior enlisted Marines, behind a desk in a massive tent, keeping communication up for the battalion, monitoring data net-works, phones, and radio connections.

When systems were up and running, and the senior officers had long since disappeared, one Marine monitored traffic while the rest of us took it easy. It was an opportunity for a young officer like me to shoot the shit with my gunny, or join him in watching Dwayne "The Rock" Johnson lay waste to enemy bodies on an imaginary battlefield in a bootlegged action hero DVD collection.

Two lieutenants in our battalion spent much of their downtime in one of the communications vans that was attached to the tent. It was an odd place for a break. One day, I got curious.

"What are you doing?"

They exchanged dubious looks, nodded their heads, and brought me into one of the vans. They shut and locked the door and turned on a monitor.

I wasn't sure what to expect. Video games?

From dozens upon dozens of files, they chose one and clicked play. It wasn't Donkey Kong. It wasn't Mario Brothers. Whatever digital shit boys were blowing up before *Call of Duty*, it wasn't that, either.

It was worse than I could've imagined: some poor blond woman, buck naked and stretched out on a bed, moaning *hard*, her sound some strange primal mix of agony and pleasure, as a glorious German shepherd entered her again and again and again.

"Fuck yeah!" howled one lieutenant.

A strange sensation came over me. I mean, Jesus H. Christ, I'd never seen a dog's penis in action, and it was *huge*. But as I sat there, my face turning the shade of raw bacon, I sensed something worse: titillation, and a horrifying hint of wetness. Then quickly, embarrassment and disgust.

As if the dog panting like a champion, enormous tongue sending pools of drool across this woman's belly and breasts, wasn't hideous enough to impress me, the lieutenants decided to show me the depth and breadth of their subject matter by clicking on additional videos. They introduced me to a rich panoply of animal penises entering all variety of female human beings. A wide cross-section of the mammalian kingdom was on display, as if the Westminster Dog Show, Animal Planet, and pay-per-view had joined forces for a marathon viewing extravaganza. The larger the penis, the more delighted the lieutenants were. They alternated between creepy silence and demented laughter. For all I knew, these officers were as hard as these working animals. For all I knew, these van walls were covered in semen.

I wanted to run and scream, but I sat there, body frozen, stuck in time. I took it all in, frame by frame, my mind trying to summon the right reaction, trying to understand why my ass was still sitting on that chair, in that pathetic little metal container. Why I hadn't marched out of there in a huff, or even surreptitiously wandered away, or come up with some fantastically witty comeback to put down these married-with-children, award-winning Marine officers.

My mind blocked out a good portion of this experience, each animal thrust causing some kind of dissociative state for which I would later be grateful. Eventually I left the box, forcing out some lame excuse about not leaving the gunny alone at the desk, as if the gunny now or ever needed a lieutenant's assistance.

We never spoke about this again. My education about the Marine Corps' underworld was just beginning.

•　•　•

On nights in Thailand, between twenty-four-hour shifts in the tent, groups of us climbed into baht buses—open-air pickup trucks that served as taxis for tourists—and headed toward Pattaya Beach at high speed, cool wind tearing through the tropical heat, lifting the weight of responsibility back on base. When we offloaded, we split instantly, vanishing through crowded streets toward bars, restaurants, shops, and clubs.

I spent most of my evenings wandering the streets by the beach, getting Thai foot massages for just a few dollars, or sitting at any one of hundreds of open-air beach bars that catered to the seedy white men who had come there for one thing only from thousands of miles away, as if called by some planetary homing device. I sat for hours at these bars, chatting with the local girls about their lives, drinking just enough to not feel my shyness. It was hard to tell how old they actually were. Calling them women was too convenient. Some were in their teens, some, I'm sure, not even.

Their voices were sweet and soothing, like the feeling of forgetting, but all of this struck me as a tropical hallucination, too syrupy to be genuine, and too kind to be rehearsed. They were young, but they were not new to hustling. Occasionally, when they weren't too busy with customers, they would play a board game with me and let their guard down a bit.

"You soldier?" they asked.

"Yes," I said. "Marine." I got a wide-eyed response as they arranged shot glasses on the shelf. They seemed to know the difference.

"Ohhhh. Mah-rine." There was always a pause. A reflection. Then, "You not look like Mah-rine. Why you Mah-rine?"

Evenings passed like this. I came to know their rituals, the way they enticed and welcomed foreign men to their bar stools with gentle laughter and hard alcohol, the way they prayed to and bowed before statues of the Buddha before taking leave of the bar matron and satisfying the client at some off-site location. I don't remember the faces of these men, but their eyes were lifeless, their livers weary, and their voices heavy with exploit. There were endless throngs of them, wrinkled European men and virile American service members, roaming the streets like craven hordes, occasionally alone, but often in packs, hunting for cheap, young Thai pussy.

I'd had a few weeks of this, this lonely dance beneath the surface of reality, and I was longing for company. One afternoon, as we ended our shift, I asked a buddy named Jones if I could join him and some other lieutenants for the evening. Looks were exchanged, not very subtly, that seemed to say, *Are you sure?* I'd never know what made them yield. Did I have a glint in my eye that even I didn't yet recognize? Was I becoming one of them?

That night, I hopped off the baht bus with my fellow officers and followed them down a side street that I hadn't explored on my own. We entered a busy parlor with several benches and tables laid out in rows. Young Thai women were strutting up and down these tables in heels, inserting and expelling various objects between their legs. My fellow officers took seats ceremoniously, as if pews had appeared before them. They were suddenly silent and locked in, like they had just acquired a target.

This collective focus, which required no spoken communication, scared the shit out of me. My discomfort was balanced by my unfortunate desire not to make a big deal out of the whole thing. Right now, in this world where the lines between male and female were as thick and obvious as a sledgehammer over my skull, I summoned an existence, if there was such a thing, beyond gender, and beyond

lines. I didn't want to be that girl who raised a ruckus every time the
boys misbehaved. Every time was looking a lot like all the time, and
I wasn't sure how many ruckuses one Marine could get away with
raising. Perhaps it was time to just stop caring.

Somehow, mercifully, a way out presented itself. In the middle of
a particularly pelvic-heavy set, Jones turned away from the stage, eyes
glazed over, and said, "Let's go. I'm bored." Jones and his bros seemed
to realize there were only so many things a girl could jam into her
private parts. I couldn't get outside fast enough.

We headed down the street to a nightclub called Tony's. The
place was huge, the lights were garish, and the floor was packed with
hundreds of high and tights. Marines were drunk off their asses and
throbbing on the dance floor, lip-locked and tongue-tied with an
assortment of waify, working Thai women. I spotted a handful of
senior enlisted Marines I knew, dudes who worked for and with me,
married men who would disappear down narrow alleys with these
girls before the night was up.

I wondered about my place in this uniformed world, where
there were enough written rules outlawing sex to make any human
being repressed for a lifetime, and where few of those rules were ever
enforced—at least, not when they challenged men's ability to get off.
I wondered why these rules even existed, why laws evoking grand, poetic notions like *good order* and *discipline* prevailed in a world where
everyone was breaking them with abandon. I wondered how secrets
were kept, and for whose benefit.

I tried to avert my gaze as I worked my way through the crowd,
but I couldn't help but lock eyes with guys whose careers I could end
in a moment if I wanted to. Without words, something was com-
municated in looks between us—surprise, pleading, resignation, or
indifference—a new connection and a new set of rules being formu-
lated, by them, by me, almost unconsciously, across this thumping,
hallucinogenic club music. The alcohol, the beats, and the grinding
bodies on the dance floor softened the realization that maybe I didn't

really give a shit anymore about who was doing what with whom, that why should I care if no one else did.

"Holy shit, that's Smith," one lieutenant said, his eyes shifting. I looked up on stage, and saw my friend, the only other female officer in the battalion, bent over toward the crowd, swinging her head like a lasso, her long hair making giant windmills in the air. Next to three other women on stage, Smith was whooping the dance floor into a frenzy. Apparently, there *was* a place for us in this world.

I couldn't watch her anymore. I turned around and walked out.

. . .

It turned out that while Bristol was kicking my ass in Quantico, some of my fellow lieutenants back in Okinawa had turned their backs on me. They didn't understand why I got to go play ninja girl, while they had to stay behind supervising their platoons. The fact that I had volunteered for the training while they had not was completely lost on them.

I'd earned my black belt. I'd bled and sweat and popped a knee-cap out of the socket over it. I'd been knocked out. I'd taken enough painkillers to put my liver through hell. I'd accumulated enough scar tissue in every joint in my body to make me dependent on a lifetime of MRI tubes, orthopedists, physical therapists, and body workers. This belt was part of my uniform now. I didn't need to prove a god-damned thing to anyone. Except that of course I did.

I ran into Quinn on the streets of Pattaya one night. He'd been drinking for hours. Quinn was an okay guy, as far as fellow lieutenants went. He put together a swim team from our battalion, and even though my amateur freestyle left a lot to be desired, he coached us through a couple of meets, where much to my surprise I earned my-self a few ribbons. (This was more due to the fact that I was the only woman stationed on the island who had signed up for the meet.) I knew his wife. She was a sweet, pretty woman who was taking sushi classes out in town. They seemed like a happy couple.

I didn't know what it was about that moment that made Quinn

nuts. Perhaps it was the heat, the booze, something I was wearing, or the way I looked at him as we headed toward each other on the street.

He wanted to know about the black belt course. I said something unremarkable. *It was tough. It was great.* Who knows? Maybe he'd heard that I was prepping for an international amateur fight now under supervision of my martial arts instructor, the broad-chested karate sensei. I'd been training in Thailand during my free hours with a fellow Marine, a tall blond dude, a green belt instructor who in another lifetime would have made a great surfing partner. We'd spar after work hours in the Thai base camp with pads and other equipment that had been brought over with us from Okinawa. When I got into town I'd watch real-life Muay Thai fighters sparring in a ring in the middle of one of the seedy tourist bars. I was feeling happy for the first time in my life.

But Quinn had a bone to pick. I did not realize I inspired this in people.

I didn't expect it. I didn't know I needed to. He threw a punch at my right cheek before I realized it was coming.

That quiet, personal kind of violence wasn't new to me, but it still took me by surprise. At The Basic School a year before, a fellow student, a massive bodybuilding type, threatened to pound my head through his car window as we drove full speed down the highway—he'd said something demeaning, I'd challenged him, and he didn't take my rebuttal so well. He never followed through on his threat, but it shut me up, fast. He was enraged, and behind the steering wheel, with the mass to easily crack my skull in half. I'd forgotten about him until now.

The overt ragers, the lusty drunks, the manically emotional guys—they were easier to handle somehow, they threw obvious swings. Their insecurities about manhood were tied into their language and swagger; they moved deep into their steps. But Quinn's swing at my jaw came from nowhere.

Marines had gathered around us, waiting for something to happen. A physical reaction. A verbal response. I took a moment. I didn't feel much in my jaw. My tongue made a quick sweep of my teeth. Nothing was missing. Gums were intact. Maybe he'd thrown a sissy punch, just to mock me.

I looked at him, dumbfounded. He smiled at me, assessing my next move, my next word. I had no plans. The shock of being smacked down by a colleague on the streets of Thailand was too much for my system to process.

I didn't swing back. He wanted to see what intricate skills I'd absorbed, what superhuman physical prowess, what new miracles I thought I could work on his body because I'd earned a title he didn't think I deserved.

I walked away. He muttered, snickered, did the things men do when they think they've proven a point. I imagine the next morning Quinn had some hint of a memory about this moment. That perhaps some shame would surface when his wife asked him next about how I was. We never interacted again.

Gunny Cain and I were walking through the Thai base the next day, and I told him about the incident. He was surprised by Quinn's behavior, but also concerned about mine.

"Ma'am, you should have swung back."

"What? Why?" I was all ears.

"He needs to know you won't take that kind of thing lying down."

"I didn't know I was defending my honor."

Gunny Cain wasn't impressed. There was still so much he had to teach his young lieutenant. The world I was immersed in now had no place for the art of diplomacy. Forgiveness was a weakness and kindness a sign of some pathological femininity.

Only I wasn't sure about these rules. It wasn't that I wasn't man enough to fight back. I just didn't buy that my worth was based on drawing blood from a guy who was being an asshole. These rational tendencies would mark me in the end, but I guess I didn't care

enough to change. I knew I could bruise some balls if it was damn
well needed.

.   .   .

One morning things were unusually quiet on base. I ran into a fellow officer between racks in the female housing area. It was Biel, the
wobbly voiced candidate from OCS.

"Did you hear about the Army colonel?"

I hadn't.

"He hung himself last night. They found out he'd slept with an
underage girl in town."

She was neither shaming the colonel nor commiserating with the
Thai girl. Biel was simply stating the facts, as plainly as she'd told me
the weather. As I wandered to my post, I seethed inside. Who were
these men?

.   .   .

Several weeks into Thailand, I had fully acclimated. I was hammered
on the dance floor at Tony's. I was off to the side of the club, minding
my own groove, no longer self-conscious or caring about anything or
anyone my fellow jarheads were doing. A local woman approached me.

"You want dance?" she asked. I looked at her. She was tiny, with
dark brown eyes and long black hair.

The woman and I hardly spoke, her grasp of English not much
better than the emergency Thai I'd learned. We danced.

"You want outside?" She pointed over the bodies on the floor
toward the exit.

"Okay."

She firmly took me by the hand, knowing I was several shots in
now, guided me off the floor, past my colleagues and out of the club,
around lesser-beaten, winding Pattaya roads. Only locals seemed to
walk these streets. I was leaning on her completely, and despite her
smallness, I felt invincible, and above reproach, and safe. I paid for
a hotel room, and minutes later we were in bed, our bodies locked
together.

When she fell asleep, I showered and got dressed. There was a moment where the alcohol lifted a bit, and standing against the sink in the bathroom I was faced with the question of whether or not I was dreaming, and what, if any, consequences awaited me. And there was the flicker of this thought: for the first time in my life I was really living on the edge.

It's clear to me now that I had given up on the Marine Corps long before this. If everyone else was above the law, then why shouldn't I be? I wasn't married. I didn't have kids back home, crying themselves to sleep at night. I didn't have some homebound wife I knocked up straight out of high school, the victim of my pathologically seductive dress blues, oblivious to the Corps' day-to-day realities about monogamy, misogyny, and marriage.

So fuck the rules. Fuck convention. And fuck the Corps, too. I returned to the club that week, but I never saw her again.

A few nights later, a fellow lieutenant, a short, nerdy colleague with a knack for science, took me aside at Tony's. He looked at me like he wanted something and we shared a sudden, drunken kiss, each shot and exchange of bodily fluid in this place adding to my growing sense that I had no idea who I was or what I was doing anymore.

"We should hook up when we get back to Oki," he suggested.

He was not my type.

"Sure. Okay."

After a long pause, he said, seriously, "I need to tell you something."

He told me I was becoming the object of a witch hunt by fellow officers who took issue with my recent activities with a local woman. The pounding club music, the throngs of drunken, sexed-up warriors, the fog of alcohol, inside me and everywhere, dulled my fear.

Silently, I thought, *What do they know?*

His eyes were gentle, even through the alcohol.

"It's all bullshit. They're trying to fuck with you." And then, warmly, "Watch your back, Bhagwati."

I was still feeling bulletproof, and more than a little arrogant. I was too young and drunk to realize what this really meant, until one morning I was required to report to my commanding officer in a private tent on base.

I should have been terrified. But I had never seen an adult squirm quite like this man was squirming now. Over the course of the next few minutes, any authority Captain Franco had acquired by rank and any anxiety I felt as the junior officer faded.

With his eyes avoiding mine, he said, "The battalion commander asked me to talk to you. About your, um. Behavior."

I knew deep down what this guy, my boss, the man I had to *Sir* regardless of whether or not I respected him, was trying to say. But I really wanted to hear him say it, because I knew how excruciating it was for him to put the words together, and because I could not wait to throw down after he did.

He said, "You were making out with another woman in a club." Well, he wasn't entirely wrong, but I didn't remember the specifics, so I probed a little.

"What was I doing exactly, Sir?" I asked, with a straight face.

Franco still couldn't look me in the eyes. Wriggling in his seat, he answered, "They said you were feeling her up."

This term I learned from prepubescent girls and boys long ago sounded all sorts of wrong coming out of the captain's mouth. In this moment, I hoped he didn't have any daughters. There was some language grown men should bury and never use again. Beneath my calm exterior, something I had learned to hone well after two years of suppressing responses and obeying orders, I felt the familiar sting of humiliation rise. I refused to let it take over. I decided to have some fun with him.

"Well, Sir, I don't really remember. I was pretty drunk."

In part, it was the truth. But whether I was playing more with Franco or with my own life was uncertain. I had just set myself up for an additional chargeable offense, and I was throwing it in his face along with my *homosexual conduct.** The notion that conduct unbecoming an officer—being wasted in a public place—might be the next possible threat to my career had occurred to me, but what the hell, there wasn't a sober American service member within a hundred miles of Pattaya Beach, and I was taking my chances that sheer audacity and some sixth sense about justice were going to steer this talk in my favor.

For some reason, maybe it was the thought of having to crawl back to the battalion commander empty-handed, the captain finally found his cojones and launched into a lecture about the inappropriateness of same-sex relations. I put up with about twenty more seconds of his Bible-thumping before I couldn't take it any longer and decided to end his misery and mine.

Square in his eyes, I told him, "Sir, if you have a problem with my alleged behavior, you should have a problem with actual adultery, too. And if you want to make a big deal about what some lieutenants said they saw me do in some nightclub, I'd be more than happy to make a big deal about every single married Marine in the battalion screwing Thai hookers every night for the last three months."

The painful silence and the unrelenting flush of Franco's face were long and satisfying. He had no response, no *Are you threatening me, Lieutenant?* because it was obvious that I was, and what was more, he knew I was right. Marines were breaking marriage vows and military law in every seedy corner of Pattaya. I could practically read his mind: *What does she know about me?*

He wasn't willing to find out if I was bluffing.

"That's all, Lieutenant Bhagwati."

I ended up on the first plane back to Okinawa. Rumor was it was

---

* Under "don't ask, don't tell," "homosexual conduct" was a punishable offense that could get you kicked out of the military. It included verbal statements about one's sexual orientation, as well as same-sex encounters like holding hands, kissing, and soliciting sex. Really, it amounted to anything, even intent to commit such acts. And your fate was entirely up to your commander.

because they didn't want me causing any additional trouble. Whether it's because they thought they'd have hundreds of raging wives and impending divorces on their hands or a "don't ask, don't tell" incident in which I was their primary character, I would never know. But I wasn't done with this homophobic stunt, even if I wasn't on the right side of military law.

Back on the island, I took aside one of the married officers who had reported me to the battalion commander and gave him a piece of my mind. He'd spent twenty years in the Corps, but I couldn't have cared less.

"It's none of your goddamned business what I do or do not do with another woman. Got it?"

He looked at me, appalled. He did not expect to be confronted. Something changed in his face, as if he'd been exposed. He smiled.

"Yeah, Bhagwati." He didn't apologize, but he never fucked with me again.

. . .

Now that I was settled back in Okinawa, it became obvious to me that the Constitution I'd sworn under oath to protect and defend was supported by a culture that was indefensible. Marine bravado was fragile. Our ego was barely held together by various well-rehearsed slogans about men's strength and heroism. Some part of me stopped giving a damn. Only I wished what came out of me as a result of my not giving a damn was something worth fighting for, an ownership of my body, a genuine pride that arose from realizing my own value.

But my choice to play the girl gone wild because everything was so unfair did not contain any artistic sensibility, any grand sense of history or timing, or foresight about the moral arc of the universe. My universe was tinged with a real adolescent nihilism, a kind of *You wanna screw me? Fuck you then, I'll just screw myself.* I played with fate like I'd just pulled the pin on a grenade and held on, waiting to see which parts of me wouldn't blow up.

My self-destruction hurt me more than anyone else. I was naive and sexually inexperienced, but even more than that, I was lost and sad and so alone I could barely get through the average day. I had no skin to protect myself from people's language, and no moral reference that counted for shit anymore. Men's words about women, the filth that was said to keep us from realizing our potential, became the core of what I believed about myself. There was no way out of these years to which I had signed my life but through them. I did not make it any easier for myself.

Though it scared me, though I was sick to my stomach with self-loathing, I found myself, slowly and unbearably, sleeping with a small assortment of Marine men, each one more indifferent to the consequences of being with me than the last, wretched lost souls who like me were so off course from living fulfilled lives that I wondered if anyone who joined this institution had anything going for them aside from the idea of belonging to this place.

There was no such thing as respect for a woman in this uniform we wore, so it should come as little surprise that they had little respect for me. Some were in awe, or in lust of how different I was from the women they had known, but mostly I was their receptacle, their distraction from a mediocre existence, the thing that kept them from hating themselves completely.

We were codependent in our misery. I felt contempt and disgust for most of them. This was exceeded only by my self-hatred for choosing to be with them. I convinced myself that these men couldn't possibly understand anything about me, and didn't on any level deserve me. I must have figured a few moments of meaningless human connection and a convenient orgasm would wipe out the loneliness and alienation I felt. I was using them as much as they were using me, to get closer to oblivion, to being nothing and no one.

One lieutenant, a young infantry jock with wide shoulders, an enormous back, and legs like tree trunks, introduced me to a new kind of sex, an emotionless, detached fucking that complemented his slightly sociopathic personality and obsession with black ops missions. One day he had my legs high over his shoulders. There was a dead look in his eyes as he stared through me, like he killed small animals for fun, which he no doubt had done.

"I want to blindfold you."

I didn't want to go down that road, but I went along, mindlessly submitting, letting him wrap the cloth around my head and enter me. I don't think I said a word the whole time.

Minutes later, he wanted to film me. I paused as the issue of trust hung before me, my instinct to protect some part of my self-worth or some notion of my public reputation having not yet completely vanished. Somewhere in my memory of how things used to be, I found the courage to tell him no.

"Come on," he insisted.

I said no again. But truthfully, I have no idea whether he got me on camera while my eyes were covered, whether some ancient footage of my motionless, naked body is floating around the Internet somewhere.

"Come here. I want to do something." I put my arms around his back. He lifted me effortlessly off the bed, carried me through his barracks room, and placed me in the tub like a bath toy. I'm not sure where this fantasy of his stemmed from, or where it would go, though it seemed an awful lot like he was orchestrating the home version of a rape-drowning scene from some porno he'd seen one too many times. I was grateful when his time on the island came to an end.

Some connections lasted for moments, others for days. These relationships horrified me, compounding my self-loathing each time I removed my clothes or closed a door. I lived in constant terror of being discovered. Even after the encounters were over, my fear and the shame of being found out were devastating.

Some men whom I thought were single hid the fact that they were married. Those who were married would gladly have disappeared their own wives. Divorce would have been a sensible out for them, but few had the courage for that kind of change. The first time it occurred to me that a man who had a wife and kids back home was hitting on me, was trying to get me into his bed, I politely excused myself, made a beeline for the bathroom, and gagged into the toilet. I should have stayed in that bathroom. I should have found a way out. I didn't. This pathology, this sexually driven self-hatred in which the part I played was to just go along, seeped slowly into me and stayed put. There was nothing left in me to recognize. All that remained was a pervasive nausea. This was the beginning of the end of my self-esteem. I spent weeks letting him inside me, hating every minute of his catlike moaning, as he assured me that his wife wouldn't mind. Like hell she wouldn't.

Most Marines came with baggage. One very senior guy had set aside plans for Catholic priesthood to become a Marine and prove to everyone around him that he was a badass. He was book smart and gorgeous, but detached and seemed far too gay to be anything real to me. Still, I was convinced he could save me from the torment of my lonely existence, and I clung to him, hard. He must have realized my desperation, or his, as he didn't stick around too long.

Another officer I knew had worked his way through Thailand's prostitutes, year after year, while his demure, obese wife sat at home thousands of miles away, taking care of their kids. I found all of this out after he had fucked me, and like a fool I was actually surprised he had a family. I must have been one of dozens of women he was banging on this deployment.

These men were in all sorts of deep personal shit, wearing various layers of denial. Some were simply setting aside adult responsibility, or feeling the rumblings of early midlife. Others had personalities that were split in two. Most of them were senior, career Marines in the kind of emotional turmoil that required extensive soul searching and a fire team of therapists to sort out. Most of them would never bother.

How I ended up crossing paths with them, naked in bed, was something that would take ages to understand. Years later, a trauma counselor would make the grave mistake of suggesting that perhaps my foray into these forbidden relationships was titillating for me—

my version of living wild and free, and testing the limits of the law, like Thelma and Louise. I was appalled and enraged by her analysis. I only wished I could live for my next sexual conquest. I wished I could love flaunting the authorities like some maverick woman. But I was too guilt ridden for all that. I was conquering no one with these escapades, least of all myself.

My fear stemmed from many places. I wasn't just a sheltered Indian girl who hadn't had much sex in her life, who wouldn't have known what you meant if you'd talked about men's ulterior motives, who'd spent so much time studying and fussing over grades that sex wasn't even the luxury of daydreams. Whatever sexual awakening I was having now, there was much more at stake. Half the shit I was doing could have landed me in military prison.

The military regulated sex with puritanical zeal, all in the name of good order and discipline, but that was hardly the reason. You could get court-martialed for all sorts of sexual acts. Rape was thankfully on the books (in words, at least, it was criminalized). So was bestiality. So, ironically, was sleeping with a prostitute. But so were homosexuality and sodomy—that is, oral or anal sex with someone of either sex. You could also face jail time for adultery and fraternization. The military's antisex laws stretched far and wide, criminalizing far more consensual sex acts between adults than nonconsensual ones.

Though I wasn't married, I could have been court-martialed for sleeping with a married service member. It occurred to me years later—it seemed obvious to anyone but me—that I was playing out some childhood narrative, that all of these men were way older, in most cases a decade or two more experienced than I was and well versed in Marine Corps culture, meaning I could work through all my crippling insecurities about needing Dad's approval by taking off my clothes for them and pretending they cared about me.

I quickly discovered there were enough adulterous officers in the Corps to form their own regiment, but I was playing with fire well beyond that. The gay priest was a first sergeant. In military parlance,

that spelled fraternization. Although he was older than me by several
years, he was technically junior in rank. Senior enlisted Marines ran
the show on the ground—heck, they ran the whole Marine Corps—
but ultimately they reported to officers, which meant if he and I
crossed paths on base, he was calling me Ma'am and saluting me.

I was being reckless, and I knew it. Sleeping with someone I outranked, even if he was ten or fifteen years older than me, wasn't worth
it. The stress was more than I could handle. Fraternizing made me a
pathetic leader in the eyes of the Corps, or so we had all been told. I
remember spitting vitriolic judgment toward officers whom I'd heard
had engaged in relationships with junior personnel. They were men
who clearly had taken advantage of lower-ranking women, right? And
yet here I was, doing something I had sworn was unthinkable just a
year ago. The shame burned.

It would be a long while till I realized that military law wasn't so
black-and-white. These rules were rarely enforced. As if Pattaya Beach
was not proof enough, few people in uniform cared if two straight
adults were having consensual sex. In fact, it appeared that every man
who was having sex with a woman he wasn't supposed to be having sex
with was well protected by other men. The military's rules amounted
to scare tactics on paper, vestiges of a time when perhaps religion ruled
more than common sense, but irrelevant to day-to-day life in the Corps.

However, if one of the parties was disliked, things got risky. And
as I was learning firsthand, on the rare occasion when these rules were
enforced, they were usually brought to bear against women. I heard
stories later on about how deep the shaming of service women went;
one female officer was marched off in handcuffs for sleeping with the
wrong man, a woman who had given years of her life to serving in
uniform. I felt horrible for her, and for him. Why was sex or love between adults anyone's business if it didn't get in the way of their jobs?

If neither party was being harmed or exploited, I wasn't sure what
the military gained from criminalizing consensual adult relationships.
Couldn't the services handle these inevitable human connections in

some way that didn't cause so much unnecessary shame, hiding, and permanent damage to people's careers? Couldn't folks just be transferred to other units if relationships got in the way of people's work? Why was the military playing priest and judge in the bedroom?

Most of the men I connected with were living double lives. Some combination of smooth-talking con men and sad, alienated loners, they were very, very good at this. I, who had no secrets to keep before wearing this uniform, now had everything to hide and something to lose, even if I didn't recognize its worth to me at the time. I was not good at this. I was in over my head, and drowning.

I had every reason to step outside of this pitiful, self-hating cycle. But there was no way out. I felt like I was in too deep. I didn't know who I was anymore. I didn't know what would snap me out of this. A homicidal wife. HIV. The brig. I didn't know what would hurt me most. Some part of me wanted to find out. Some part of me wanted to be punished for all my transgressions. Maybe it would prove I didn't belong in the Marines after all.

CHAPTER 7

Joining the Grunts

Two months after Thailand, I stood before my battalion executive officer with a copy of my fitness report in my right hand.

My company commander, Captain Franco, whom I saluted at this point only because military custom required it, had given me the lowest possible marks on my report. In the real world, it would have meant looking for another job, but a contract was a contract. There was no justification for these marks other than retaliation, and I told my executive officer just as much.

Franco and I had butted heads over far more than the anonymous Thai woman. A mediocre officer who was socially awkward and a clumsy manager, he led our company by forcing people to obey him rather than seeking counsel from his subordinates and listening to good ideas.

But worse than this, Franco had clearly missed the memo on sexual and physical boundaries. Inexplicably, I became his pet when I returned from black belt training in the States. At one staff meeting, Franco wanted to nominate me for a young leadership award, though no one, including me, seemed to be sure what I'd done to earn this recognition. In front of Jones and the lieutenant who'd swung her hair in Tony's, in front of Gunny Cain and the other senior enlisted leaders in the company, Franco began swooning over me, like a man with a schoolboy crush. I turned beet red, trying to hide in my seat as the Marines in the room grew silent. Franco's first sergeant, a wiry Black woman with twenty years in the Corps, sensing that a temporary paralysis had set in in the room, responded to the captain's excesses by moving the meeting forward at lightning speed. I dealt with his attention by silently fuming and then avoiding him completely.

One week I was in the company office to grab some paperwork, stopping to say hello to one of my Marines, a young kid who was injured and assigned to help with admin. The captain came out of his office and sidled up to me, telling me he was feeling cold. Before I could even conjure the thought *So what?* he placed his hand on my cheek to demonstrate his body temperature.

"See?"

I didn't respond. I had no idea whether my Marine had witnessed the interaction, but I backed away and out of the office, with a deadly look in my eye.

Captain Franco had no clue about personal space or contemporary gender norms, so when he'd taken his lieutenants out to dinner in town one evening, I shouldn't have been surprised that he gave my fellow woman officer and me long hugs, while he firmly shook Jones's hand. Locked in his slimy embrace, I wanted to hurl. My skin itched all the way home.

Franco didn't restrict his harassment to young officers. One day toward the end of my time on Okinawa, my new platoon sergeant, a stellar young Marine with bright red hair, approached me, telling me the captain had been giving her a lot of attention, and that it made her feel uncomfortable. All I could do was tell her I was watching him closely. Being a lecherous Marine wasn't enough to move the Corps to action.

I had one brief moment of vengeance, when I was teaching the company their introductory martial arts requirements, and the captain was now my student. Approaching me with flirtatious eyes, he asked me how to execute a particular jab to the skull. Without hesitating, my palm struck his head, knocking his helmet into his forehead and sending him back a couple of feet. He looked at me, stunned, resentment building in his eyes. I did not apologize.

"Got it, Sir?"

But all that paled in comparison to the final blow I dealt him, on behalf of one of my Marines.

At six feet four inches, Lance Corporal Ibrahim was the tallest Marine in my radio platoon. He was just a kid, eighteen or nineteen tops, with soft eyes and a gentle demeanor. He was Black, and he was Muslim. Ibrahim's faith had deepened over the last year, and he wanted to observe Ramadan for the first time in his life. We were not deploying anytime during the monthlong fast, so there was no good reason not to support him. It would be his responsibility to do his job in the platoon during the day, including participating in physical training each morning, in extremely hot conditions.

Ibrahim had submitted a request through the chain of command for Comrats—Commuted Rations—which would give him the extra pay to purchase food at the commissary so he could eat his meals at night during Ramadan. The fast prevented him from eating the free breakfast, lunch, or dinner offered to Marines at the chow hall during the day, so this simple solution made sense. It meant his survival.

Captain Franco received the request for Comrats and swiftly denied it. Gunny Cain came to me with the news. I couldn't believe what I was hearing. I had no idea to what extent Franco's stunt was some Catholic power move to harass a young Muslim Marine, but I didn't waste too much time thinking about it. I talked at length with my gunny about Ibrahim's options, and then spoke to Ibrahim, who nodded his head with plenty of *yes, Ma'am*s and *no, Ma'am*s while I told him his options. Ibrahim thought about it and made his decision.

It was ballsy for everyone involved, but given the captain's general level of incompetence, I didn't care about the consequences to me, and more important, Ibrahim had nothing to lose. I was firmly backing the kid. Ibrahim requested mast to the battalion commander, an administrative move that allowed a junior ranking Marine to speak to an officer several rungs up the chain of command when he perceived his grievance was not being addressed by more immediate supervisors. Ibrahim walked the paperwork straight to the battalion office, as I instructed him, bypassing the captain altogether.

A day later, I was summoned to see Franco.

"Good morning, Sir."

The captain said nothing in response. Barely looked at me. I could have cut the tension in the room with a samurai sword. Then, suddenly, he barked, "I could charge you for what you did, Lieutenant!" I guessed I was no longer his favorite platoon commander. He reached into his desk desperately, knocking over papers, and pulled out a *Manual for Courts-Martial*, the military's tome on criminal justice. He flipped open to a page that had been specially marked for this particular ass chewing, and read a paragraph with great emphasis.

I listened intently till he stopped reading and looked up at me, triumphant, as if he'd just pronounced me guilty as charged.

I inhaled.

"Sir, it's Ibrahim's right to speak to the battalion commander. There's nothing illegal in requesting mast."

"That paperwork should have come directly to me, Lieutenant," he growled.

"Sir, his Comrats request did come directly to you. You denied it."

He stuttered, seething. I could see him evaluating his next move, and mine.

"This isn't over, Lieutenant. You're dismissed."

"Aye-aye, Sir." I about-faced and took off. I walked back to Gunny Cain's office, telling him the news. He received it with typical calmness, but I could tell he was concerned about me.

Three days later, the battalion commander called me in to see him. The captain was waiting inside the office. My belly tightened.

"Lieutenant Bhagwati, have a seat." The lieutenant colonel was all in senior officer mode, gathering his flock together. I sat down next to Franco, who was silent and grim.

"I'm approving Lance Corporal Ibrahim's request."

"Thank you, Sir."

"Is there anything else the Marine needs? Or anything you want to say?"

I thought hard. Then I went for it.

"Well, Sir, I think it's really important that we let our Marines know we care about them. Especially since 9/11. I think we've got to be very careful to let Muslim Marines know we aren't going to discriminate against them, considering all the anti-Muslim sentiment in the world right now."

"That's a great point, Lieutenant Bhagwati."

The battalion commander's support was the last I'd get from this unit. Standing now before my major, armed with these anecdotes of bullshit behavior by Franco, he had nothing left for me. He didn't care about Franco's harassment, of me, of other women, or what clearly was Franco's attempt at punishing me for making him look like an ass before the battalion commander. Instead, he said, "I wouldn't be surprised if you wanted to start over."

He was right. I'd been looking at next duty stations. It was 2002, and while a friend in a neighboring unit had joined one of the first deployments to Afghanistan, and I wanted to be in the thick of it, it was a long shot that my platoon would have the opportunity to go there anytime soon. Leading enlisted Marines was fun and challenging, and worth it every day. But the officers in this battalion were another story. There was no point sticking around here.

At a final officer dinner I attended, I rose to my feet and thanked everyone—the porn addicts, the adulterers, and the homophobes—for everything I'd learned. I think I said it more to be seen than anything else. None of these officers were going to miss me, and I sure as heck wasn't going to miss their backstabbing and jealousy.

I wanted to be somewhere exciting, and I'd found an opening back stateside, at Camp Lejeune. Like the black belt billet, it was a unique position that had recently been opened to women officers. I'd be an executive officer at the School of Infantry, helping instruct brand-new Marines from Parris Island in the combat skills they'd need to know in the operating forces. I'd be working almost entirely with infantry Marines, on both the officer and enlisted side. I'd actually have an infantry officer's billet. It would be the closest I could get to the infantry, something that was still irrevocably off-limits to women.

My then sexual partner, the infantry officer who'd blindfolded me, looked at me like I was nuts.

"Why would you want to work there? All grunts think about is killing, drinking, and sex." He would know. Still, if the infantry was where the real Marine Corps was, I wanted in.

Franco ended up getting promoted to major. A few months after I left Okinawa, a friend told me he had gotten in trouble for harassing a bunch of officers' wives. I just shook my head. I'd already moved on.

· · ·

North Carolina was as Deep South as I'd ever lived. And Jacksonville, North Carolina, made Quantico, Virginia, look like the liberal Northeast. Jacksonville was my first full immersion in conservative backcountry living, a sprawl of strip malls, fast food chains, tattoo parlors, and bars surrounding Camp Lejeune, the largest Marine Corps base in the world.

The School of Infantry had its own location off to the side, at Camp Geiger. I was assigned to Echo Company, and when I went in to meet my new boss, I could already feel something different in the language and look of the Marines in his charge. He spoke with an intensity and seriousness that defined Marine Corps infantry. He called the troops in to meet me. There were about thirty men, mostly sergeants, a few corporals and staff sergeants. They were all infantrymen. The gunny had just whipped them into silence and stood to the side, ready to tear out the tongue of anyone who spoke out of line. They looked up at me expectantly, as if I were about to deliver them from death or kick the crap out of them.

Their discipline was impressive. If there was any question about working for a noninfantryman, and a woman at that, I picked up nothing from this group. Most of them had never worked with or for a woman. And they were training only male Marines in this company.

Unfortunately, just as I was getting settled, my new battalion commander had me reassigned to a neighboring company that was training both male and female Marines. Apparently the infantry captain there had two young kids and he needed some extra support in the field while he helped take care of his family. Though most of the staff was infantry and male, we had a handful of female corporals and sergeants, as well as a female first sergeant.

I drove out to the field to observe my first training evolution. The NCOs were scattered in various stations, each with fifteen to twenty young Marines, bright-eyed, awkward, and mildly terrified, learning about cover and concealment. My goal was to meet the instructors and get a sense of the schedule.

I walked over to one squad. Their sergeant was small and loud. She skipped over to me, her yellow bob bouncing off her shoulders.

"You must be our new XO, right, Ma'am?" She was as much cheerleader as squad leader. She spent the next couple of minutes rattling away about the personalities in the company like she was preparing me for my entrance at a frat party. I'd never heard so many "likes" uttered from the mouth of a Marine. But nothing prepared me for the shock of seeing her pull up and re-roll the cuffs of her trousers while she tied her laces and then bloused her boots, snugly wrapping boot bands around her trousers to keep them in place.

The sergeant was wearing knee-high yellow-and-black-striped socks underneath her camouflage uniform. She didn't even try to hide them.

"You always wear those, Sergeant?"

"What? Oh, these? Yes, Ma'am. Aren't they, like, great?"

She bounced back to her squad while I stood there in shock. What the heck kind of company was this?

When I saw the troops with the company commander, Captain Jacob, they treated him like he was their pal. He not only didn't mind, he seemed to encourage it. It was clear he had no idea how to manage women. A couple of the younger women looked at him like they were lovestruck. They all called him Sir, and it was clear that the infantry guys would have gone to bat for him, but the group was way too relaxed around him. I wondered if the presence of women there had made everyone nuts.

Back at the company office, I took my new CO aside.

"Sir, do you know what your NCOs are doing out in the field?"

Captain Jacob chuckled. "Lieutenant, feel free to fix whatever needs fixing. It's all yours." He was serious. With two young kids back home and a wife who was apparently giving him hell for his long hours, the captain gave me full license to rein in his troops. I was in charge whenever he wasn't around.

The bumblebee socks were gone within a day. And the NCOs started straightening up when they saw me. The SNCOs, senior enlisted infantrymen who essentially supervised training in the field, were surprised. I developed a reputation as a hard-ass XO, the one who wouldn't let the troops gaff off. There were some talented junior women in the company, and the lackadaisical standards hurt them the most. Lost in a sea of hard-core infantry guys, they had a lot to prove, but no one was holding them to a higher standard, or taking them seriously. All their senior enlisted mentors and officers were infantry guys who had neither the experience nor the courage to treat them as hard as they would the men.

My infantry learning curve on matters of sex and gender was steep, and I was rapidly taking mental notes. During one top-level briefing among officers in the school, my captain diagnosed the problem of several young Marines in our company not performing up to the Corps' standards as *vaginosis*. It was another level of slur, as if the darkest, foulest thing one could be, furthest from the tribe of real men, was the smelly, itchy mess of infection in the damp nether regions of a she-human. I sat there in silence as he plowed forward with his briefing to the colonel. No one said a word.

Other breakdowns in training occurred along gender lines. The guys just simply were not training the female students hard. Whether it was fear of hurting them, or being hurt by them, I didn't know. And I didn't care. With the war in Iraq now under way, many of our students were going to be deployed to places like Fallujah. It didn't matter that our students weren't infantrymen. There were no more front lines in America's wars. Everyone was fighting out there, regardless of their jobs. These infantrymen could no longer afford to treat our students like Barbie dolls.

I threw the female students up on pull-up bars, and I insisted to my captain that we integrate squads to the lowest possible level, ensuring that women were not being sheltered in all-female units. The women would have to find a way to come out of the protected shells they'd grown at Parris Island, where boot camp was still segregated and completely unequal. And men would have to get used to women training alongside them.

I was on my belly one day with one of the squads, low-crawling alongside them, when a private came up to me, starry-eyed.

"Ma'am, you're in better shape than most eighteen-year-olds!"

I looked at him briefly before an NCO howled, "Shut your pie-hole, devil dog! Get your ass back in gear. Now!"

I shook the company up. Remembering my training from black belt school, I wore combat boots on company runs while the others wore sneakers. I wanted them to know women didn't deserve special treatment. In fact, we could handle more than they thought.

Immersed now in infantry culture, I was getting to know some real characters that didn't exist in the integrated world of support units. The infantry guys treated me with an odd mixture of curiosity, fear, respect, and befuddlement. Sergeant Murray was a typical infantryman: average-looking, skinny, and tenacious as hell. I remember holding an empty Gatorade bottle one day, asking him where the recycling bin was, and he looked at me like I'd personally offended God, Country, and Corps. Warfighters did not recycle.

He was a know-it-all, but he had the skills to back it up, so during my first week with the company, Murray gave me a personal tour of the training area at night to break me in. He took me through miles of woods under the black sky. He was happily aiming for the thickest brush. Flashlights were out of the question. He barely made a sound while I stomped behind him like an elephant in the jungle. I silently cursed him, wishing I had a machete, and maybe the gall to kick him in the nuts. I could hear him chuckling ahead of me every now and then. My legs were covered in chiggers for the next month.

Murray was arrogant to a fault, but utterly reliable, and the guy you wanted by your side in a scrape. I'd been there a few months when the captain mentioned to me that Murray and his wife were in dire straits, and that Murray was now on thin ice for dating another woman. It seemed his wife was raising hell with the command, and the battalion commander was getting tired of the drama.

Murray found himself reporting to me in the company office one day, looking petrified. I'd never seen him look nervous. It did not go down the way he expected.

"Sergeant Murray, you're human. But you've got to be a little more tactful, yeah? Look, you're an adult. Just remember you've got to respect how delicate this is, not throw this in anyone's face. Treat this with caution until the divorce goes through, okay?"

I'd never policed people's hearts, and I wasn't about to start doing it now. He was terribly shy all of a sudden. The grunt in him was nowhere to be found.

Quietly, he said, "Yes, Ma'am. Thank you, Ma'am."

Murray acted like I was some kind of angel after that. He'd expected me to crucify him and pronounce him a fornicator. I had no interest in all that. He just needed some time to sort his life out and grow a little.

The head of the School of Infantry was a colonel with a storied infantry career. He'd survived a legendary injury in his younger days, which added to his notoriety as the real deal. On one of his jumps, he apparently hit the ground so hard that his femurs shot up through his hips. He was one of very few men who was thrilled to have me in his unit simply because of my résumé. He had a college-aged daughter to whom he wanted to introduce me, because she was interested in the Corps. He saw me, with my Ivy League creds, as some kind of role model. My fellow infantry officers were stuck halfway between disbelief and jealousy over this extra attention. Civilian smarts and women's inherent worth had no bearing on their world.

If I was doing well at work, my personal life left much to be desired. When I wasn't with my company, I spent many evenings staring at the sky, wondering what was next for me. I was desperately lonely. The few friends I'd made were stationed elsewhere around the globe. Jules was stationed at Parris Island, South Carolina, and living with her girlfriend. She was so deep in the closet I wondered how she was surviving. I had no friends in Jacksonville. There were no single officers in the battalion, and no other women officers stationed at the School of Infantry aside from an awkward attorney whom I barely saw anyhow.

Jacksonville was a wasteland that challenged me to the core. I spent my free time working out and sprucing up my house there, the first property I'd ever owned. I got one dog, a rottweiler. Then a second, a chocolate Labrador. I named them Shiva and Uma, after the mighty Hindu god of destruction and his loyal companion.

A few months into my tour, a new female lieutenant was assigned to another training company in the battalion. She was excited to be there and seemed like a nice person. I still remember her—friendly, unassuming, smart, blond. Not like many women officers I knew, who tended to hide their personalities under several layers of suspicion. I remember talking to her during her first week and answering her questions.

Two months later, she was gone, just like that. Word was she couldn't handle the guys in her company. She couldn't *hang* with the infantry. My gut told me half of this was bullshit. I knew what those infantry dudes were capable of putting her through. Her own boss was a first-class tool, an insecure grunt who still used the term "Dark Green Marines" to refer to Marines who were Black. His assumptions about her were probably just as bigoted. I was ambivalent about her fate. Part of me wanted to rally on her behalf. And part of me was tied up in my own fragile ego, which had been suckered and manipulated since my first day in the Corps. *I* had survived working with these grunts. *She* hadn't. That made me worthy.

Hours at the School of Infantry were long and grueling—I spent three straight weeks and many long days and nights with my staff, getting four hundred young Marines through our rigorous curriculum. We had five days off before starting the cycle all over again. I spent most of that time just catching up on sleep.

Around this time, my company staff was given some kind of tactics exam by the battalion, and they failed it, miserably. It wasn't all that surprising. Most of the guys on our staff had been grunts in the fleet and knew their way around the real-world infantry like they did a porn site, but a multiple-choice test was challenging a whole new set of muscles. The boss assigned me and his senior staff sergeant, Henry Lowell, with improving the company's tactical knowledge. We came up with homework assignments for the NCOs, which felt like a personal kind of torture for both us and them. That month they were like grumpy kids, wearing pouty faces and constantly complaining.

Staff Sergeant Lowell was an emotional, hotheaded guy. He'd lunge around the training area, ripping into NCOs and students left and right for professional infractions and all-around boneheadedness. He was a tiny hellion, about forty pounds overweight, who read a worn paperback of *Anna Karenina* in his free time. He treated me with appropriate distance, but was curious about my education, asking me questions about all sorts of things from politics to philosophy.

"I can't believe you chose to join the Marines, Ma'am. You could have done anything."

Assigned to reform the company and prep them for the next exam, Lowell and I spent hours after work each day over coffee and paperwork. As time passed, we became friends. When I told him about a scumbag lieutenant from Okinawa who had dumped me for another woman, he offered with full sincerity to get a group of grunts together to beat the shit out of him.

I think if I'd had anyone at all to confide in, to share my fear and self-hatred with, a safe place to name these things that I had felt ever since the beginning, even some family member or friend back home whom I could talk to about my life in this cold, isolating place, things would have turned out differently.

One evening after we'd worked on our assignment, we prepared to drive our separate ways, but I invited Lowell over to watch a movie at my house instead. His hand brushed mine on the couch, and I knew there was no going back.

It was a mistake that, as the senior Marine, I was entirely responsible for. It didn't matter that he was several years older, or that because of his infantry background and his years of experience in the Corps, he had more authority in this unit than I did. Every day I wanted to take it back. He was not only someone I shouldn't have been with, he was also someone I didn't want to be with. Like all my questionable partners, Lowell had personal issues that were haunting him. One day he opened up about his past. Lowell's family had pimped him out as a child to men who would pay for sex. And some part of that nightmare was still haunting him. Lowell crooned to his sexual organ, wanting me to recite things to him—to it, in fact—that I now realized had probably been planted in his brain decades earlier by his abusers. It seemed to me that some part of his being with me was about healing from rape and erasing any stigma about his manhood from his memories.

Whether I was part therapist or something else to him, I wasn't sure, but here I was. And I was compromising both of our careers. It didn't matter that I wasn't in his chain of command, that I couldn't actually influence his reporting marks. We were in the same company, and he still took orders from me. Things became even more insane when Lowell wanted to tell the captain, our boss, that we were together, as if this was something we should be proud of sharing. To my amazement, Captain Jacob didn't care.

"So what?" he said. And we all went right back to work.

If I was taking on more than I could handle, I wasn't conscious enough of it at the time. At a company function, I was surrounded by grunts with their impressive stacks of combat ribbons. I had worked hard and felt like I belonged for the first time in a long time. I was drinking more than my frame could hold. Filled with booze, emotion, and gratitude, I apparently planted a kiss on my captain's lips. Thankfully, I don't remember it, and when I found out months later, I was horrified to discover I'd done such a thing. The captain had just told Lowell to get me home safely.

This was a dysfunctional arrangement that worked for a few weeks. The problem was, I was sick inside with fear. Petrified by my own self-destructive behavior, I reached out to a family friend back home, who sat me down, sternly pleading with me to break up with Lowell to avoid ending up in military prison. *I know*, I said. *I know*. But I did nothing.

Neither Lowell nor I were being careful. I was starting to get soft around him, and it showed. One day he drove me into work when our Marines could have easily seen us exiting the car. And on another day, after a company physical training session, I changed my clothes in the company office while Lowell was in there as well, with our junior Marines wandering back and forth outside the door. It was clear I'd lost my mind.

The captain noticed this, or perhaps guessed it. He called us in and told us firmly it was over. I was relieved. I couldn't handle the pressure anymore. But Lowell was furious. He felt the captain had embarrassed him. Lowell was stubborn and naive, and determined to screw the system. I had no interest in burning up alongside him. Eventually he got stationed elsewhere, but I had come awfully close to blowing it.

Captain Jacob may have saved our hides, but I couldn't save Lowell. It turned out this whole time Lowell wasn't recovering from child abuse as much as reliving it. One morning, long after Lowell had transferred to another unit, I was scheduled to supervise a live-fire range. One of my favorite SNCOs was chatting with me during a break.

"Ma'am, did you hear about Lowell?"

I tightened up.

"No. What happened?"

"He went home to be a recruiter. He was busted for messing with his female recruits. His wife left him." My insides froze, but I tried to play it cool.

"You're kidding." I knew Lowell was dealing with ghosts, but I had not expected him to prey upon a bunch of doe-eyed teenagers. Disgusted, I did not want to know how old these girls were. And I had no idea he had been married. I felt like I needed to be purged. I was relieved and grateful that my boss had separated Lowell and me when he did, and with so much mercy. There was no time to be shocked or to get sentimental. I had a job to do. I tried to forget I'd ever met Lowell and pressed onward.

• • •

Things back at the office shifted when a new staff sergeant was assigned to our company. A seasoned grunt, Fox was often bitter, his skin turning yellow with sarcasm or anger. He did not like answering to anyone, least of all women, and was once so fed up when I gave him a simple order that he mouthed off to me. I wasn't offended as much as shocked. He got his ass nicely chewed by the captain.

After each three-week training cycle, we received student evaluations in which we'd find out who among our instructors had made a difference in the lives of young Marines. It was an opportunity to assess student morale and improve staff performance. The captain called me early one evening after I'd driven home from our ten-mile hike in the field. He told me to come back to the office immediately.

Captain Jacob looked haggard and strangely depleted for a guy his size. Four hundred student evaluations were stacked on his desk.

"Lieutenant Bhagwati, sit down. We've got a problem."

It felt like someone had died. It turned out to be much worse. Staff Sergeant Fox had been accused of sexually assaulting female students in the field. And they had spoken out en masse.

Sexual predators thrived in places like the Corps, especially when they had rank. Privates, most of them straight out of high school, had no power here. Female privates, even less. These anonymous student evaluations were the only way of getting word up the chain of command that there was a sex offender on our staff.

The captain placed our students on graduation hold, preventing four hundred Marines from flying around the country to their follow-on training schools. He prepared to get official statements from the students, which would be critical in military judicial proceedings.

The next couple of days were a haze. Overworked, stretched thin, and needing to attend to his two small children back home, my boss asked me to step into a meeting with our battalion commander. I reported in. The BC was in the middle of a phone call and pointed at me to sit down.

He had a Marine's mother on the line. The mother was in hysterics, threatening to go to CNN and tell reporters about Fox and the sexual assault scandal. My BC remained calm and focused. He insisted things were being handled, that she need not worry, that her child would be fine.

I was mortified, hearing this man spin a tall tale for an American mother. How did he know her child was fine? Did he have any idea what Fox was capable of? Did any of us? And why the hell was I there to witness this thing? Was my presence enabling this charade?

Monday morning came quickly. I checked in with the captain. He looked pale.

"They transferred Fox to the fleet. He's back with an infantry battalion. They're getting ready to deploy to Iraq."

"Sir?"

"He's not being charged," he explained. "They let him get away with it."

"Holy shit."

"All those kids." My boss looked devastated.

"There's nothing we can do?"

"Lieutenant Bhagwati, when a full-bird colonel makes a staff sergeant disappear like he never existed, it means it's been handled."

It was almost impossible for me to reconcile that the school colonel, who prided himself on promoting women, on mentoring his own daughter into the officer Corps, had just covered up a sexual assault scandal and willingly sent a predator back out into the Marine Corps. Was this really happening?

There was little time to think about any of this. Captain Jacob was transferred a few days later to another company. It looked an awful lot like they needed him to disappear, too. I got a new company commander. We continued to train Marines like nothing had happened.

CHAPTER 8

One Last Oorah

In 2003, my battalion commander gave me an early promotion to captain, and I became the only woman to command a training company at the School of Infantry. Before the change of command, I sought guidance from the best expert I knew on drill and ceremony: Brenda Baughman. My old drill instructor was stationed at an adjacent unit, and she was more than happy to give me some feedback for my new position. She adjusted the pitch and volume of my voice, and the inflection of my words as I called my mock company to attention. We went back and forth, call and response, until finally, I was ready.

Being a company commander was a privilege that not every officer was given. At twenty-eight, I had a ton of responsibilities, not least of which was making sure no one got killed on a live-fire range. I had a brand-new set of staff instructors, and a group of incredibly talented NCOs, including two young women who were changing the game for all of us.

Miranda Hamby was Alabama born and bred, with a thick accent and quick wit. She was twenty-one years old, a die-hard Marine who took her job seriously and never, ever complained. She was the first to volunteer to help someone in need, and had the humility of someone who'd never had anything given to her without hard work. To the delight of her senior enlisted supervisors, she drank up new infantry skills and taught them to her squad with a clarity and enthusiasm that others envied. She was determined to get them to learn, and she had no patience for slackers. At all of five feet four, she had the spirit of a giant. In many ways, she reminded me of a younger version of Baughman.

By the time I was settled into the company, I had a slight Alabama accent myself and was y'alling up and down the live-fire ranges. There were moments during the twelve- to sixteen-hour training days when Hamby's relentless energy and hysterical commentary would have the entire leadership staff in stitches. I felt proud that this many grunts acknowledged her raw talent.

Jennifer Katz was the other phenom in the company. She was a physical stud and a fiercely determined NCO. She had fire in her belly that came from a desire to prove the guys wrong, something I understood intimately and admired in her. She strode around the training field with a formidable presence, rallying her troops to excellence. Occasionally we'd cross paths in the gym during our off-hours, and she'd tell me about her training goals and the trajectory of her career. She was a serious Marine.

Sergeants Hamby and Katz delivered squad after squad of solid new Marines. Their talents got some of the SNCOs in our company discussing women in the infantry. They'd spend smoke breaks talking about sending Hamby and Katz through Infantry Squad Leaders' Course, if it were only allowed, and shutting up anyone who thought the women weren't strong enough to make it. I quietly beamed.

Aside from these women, my biggest influence during this time was my company first sergeant, Ray Mackey. Mackey had spent over two decades in Marine Corps infantry, and had survived the Beirut bombing as a teenager in the Corps. He had the steely, I-don't-give-a-shit attitude of a man who had seen it all. But his no-nonsense style was balanced by enormous compassion. He cared as much about our Marines as he did his own kids. None of them—none of us—wanted to disappoint him.

Mackey and I were an odd couple, he the stubborn and big-hearted first sergeant whose word was gospel to the troops, and I the firm and passionate commander whom he wholeheartedly supported. As the company boss, I never tried to be something I wasn't, or get involved in details Mackey or our instructors could clearly handle. I learned from my staff, guided them where I thought they needed guidance, and listened to Mackey's counsel. He didn't hesitate to tell me what he thought, but always respectfully. We earned a reputation of taking care of our people. We were a happy, hard-working company, and many of the troops in the battalion wanted to serve with us.

Week after week, we trained thousands of Marines in the combat skills they'd eventually be using in Iraq and Afghanistan. The world was changing, and training took on new meaning. These Marines were going to war, whether their recruiters had told them or not.

Abu Ghraib was a turning point for me. I was in the company field office with my SNCOs one morning as the news rolled in about Iraqi prisoners being tortured and sexually humiliated by US soldiers.

Everyone chimed in. The Army was *undisciplined. Nasty. Weak.* This was their problem. And that was the end of that. I took things a bit more to heart, gathering the four hundred students in our company in formation, telling them that we'd done something unacceptable, and that the entire world was watching us.

"We have to take the higher ground. We have a moral responsibility to treat all people with dignity."

As with all lectures from officers, I had no idea if this speech of mine touched anyone. Most of these Marines would see the Middle East in the role of invader and occupier. Whether they would end up calling Muslims and Arabs ragheads, sand niggers, or hajjis like far too many of their fellow Marines, I wouldn't know. In the week after

9/11, I remembered listening to an unhinged master sergeant rattle on about wanting to kill every man, woman, and child in Afghanistan. With these younger Marines, I could only plant a seed.

Officers usually only knew as many details about personnel issues as their senior enlisted advisers chose to tell them. One day Mackey informed me that a white kid in our company had called a Black kid the N-word, and flat-out refused to train with him. With Mackey observing his every move, the white Marine reported in to me first. Stood before my desk at all of 120 pounds of skin and bones.

So, you're the big, bad racist, I thought.

"Did it ever occur to you that you're going to be deploying with Marines from all different backgrounds who might save your life someday?" This was mostly a rhetorical question, and he sensed it, staying locked at attention.

"Did it ever occur to you you're actually working for Marines who aren't white?" Again, a blank stare.

"There's no room for bigots in my company. There's no room for bigots in the Marine Corps. Get out of here. You're dismissed."

"Ay, Ma'am," he exhaled, pivoting like a wet mop.

"No! Do it again!" Mackey gave him a look of death.

The kid about-faced one more time, then ghosted.

The Black Marine, Private Johnson, reported in a few hours later.

"At ease, Marine." God, they were so damn young, these kids. He was the same size as his racist counterpart. I could have drop-kicked both of them to the other end of the room without even trying.

"Private Johnson, there are a lot of morons in this world. And unfortunately some of them make it into the Marine Corps."

"Yes, Ma'am."

The kid was looking at me softly.

We'd already written up and scared the living hell out of the bigot, so I figured making a lesson out of his ignorance might help everyone in the company. I asked Johnson if he was okay staying in the white Marine's fire team and showing him that just because his parents didn't teach him right from wrong didn't mean we couldn't. Johnson nodded his head and reported back to his squad.

I turned to Mackey and sighed. "Have the NCOs all over that racist punk, First Sergeant. I don't want Private Johnson to put up with that shit ever again."

"You got it, Ma'am."

• • •

We heard that the battalion was getting a new lieutenant months before it happened. Neil Thomas had just won a Bronze Star in Iraq for saving lives on the battlefield. The grunts in the battalion sensed that despite his junior rank, Thomas was going to have an ego that would displace everything. And they were right.

That fall, Lieutenant Thomas arrived. Because I didn't have an executive officer, he was assigned to my company. Before meeting with me, he'd made a beeline for Mackey. Mackey told me promptly that Thomas had griped about being assigned to an integrated company, and what was a woman doing commanding one of these companies anyhow?

So the man didn't like women. Heck if I cared. He was going to have to adjust.

Thomas was older than me by a few years, and a prior enlisted infantryman. Still, he was just a lieutenant, and it meant he had to take orders from me, a lowly noninfantry captain, whether he wanted to or not.

I made sure Thomas stayed busy. Training four hundred Marines every day meant a lot of supervision, so I split the live-fire ranges and classroom time with him and carried on as usual. Thomas fell into a routine. He tried to buddy up with the grunts in the unit, but I wasn't the least bit threatened. They still knew I was in charge, and they continued to answer to me.

During one of our slower months, our company requalified on the rifle range. To no one's surprise but Thomas's, I was shooting better than him.

"Ma'am, the guys in my old unit would never let me hear the end of it." I shrugged my shoulders.

A few months into Thomas's time with us, Mackey called me in from the field. He never did that unless there was an emergency. I closed his door and sat down.

"First Sergeant?"

He spoke slowly and calmly. Sergeant Katz had accused Lieutenant Thomas of sexual harassment. He had called one of her female students a slut. She confronted him. The lieutenant responded by spreading rumors that Katz had given him a blow job. Katz was livid, and was not taking Thomas's words without a fight. Sergeant Hamby immediately came to Katz's defense and challenged Thomas. The whole thing then erupted throughout the company.

None of this was hard to believe. Thomas had practically broadcast his misogyny on a jumbotron. But after his initial temper tantrums about women in the Corps, I was hoping he would acclimate to our company. Instead, he'd just been wreaking havoc.

"Oh fuck. How's Katz?"

"She's upset."

Yeah, no shit. I sat there, thinking. The clock was ticking, and my head began to ache. "Options, First Sergeant?"

There was nothing easy about this, but I knew what I had to do. Thomas was like a leaking oil tanker. I decided to keep him away from the company till I spoke with the battalion commander. I called Thomas in from the field, leaving my staff sergeants in charge of training.

An hour later, Thomas came into my office, tentatively.

"Sit down, Lieutenant Thomas." He sat.

I relayed what I'd been told, without emotion. I saw his face rapidly turning red. He barely let me finish.

"That's bullshit. They're lying!" he snapped.

"Listen, Lieutenant Thomas, I want you to stay home till we sort this out."

This sent him over the edge. He lashed out hard, yelling, calling them liars, again and again. I raised my voice, once.

"Shut the hell up."

He did.

I wasn't budging, and he knew it. A menacing look appeared in his eyes. He narrowed them, curled his mouth to one side, and said, "I know you had a relationship with a staff NCO. Sergeant Gornik told me." Oh great. Bumblebee Socks was spending free time with the lieutenant. That could only spell disaster for both of them. Thomas's sudden attempts at deflection and mutiny didn't work. I met him head-on, looking him in the eye.

"Is that right? With whom?"

The lieutenant was searching for names in his head. He didn't know. He let it go.

"Go home, Lieutenant Thomas."

He got really quiet then. And calm. Which just made him look sinister.

"I'm gonna request mast to the colonel," he said, invoking the same protocol I'd told Ibrahim to use when he wanted to speak to someone several levels up the chain of command. Our current school colonel, Gary Keller, had replaced the jump-master who had officiated the sexual assault cover-up. Keller was one of Thomas's old commanders and had recommended Thomas for OCS, paving the way for the infantry sergeant to assert his misogyny with the rank of an officer. The new colonel lacked any of his predecessor's gravitas. He was the kind of socially awkward guy you could tell was bullied as a kid. But none of that mattered now. He had rank. Over me and Thomas, over Katz and the battalion CO.

"Go right ahead. You can submit the paperwork to Sergeant Katz. She's working at the battalion office today. I'm sure she'll process it efficiently." I looked at him, unblinking. That had hit him square between the eyes. He stormed out of there.

My battalion commander, Lieutenant Colonel David Hubbard, was also new to the job. His predecessor, the one who'd talked the Marine mother into keeping quiet about the sexual assault scandal, had just retired. Hubbard had returned stateside after a lengthy combat tour. He seemed to be a fair, levelheaded man. At an officer function he'd recently hosted at his house, I met his wife and his teenage daughter, a bright girl who was a competitive swimmer. I had given her a copy of Lynne Cox's open-water swimming memoir. They were a picture-perfect family.

I'd handled dozens of personnel issues in every unit I'd served in. But handling a renegade subordinate was something new. I couldn't wait for my battalion commander to knock some sense into Thomas and send him on his way. Sitting on the edge of my seat in his office, I told Hubbard the details of what Thomas had been doing to the women in my company. I felt relieved. It didn't last long.

"Captain Bhagwati, Marines accuse officers of all kinds of things."

"Excuse me, Sir?" He must not have heard me.

"Marines say things. Accusations like this can ruin careers."

Oh god, he *had* heard me. I looked at Hubbard, searching for some sign in his blank expression. Someone must have gotten to him before I did. He didn't even feign shock. He didn't even pretend to need time to gather the facts.

"Sir, we're talking about Katz and Hamby. They're the best NCOs in our company."

Hubbard just stared at me. Shit, this wasn't working.

"You just gave Hamby a NAM.* Are you saying they're *lying*, Sir?"

"Marines get frustrated, and they lash out."

My head was reeling.

"Sir, you know Thomas has issues with women. He never wanted to be in an integrated company. He made it known. Loud and clear."

"Look, Captain Bhagwati, you gave Thomas good marks on his last fitness report."

---

* Navy and Marine Corps Achievement Medal.

It was true. It was after he calmed down a bit and I felt he'd gotten the swing of things. But one good evaluation didn't mean he wasn't a serial harasser. It didn't mean anything.

"Sir . . ." I paused. God, I felt like I was stuck in some never-ending loop where senior officers were completely confounded by Marine men doing awful things to women.

I couldn't read my BC. Was he buying that two of the best Marines in his battalion had some personal vendetta against Thomas, a man who'd established a solid reputation for undermining women? Katz and Hamby had everything to lose by making a stink about a Bronze Star–toting officer who was chums with the school colonel.

"Captain Bhagwati, I've been in situations like this before, where two Marines just look like they want to knock each other out." Hubbard meant Thomas and me. What was he playing at? Thomas hated me because I was a woman. It was just that simple.

I had to try something else. Something personal.

"Sir, if your daughter was in my company, would you be okay having Lieutenant Thomas as our executive officer?"

The mood in the room was somber, but a smile unfolded on Hubbard's face. He was in another world.

He said, "Yes, Captain Bhagwati. Because you're in charge."

I had officially entered Crazy Town.

"Sir, I urge you, at the very least, transfer Thomas to another company. Send him to ITB.* He can't work with women. It's not a good idea for anyone."

My plea must have sounded like a child's whine, because for whatever reason, Hubbard was not budging. I had no cards left to play.

"Captain Bhagwati. Thomas is staying in your company. And you're going to fix this situation."

---

* Infantry Training Battalion, the unit where all enlisted infantrymen are trained. Because of the ban on women in the infantry, there were no female students or staff at ITB at the time.

. . .

Over the next few days, I learned that the Marine Corps had its own methods of dealing with sexual harassment allegations, particularly when the accused was an officer.

Soon after my conversation with the battalion CO, the battalion executive officer forced me to play along in the military's most beloved method of ensuring harassment like Thomas's went away quickly, without any paper trail: informal resolution.

This amounted to the major sitting me down with Thomas for a casual conversation. Thomas sat there calmly, like a well-prepped criminal defendant. God, the guy could really act. I was in no mood to play. I was horrified by the school's attempt to squash Katz's complaint yet again.

"Captain Bhagwati, Lieutenant Thomas, this meeting is designed to address any misunderstandings between the two of you."

I was dumbfounded. Since when did this become about misunderstandings between Thomas and me? I could barely sit still.

"Sir, I'm not participating in this. Thomas shouldn't even be here. It's inappropriate." I stood up suddenly, bid the major a good day, and walked out, leaving them both stunned.

I thought hard about what to do next. I headed for the school headquarters on base. I asked to see the school XO. He worked for the school colonel, Keller, who was surely protecting Thomas, but perhaps he was more reasonable than his counterparts.

I was right. The man listened to me. He nodded his head. Sympathized, commiserated. It was looking good for Katz. But at the end of the day, I was just a lowly captain, and senior officers had loyalties only to one another. Within hours I was summoned to report into my battalion commander's office.

Hubbard's face was bloodred. With the fury of twenty years of infantry experience behind his voice, he told me, "You will not speak to anyone outside of your chain of command about this incident. Do you understand, Captain?"

I understood. With this gag order in effect, I went home, shaking.

I was dragged into the battalion commander's office again the next day, with Thomas in tow. We sat down beside each other uncomfortably, like two children awaiting punishment after pissing off their dad. Hubbard looked at us both sternly. Before he could get two sentences out, Thomas interrupted him.

"Sir, I have proof that Captain Bhagwati is in an inappropriate relationship with a—"

"Not another word, Lieutenant." Hubbard's blue eyes darkened. Thomas stayed quiet.

"Captain Bhagwati, I want you to go over what you expect of Lieutenant Thomas going forward. Lieutenant Thomas, I don't want to hear any nonsense about you from your company commander or anyone else. Is this understood?"

"Yes, Sir." It was the first time I'd seen anyone aside from me smack Thomas down. It seemed to be the only way to get him to do the right thing. That was not comforting.

Hubbard dismissed us. Thomas followed me into an adjacent conference room as I mustered whatever poker face I could, Hubbard's words still echoing in my head. I was terrified. Of Hubbard. Of Thomas. Of what I knew was happening. Of what I didn't know was happening. Without any way out, I started performing.

"Lieutenant Thomas, I need you to make sure you're not sexually harassing anyone in the company. Saying sexually explicit things about any staff member or student. Using words that could at all be construed as being sexual in nature. Demeaning women. Speaking about women's bodies . . ." I could barely believe the words coming out of my mouth. In what bizarre world did this need to be said?

The guy was really playing along. Two minutes before he was threatening bloody mutiny, but now Thomas was taking notes—or possibly, drawing a picture of me with a bayonet in my chest—as though I were giving him an op order. This was not lost on him, the recipient of a combat valor award and a guy who'd spent so many years kicking down doors and shooting Brown people around the world that he looked twice my age on a good day. I don't know for whom this administrative humiliation was intended more, him or me.

"Got it? Any questions?"

"No, Ma'am." He looked at me with the corners of his eyes signaling triumph. As if nothing had happened. In that moment I realized I was dealing with an experienced sociopath.

I went back to my company. We were in the middle of a training cycle while this drama was unfolding. First Sergeant Mackey got our Marines together in the company hut out in the training area. Thomas was not present.

"Guys, I tried my best to get the battalion commander to understand what the lieutenant has been doing here. The BC's not listening. He doesn't seem to care. I'm really sorry. Sometimes you can be right and it just doesn't matter."

I heard some gasps and some what the fucks. The guys, all grunts, had Katz's back. That was good to see. That support was probably all she was going to get, but it meant something. We sat there for a few minutes. A couple of folks had questions for me, while the rest looked like someone had just kicked their teeth in. One of the NCOs rose to his feet, impatiently.

"Come on, we have work to do."

He was right. We couldn't let these morons derail training. Life went on. I gritted my teeth. Thomas went about the training area the proud victor. I said little to him, and he said little to me. The Marines just did their jobs. But any feeling of joy in the company was gone. This was no longer a safe space to work, and I didn't know what to do about it.

Fourteen years later, Mackey would tell me vividly that during those tenuous months, he followed Thomas around the company training areas. Shadowed him in the field. Even before the harassment scandal erupted, Mackey didn't trust the lieutenant with any junior women and knew I had no power to stop Thomas. Mackey had seen everything during his career. The idea that the Marine Corps was so impotent in dealing with sexual predators that Thomas had to be watched like a sex offender around a schoolyard floored me.

One day, two of my staff sergeants approached me in the company pickup truck. They looked at me expectantly through the window.

"Ma'am, the lieutenant is at it again. He's talking shit about women. About you, too." I felt an all-too-familiar rage arising inside me as they told me the latest details. But I started to wonder, why the hell hadn't *they* said anything to Thomas? So what, he was an officer. But he wasn't *God*. When were they going to realize that they, too, had a say in right vs. wrong?

Later that day, the battalion commander was walking through the training area. I remember it was hot outside. I saluted Hubbard, and he returned the salute.

"Sir, Thomas is back to his old tricks."

He paused. "I'll get the XO to sit you two down again, sort this out."

"No, Sir." He hadn't meant it as a choice, but I didn't care. "Thomas hates women. I'm not letting him get away with this again."

I left the BC standing alone in the dirt road, blinking. After a sleepless night, I drove across town to Camp Lejeune, the site of legal headquarters. It was my first brush with military lawyers since Horse Face had been dropped from OCS. Judge Advocate General (JAG) Corps was another world inside the military.* Marines generally spoke about JAG as though it were in some ivory tower and removed from the realities of the Corps, but it was often the glue holding the institution together.

A colonel invited me into a plush carpeted room, sat me down in

---

* Attorneys in JAG Corps handle legal matters for the military.

a leather chair, and listened. It felt good to be able to speak without being told that women were plotting to ruin a good man's career. A senior military lawyer, the colonel suggested I meet with Base Equal Opportunity (EO) to file a complaint. I'd received dozens of force-fed EO briefs over the years, death-by-PowerPoint Marine Corps presentations on the politically correct regulations that were feminizing and weakening the Corps, none of which actually protected vulnerable Marines from bigots in uniform. EO allegedly covered the full gamut of discriminatory treatment, from Thomas's blow-job rumors to Marines not getting promoted because they were Black, female, gay, or Muslim.

I decided to give EO a shot. I was tired, driving myself forward by the growing sense that if I slowed down at all I'd realize how powerless I was in the face of these senior officers and either freeze or fall apart. A staff sergeant—a white woman with short brown hair, impeccable manners, and a warm voice—sat me down in a folding chair before a wooden table, a setup that reminded me of public schools back in New York City.

In the next few hours that the staff sergeant spent with me, it became clear that her assignment was not the soft, cushy billet for POGs that most Marines said it was. I was throwing everything at her from sheer outrage to details about who had done what to whom and where, and she dealt with it like some kind of therapist-cum-crisis-communications-expert while maintaining the calm bearing of a monk.

"Ma'am, it's a clear case of sexual harassment. There's no gray area here."

What? If it was so clear-cut, why was I sitting here like some kind of asylum seeker, waiting for the other shoe to drop?

She went on.

"Ma'am, it's not just the lieutenant's actions. You have clear grounds for charging your battalion commander for failing to address the ongoing harassment. He was derelict in his duties."

I grew terribly silent. Almost numb. She left for a moment to talk to her boss. We joined him in his office a moment later. He was a full-bird colonel, the officer in charge of EO for all of Camp Lejeune. He was the only Black officer I'd met in my entire career above the rank of captain. I don't know what happened exactly. I just crumbled.

As tears and snot dripped down my face, the colonel invited me as gently as he could to take a break. I sat there, shaking. Somehow I mustered the words, "Sorry, Sir, I've never lost my bearing like this in front of a senior officer."

"Staff Sergeant, get the captain some Kleenex." Those words were meant to offer compassion but they stung, as if Thomas himself had said it. They waited for me to find my breath.

"Sir, you want me to charge my battalion commander? He has a daughter. And a wife." They let me breathe. Softly, I said, "I'm only a captain."

"Captain Bhagwati, it's your choice. I know it's not an easy thing." The colonel was the king of understatement. This ludicrous proposition undermined the very order of the Corps. We always took orders from senior Marines, or faced terrible, life-altering consequences. A Marine was not meant to charge her boss, particularly after being threatened by that boss, who was clearly taking orders from his boss. It was just not done. I was protecting Katz as best I could, but there wasn't a soul protecting me. The system was broken, and we all knew it.

I sat there in a quiet, timeless bubble that I came to know years later as a dissociative response. How I survived despite it—or that I survived because of it—might have said something about my genetic makeup, or a steely inner disposition, or luck. It sure as hell wasn't my training. The Marine Corps prepared me for none of this reality. It hadn't prepared any of us.

I wished time would stop, so I could stay there in the relative safety of these two Marines, who so clearly, unequivocally affirmed that the officers at my school had staged a united cover-up to protect a junior infantry officer.

I went back to my company. I needed counsel from someone I could count on. I sought it from Sergeant Hamby, who lacked guile and would talk to me straight, even if it was going to be uncomfortable or difficult. We sat on a bench outside the battalion office. I caught her up on my legal conversations and laid out my options.

"Sergeant Hamby, what do you think? Do you want me to move forward with this?"

Hamby thought quietly. She finally said, "Ma'am, you're the only one who can do something to stop him."

It was settled then. The same day, I filed an official investigation into the incident with EO. It would be completely independent from my chain of command at the School of Infantry. EO would appoint an impartial investigator to step into the school, interview witnesses, and come up with recommendations as to what to do with Thomas.

As for criminally charging my battalion commander, I was terrified enough of the repercussions of the EO investigation without the additional pressure of throwing my boss behind bars. But there was more to it than that. Even though he had done the wrong thing, I still felt a dizzying sense of something that felt like loyalty. This was not actual loyalty—like the kind I felt for Katz or Hamby or Mackey. It was a warped loyalty based on abuse of power and lies. If my parents had introduced the concept of love being entwined with force, manipulation, and authority, the Corps had drilled it into my sense of the world. Affection was wound up in power, and even though Hubbard had abused his, I was on some level still the obedient Indian girl who could not fully challenge my father. Hubbard may have ended up being the unintended beneficiary of my unresolved daddy issues.

Upsetting the order was necessary in order to free my NCOs, and in order to free myself, but I was barely functioning at work anymore. Sleepless and anxious, I put on a game face that required emotionally shutting down. Every minute I was on that base felt like suffocation.

I followed the advice of the JAG colonel I'd seen and got a

restraining order filed against Thomas. I didn't know what he was capable of, and the school sure didn't have my back. I had visions of Thomas showing up on my doorstep with a loaded shotgun and blowing my head off. The battalion responded to my restraining order by getting a restraining order against me on Thomas's behalf. When Hubbard, the man I could have charged, called me in to sign the paperwork about the distance I'd be forced to keep from Thomas, I laughed out loud in disbelief.

I now made sure that I never entered the battalion commander's office without a witness, and took careful notes of everything he said. I wasn't going to risk being threatened by him again in private.

The next month was a haze of waiting. I had come up with a list of about fifty witnesses for the investigator to interview. Thomas's comments spanned the spectrum of gossiping about who might be a lesbian—he'd focused his attentions on one corporal in particular—to scrutinizing the dimensions of our young female students to inventing illicit relationships between female and male staff in the battalion and spreading sexual rumors about me and countless other women in uniform. Apparently this was stuff he'd been doing for a while.

Some part of me knew that seeing justice in a system where men wanted nothing more than to shut doors to women was not likely, but I was a hopeless optimist. I had some sense that had stayed with me from the outside world, a world I was increasingly seeing as the real world, while this was one of fantasy and nightmare.

• • •

As my faith in the Marine Corps plummeted and the lieutenant's sexual harassment morphed into a full-fledged battalion scandal, I began to seek refuge in unexpected places.

I was living in Wilmington, North Carolina, now. It was an hour-long commute from base but well worth the hassle because it reminded me that there was a vibrant world outside the Corps. I was surrounded by college students, shaggy-haired surfers, multigeneration Black families, even a gay bar that pulled in crowds of colorful queers from all around the Carolinas.

One evening on the drive home I stepped into a yoga studio just off the highway. Yoga wasn't new to me. I discovered it back when I was a second lieutenant, navigating Captain Hoffman's rape jokes and my friends' strip club tales at Communications School. On a whim, I had spent two weeks of leave at a yoga ashram in the Catskill Mountains.* I left feeling giddy and peaceful, but when I returned to Quantico and put on my uniform again, I realized it was hard to practice being calm and centered and cultivate the art of killing at the same time. Being a Marine meant summoning the best of my rage and aggression. Peacefulness had no place in my survival. And as a woman in the Marines, survival was all that mattered.

Yoga was about creating space for vulnerability. Now, at the School of Infantry, I felt like I had nothing left to lose. In the studio in Wilmington, I was greeted by two women, identical twins who had sturdy shoulders and wide lats from years of standing upside down. But what I remember most was their kind eyes and warm smiles.

This was not the land of CLP. The place smelled like lavender and pine trees. The walls were soft yellow and lime green. I entered a room that faced the woods, and we stretched, breathed, rolled over, and stretched some more. After an hour or so of this, we lay down on our backs.

A middle-aged teacher, white, female, and skinny, softly encouraged us.

"Gently release."

I tried to release, gently.

"Just surrender."

I tried to surrender, but not so gently. In the silence, with my vitals now completely exposed to the ceiling above, something arose in

---

* The Sivananda Yoga Ranch is still alive and well. It is one of the few classical yoga institutes in the United States.

me, a warped, three-headed-monsterlike panic, and I knew on some primal level that I was not safe. I needed to move. I needed to escape.

I sat up on the mat, stiff all over again.

"Can you lie back down?" It was a question, but it felt like a command.

I shook my head from left to right, *no*. Avoiding eye contact with the teacher, stuttering, because words to explain what was happening inside me weren't available to me at the time, I sprinted out of the room, ran to my car, and drove off.

I didn't yet understand these post-traumatic rumblings, but they were a small price to pay for the feeling I got of being in a place where as a woman I wasn't looked at like I was a liability or an opportunity for conquest, where I could listen to the soothing voice of an instructor who had no personal agenda to work out on my body, or abuses to unload on my psyche. So I went back.

In the final few months of my military career, I was doing all I could to maintain my composure for my Marines. Each day amounted to keeping people alive, tolerating the knives in my back, and when my day was done, getting into my car and hightailing it off base, music blaring, tears falling.

The yoga twins knew something was amok in Jacksonville. My days were saturated with violence and uncertainty. On a typical day I made sure hundreds of teenagers properly threw live grenades over a cement barrier and ducked with the correct sense of urgency. If some kid didn't follow safety rules or one of our instructors wasn't paying attention, someone would be dead and my ass would be on the line.

I could handle this. I lived for this. But the sexual harassment investigation, on top of everything, was more than my body could contain. The twins gave me shelter, week after week, with an endless supply of smiles and deep forward bends. I was not flexible, but flexibility was beside the point. I learned to lie still on my back while they placed oil on my palms and feet. I smelled oranges and lemongrass.

One day back on base, I chose to teach my company yoga. I

demonstrated pose after pose, which they soaked up like hungry recruits. Yoga today was the great equalizer. Hamby and Katz were having a blast. Even First Sergeant Mackey was deep in it, although probably silently cursing me for stretching the muscles in his older, battered body. I kept a close eye on Thomas, who had no choice under my command but to reach, twist, and bend, exposed before the women he had harmed.

There were eager cries of enthusiasm when I asked if they'd like to learn some inversions. Headstand. Handstand. Scorpion. These were not poses for beginners, but Marines tended to forget there was any way but all the way. So I taught them to balance upside down against the wall of the barracks. The hell with form or caution. Laughing, heads down and forearms on the grass, they flung their legs up against the bricks as if there were no such thing as gravity, and for a moment, I was at ease and happy, forgetting about both the lieutenant's toxic presence—he had given up on these poses anyway and was standing to the side—and my contempt for the command. My Marines were having fun, and so was I.

• • •

If there was one redeeming element to my last year in the Corps, it was that I gained a close ally and a best friend beyond the Marines. Before getting command of my company, I ended up working on a special project with my old boss, Greg Jacob, the captain who had tried in vain to get justice for our students who had been sexually assaulted and who'd extracted me from the destructive relationship with Staff Sergeant Lowell. We spent several months putting together a training curriculum for tens of thousands of reservists who had just been recalled by Uncle Sam to deploy to Iraq.

Greg thought I was wasting my talent. He was one of the only Marines I'd meet who believed I had something to offer the world. Greg may have been raised in the culture of the infantry, but he was a far cry from his peers. He was well read in everything from feminist theory to world history.

A member of the Lakota Sioux tribe, Greg intimately knew the history of the US government's exploitation of people of color. He had wrestled with the meaning of gunning down poor Black people in Liberia or earning his Purple Heart while defending a Nike shoe factory from mobs in Indonesia. After the episode with Fox, the sexual predator, Greg was convinced there were few reasons left to drink the Corps' Kool-Aid. And when I told him what was going down with my lieutenant, he supported me instantly. Our shared experiences with the Marine Corps' hypocrisy would form the foundation of a connection few people could touch, in or outside of the Marines.

Meanwhile, Greg's marriage had fallen apart. He was separated, living in the barracks, and still somehow managing to get his young kids to and from school. It was a messy time to fall in love. Thomas was completely protected and coddled by his senior officers, but his threats against my personal life didn't land on sympathetic ears, whether it was because Greg had already told our higher-ups we were together or because these senior infantrymen had seen and done it all before, who knew. After my time in Thailand it was easy to believe many Marines were privately managing secret relationships while putting on masks in public.

By North Carolina law, Greg couldn't be officially divorced until one full year of separation. While he waited for the paperwork to come through, we moved together with my dogs into a house in downtown Wilmington, and I had some semblance of home for the first time since I joined the Marines.

When I told my mother I was moving in with Greg, she was horrified.

"What kind of a person are you, breaking up his marriage!" she cried. In her mind, I was the heartless vixen who had steered Greg away from his helpless wife and kids. Greg insisted that he and his wife had separated months before we'd gotten close, but my mother's shaming was more powerful than anything Greg could have said to convince me otherwise.

When shit hit the fan with Thomas and the battalion, Greg was my only support. I came home each evening from long days of commanding my company, sobbing, collapsing in a huddle, holding my animals, wishing my life away. Greg told me that what I was going through—the personal isolation, the cover-ups, the threats and intimidation—was far worse than anything he had experienced in war.

. . .

When the school commander decided to promote Thomas to captain and give him command of my company before the sexual harassment investigation was even complete, I went radio silent. I kept thinking about my mother. She hadn't raised me to put up with this shit. I remember pondering if I should bring in my junior senator, the former First Lady of the United States. A congressional investigation by Hillary Clinton's office was the next logical step. But I was exhausted. And completely demoralized. Nothing had happened to Thomas, but I didn't need to see Thomas punished anymore. I needed recovery.

I had applied to graduate school—a move that Hubbard questioned, asking me, "What are you going to do if you don't get in?" as if he cared.

At my final school function, Hubbard called me forward to speak. With sickening gall, he told the room full of senior infantrymen that my leadership as a company commander had been defined by taking care of others. The grunts in the room gazed at me with cold, detached eyes. I decided to say my last few words in gratitude to First Sergeant Mackey, who'd had my and the other women's backs despite the school trying to crush us.

All the women who were in Thomas's crosshairs left the Corps within months, including me, Katz, Hamby, and the corporal who was in fact a lesbian. One of my staff sergeants called me weeks later, after I'd driven back home to the Northeast, a guy who'd once told me I was as good a company commander as any infantry officer he'd ever met.

"You shouldn't have quit, Ma'am. You let them win."

His words stayed with me for some time. Was I really a quitter?

I felt as though I had no real choice but to break up with the Corps. My misery was starting to look a lot like trauma. Men like Franco and Thomas and Hubbard were everywhere. And I'd always be answering to or avoiding them. I'd wanted badly to serve in combat. I'd wanted to prove myself and test my limits. It was impossible to have been fed the inspiration I'd gotten for five years from the men I'd known—men like Mackey and Bristol—and not want to deploy with them overseas.

I made no time to reflect on what I'd done well in uniform. It was not possible for me to see anything but the worst of my experience, when the worst seemed to be all that surrounded me. I was drowning in self-hatred. And I was drowning in shame. Shame that I couldn't protect my Marines. Shame that I'd made so many mistakes. That I possibly wasn't good enough for the Marines, just like Baughman had said. And worst of all, shame that I may have proven that women didn't belong in the Corps.

I ran away from the Marines as quickly, furiously, and thoroughly as I'd run away from my parents. But it was becoming increasingly apparent that the person in my life I most wanted to run away from was me.

a leather chair, and listened. It felt good to be able to speak without being told that women were plotting to ruin a good man's career. A senior military lawyer, the colonel suggested I meet with Base Equal Opportunity (EO) to file a complaint. I'd received dozens of force-fed EO briefs over the years, death-by-PowerPoint Marine Corps presentations on the politically correct regulations that were feminizing and weakening the Corps, none of which actually protected vulnerable Marines from bigots in uniform. EO allegedly covered the full gamut of discriminatory treatment, from Thomas's blow-job rumors to Marines not getting promoted because they were Black, female, gay, or Muslim.

I decided to give EO a shot. I was tired, driving myself forward by the growing sense that if I slowed down at all I'd realize how powerless I was in the face of these senior officers and either freeze or fall apart. A staff sergeant—a white woman with short brown hair, impeccable manners, and a warm voice—sat me down in a folding chair before a wooden table, a setup that reminded me of public schools back in New York City.

In the next few hours that the staff sergeant spent with me, it became clear that her assignment was not the soft, cushy billet for POGs that most Marines said it was. I was throwing everything at her from sheer outrage to details about who had done what to whom and where, and she dealt with it like some kind of therapist-cum-crisis-communications-expert while maintaining the calm bearing of a monk.

"Ma'am, it's a clear case of sexual harassment. There's no gray area here."

What? If it was so clear-cut, why was I sitting here like some kind of asylum seeker, waiting for the other shoe to drop?

She went on.

"Ma'am, it's not just the lieutenant's actions. You have clear grounds for charging your battalion commander for failing to address the ongoing harassment. He was derelict in his duties."

I grew terribly silent. Almost numb. She left for a moment to talk to her boss. We joined him in his office a moment later. He was a full-bird colonel, the officer in charge of EO for all of Camp Lejeune. He was the only Black officer I'd met in my entire career above the rank of captain. I don't know what happened exactly. I just crumbled.

As tears and snot dripped down my face, the colonel invited me as gently as he could to take a break. I sat there, shaking. Somehow I mustered the words, "Sorry, Sir, I've never lost my bearing like this in front of a senior officer."

"Staff Sergeant, get the captain some Kleenex." Those words were meant to offer compassion but they stung, as if Thomas himself had said it. They waited for me to find my breath.

"Sir, you want me to charge my battalion commander? He has a daughter. And a wife." They let me breathe. Softly, I said, "I'm only a captain."

"Captain Bhagwati, it's your choice. I know it's not an easy thing." The colonel was the king of understatement. This ludicrous proposition undermined the very order of the Corps. We always took orders from senior Marines, or faced terrible, life-altering consequences. A Marine was not meant to charge her boss, particularly after being threatened by that boss, who was clearly taking orders from his boss. It was just not done. I was protecting Katz as best I could, but there wasn't a soul protecting me. The system was broken, and we all knew it.

I sat there in a quiet, timeless bubble that I came to know years later as a dissociative response. How I survived despite it—or that I survived because of it—might have said something about my genetic makeup, or a steely inner disposition, or luck. It sure as hell wasn't my training. The Marine Corps prepared me for none of this reality. It hadn't prepared any of us.

I wished time would stop, so I could stay there in the relative safety of these two Marines, who so clearly, unequivocally affirmed that the officers at my school had staged a united cover-up to protect a junior infantry officer.

PART II

CHAPTER 9

Invitation to a Beheading

Cambridge, Massachusetts
2004

Two weeks into my master's program at Harvard University, I got the phone call I'd been waiting for from Marine Corps Training and Education Command. A female master sergeant delivered the results of my sexual harassment investigation. She was smart and authoritative, and I exhaled for the first time in ages. She and the general in charge determined that Lieutenant Thomas was in fact guilty of sexual harassment. They'd advised the School of Infantry to remove Thomas from any leadership positions and to reflect the incident in his records.

Unfortunately, this decision lacked the fear-of-God impact of real Marine Corps ass chewings. Equal Opportunity rulings had no legal or criminal weight. The general's words were simply a recommendation, not a verdict. And when the colonel in charge of the School of Infantry was the bad guy who swept the lieutenant's mess under the rug in the first place, it meant nothing happened to Thomas in the end, except for a private counseling session, in which I'm pretty sure the colonel toasted the lieutenant for his good fortune, and the lieutenant thanked the colonel for saving his ass.

I thanked the master sergeant and hung up the phone. The only consolation was that I was hundreds of miles away from all that craziness, rebuilding my life from scratch.

Remarkably, when I left the Marines, I ended up in Lexington, Massachusetts, in the house that I lived in as a baby. It was empty now except for me and Shiva and Uma, who, aside from Greg, were the only two beings left over from my time in uniform.

Greg was now living in Long Island, New York, while I finished my studies. Greg had come up north with me despite a near breakup. In the middle of the investigation at Camp Lejeune, I completely shut down, and before rejecting the Corps as a whole, the first Marine I rejected was Greg. I cheated on him with a complete loser of a man, an older Marine in the school who was a serial womanizer, and like so many others, married but not revealing he was.

It was the first time I'd ever cheated on anyone. My best friend, no less. The man who'd had my back. I don't know what I was doing. Hurting Greg may have given me one more reason to think I didn't have a right to real happiness. He forgave me, even though I did not feel I deserved to be forgiven.

I'd brought my furniture from North Carolina up to Massachusetts. Greg helped me paint the rooms in bold colors: yellow, orange, and midnight blue. I might as well have painted them gray. Some nights I just lay in bed staring at the space between my feet and listening to the suburban darkness, this silence that was too silent to find peace in. On other nights my dreams took me back to the Marines.

I had a recurring nightmare in which Sergeant Hamby was struck by lightning and left at the bottom of a ditch. I was trying to bear the weight of a crackling, falling telephone pole so it didn't crush her into the mud. I was holding the log over my head while trying to dig her out of the earth. It was too much, and I could not save her.

Reality was shifting beyond me. I turned on the television to make sense of my place in the world. It was a hopeless endeavor. Every network contained pictures of proud young men with big guns, sunglasses, and tan boots kicking down doors, patrolling hot urban streets filled with throngs of sun-drenched men and head-scarved women, and small brown children with large brown eyes. I wasn't sure if I was the one holding the weapon or looking into its muzzle.

There was an unused Ka-Bar within arm's reach by my bed. It had mostly been for show, this knife. Now it was my protection from the silence of the night. I imagined taking the blade from its sheath and carving along the thickest parts of my legs, slowly, so I could hear the sound of sinews giving in, sense the warmth and wetness of this flesh. I would remember then how it was to feel. If I cut well, I was bound to leave a good scar. The blood would stain these sheets, so I would not forget.

Except I was fucking chickenshit. I left the knife where it was, watching it. Though I rehearsed it well in my mind, I did not step into any moving trucks, or jump off any highway overpasses. I kept it all inside, partially trapped, so that it seeped out just enough to keep me mad, stuck, and miserable. It was so typical. No follow-through. No commitment. I was a bad Marine, and I was even worse at ending myself. There was no way out.

• • •

Choosing to attend a public policy program at the most elite school I could imagine was my way of making sure the Corps felt small. This was my exit route, and my new beginning. The thing that would give my life meaning. But graduate school at Harvard was no reawakening. It was certainly not a homecoming. It was just purgatory, a place to bide my time, pretend that I belonged, act like I cared. My head was disconnected from my body. I was floating from moment to moment, sad, furious, bitter, detached.

The wars in Iraq and Afghanistan were rolling along, and everyone not wearing a uniform, everyone who would never, ever wear a uniform, wanted a piece of the action. Professors and students very proudly professed opinions on foreign policy strategy, diplomatic alternatives, military readiness, and new tactics developed by an ever-growing web of dark-skinned terrorists. My classmates, white men with career eyes on the NSA, Pentagon, and State Department, had a real boner for Al Qaeda. They talked about Islam like it was a woman whom they would never have. They talked about Osama bin Laden with too much personal enthusiasm, as if they were finally gonna get even with their childhood bully. Men flocked to national security classes, inspired. In a world where no one was safe, these folks had found their purpose.

I was fed up with this place where fantasy concocted in classrooms would very likely become reality in Washington. People talked about war like it was a video game. And they talked about troops as if they were either demigods or no one at all.

One day, out of nowhere, I got an email from Bristol. Time stopped for a bit and I could not recall where I was. He was spending a year at MIT, at a program for select senior military officers. He told me he had just been showing off about my black belt journey to some folks. I felt a rush of pride. I still worshipped this man. I would still crawl over broken glass for this man. I hated and loved this man. Bristol was my Kurtz, and no reality in the Ivy League could explain my pull toward him. We talked about having coffee but it never happened. This was just as well. I might never have found my way back. It was the last time I heard from him.

I was not free from the military's influence just yet. A handful of active duty and veteran students attended graduate school with me, which meant I was constantly on edge, watching my back, preparing my defenses for the next ambush. The vets didn't understand why I wasn't hanging out with them after hours, drinking beer, laughing about the dumb shit we all went through and sharing war stories. One ex-Marine, a friendly guy who'd just returned home from Iraq, was eager to share company with another Marine and wanted to connect with me. I desperately avoided him.

The former Navy SEALs among us were treated like immortals. One was working his way through the female population like he'd just been released from prison. Another military student, a five-foot-tall Navy ensign all of twenty-two years old, told me with a sadistic grin that he couldn't wait to get out there and kill a bunch of terrorists. The short schmuck rekindled whatever disgust I had for morons with access to weapons.

One blond-haired, blue-eyed student, a young Robert Redford look-alike, was doing the talk-show circuit for a book he'd written about his Marine Corps recon and infantry exploits. I wanted to like him, but he talked about war and civilian casualties and his pussy-loving, "raghead"-hating troops like he was Lawrence of Arabia. The media was eating him up, and he was massaging them right back, with eloquent sentences and cultural insight they couldn't seem to get enough of. If he had any idea of the critical role he was playing in the larger world of white conquerors triumphing over Brown savages, he didn't let on. I pushed him to open his mind to some bigger picture that I could barely put into words back then, but he was too far gone down the path to celebrity. Like most public war heroes, he was living in his own bubble and untouchable.

I had too many strong feelings and no skills to manage them around these folks, so I avoided them. I sought company in places from my past. This felt safer. More like me, somehow.

Being in an institution in which half my classmates were now women took a few weeks of acclimation. Women were no longer expected to take a backseat to men, and my system was in shock. I began to wonder if something good inside me had shifted irreparably, if the Marines had changed my wiring about how I perceived women. Had I become a misogynist?

One afternoon I was having coffee with two women in my class, die-hard activists for racial justice and gender equality, and unapologetically queer, and it occurred to me that this moment never would have been possible in the Marines. There were no activists in the Corps. The few friends I had repressed their racial, religious, and gender identities with the same intensity with which they trained for deployments. Sipping my coffee and listening to these women talk about June Jordan and Audre Lorde, I started tearing up. I told them, "I couldn't talk to anyone like this in the military. Women weren't supposed to think for themselves."

They looked at me with a mixture of sympathy and surprise. Watching women hold their own without being slut-shamed, damned, or erased for existing in the same space as men was a sweet form of therapy. Another gift was meeting students from all over the world, confirming for me that the band of brothers I used to serve with, many of whom flinched at the sight of a brown-skinned man, a burqa, or a turban, did not have the final word on who I was or how I lived my life.

I found myself here at the academic intersection of all things violent and possible. This was an exhausting place to be, where morality was relative, and everything was open to discussion.

My law school class on the rights of those seeking asylum turned one day to a discussion of Nazi tactics. There was a twentysomething Jewish law student, straight out of college, rapping fervently about the unique nature of the individual Nazi who was blindly following orders to kill. I listened closely.

This kid was too educated for his own good. Like most of his peers, he would become a corporate lawyer, with a shot at becoming a real muckety-muck, in just a few years. Few people would ever question him. And poring over all that case law, he would rarely have the time to question himself.

Still, I knew this kid could have been me, or maybe I used to be this kid, and I responded with as much care as I could, raising my hand and explaining that even good people could be trained to think and commit horrific, unthinkable acts of violence. I saw the kid, this top-of-the-class, smart-as-fuck Harvard Law student, getting riled up. He was shaking his head vigorously, *No, she's wrong*.

He could not comprehend. Law school was not cultivating this kid's imagination. He could not even pause to consider the possibility of a world larger than the books he had read, or the stories he had grown up with. The Nazis couldn't possibly have been born human. Real human beings would never do what they did. You either were or were not a psychopath. It was just that simple.

This reductive analysis of those who perpetrated violence had my head spinning for years. I had no reason left to believe that some people were good and some bad; with his combat awards, Thomas would be some kind of god to sheltered kids like this. And Fox had not only gone to Iraq after putting his hands all over female Marines, he'd gotten killed there. He would be remembered as a war hero, and all his sins forgotten.

. . .

Three months out of the Corps, I was in my university computer lab writing a paper on US torture policy. This was the kind of situation my childhood moral compass would have immediately rebelled against. But these days, I was all in.

My professor, Michael Ignatieff, a former journalist turned human rights scholar, had recently written a provocative article supporting the US war in Iraq. His reputation as a good guy was being called into question by the bleeding hearts of the Western world. They'd damned him as a traitor to the cause.

Moral relativism—let's invade for the greater good—could morph into all sorts of twisted thought experiments in the ivory tower. This was the world I currently occupied. With my academic privilege, I discovered the extent of my own sadism, and my own shame.

Ignatieff had made himself quite the target for leftists and peaceniks. He believed human rights must at some point meet the cold truth of reality on the ground, and the needs and limitations of the state. He delivered lectures with enviable charisma. He had the intellect, looks, warm eyes, and poetic voice that pulled you in and convinced you he was on your side. I was used to men like this.

At the front of the lecture hall one day, he pulled up the now iconic photo of an Iraqi detainee stripped down to a loincloth, hooded and just barely standing on a small box in the Abu Ghraib detention facility.

The headline read: "Is This Torture?" There were murmurs. Blatant attempts to impress the professor. And sighs of frustration.

Some folks dismissed the exercise immediately, calling my professor a war criminal behind his back. But I lived in the no-man's-land between right and wrong. I felt compelled to undergo the intellectual exercise of examining what I believed and formulating a new worldview, a handbook, on morality. I wasn't going to swallow the ethical guidelines of a fairy-tale universe, where people were conveniently marked as either heroes or villains.

I'd been changed. Fundamentally altered, down to the DNA. Bristol was largely to blame, or praise, for this rewiring. Because Bristol had driven home in me my relative lack of worth as a woman in this world, I had homed in on men's vulnerabilities with ferocity. Necks and groins were practically begging to be sliced open. I could do this well, even at my size. My inner monologue was a study in sociopathy. I had been such a quiet, domesticated child. I had never stood up for myself. Now the tables were turned.

Street harassment by creepy dudes would be enough to make me want to stab a man, tear his tongue out, and then make him swallow it, but my threshold had shifted of late, my bar had dropped, and so many innocents had become part of my selection pool, potential targets of unchecked rage. I found my inspiration in the extreme ends of a stale, oppressive gender binary: giggling white women with high-pitched voices, high heels, and makeup, and men reciting football stats, bench press feats, and S&P stock-bond nonsense. In my mind, I orchestrated ugly endings to them all. These assholes had no idea what was going on around them.

For years in front of my mirror, like a good Marine protégée, I had practiced reaching for my switchblade faster than the eyes could take it in, flicking it open, cutting the air, slicing neck and torso, again, and again. Even imagining it in my mind felt like a release, like the lust for conquest had been spent a little.

Now that I was out of the Marines, the lust was still there. People with strong opinions had started to bore the hell out of me. Folks at Harvard seemed like phantoms of a force-fed childhood, where you simply believed what you were told to believe.

As I was typing my response to my professor's torture question, a friend tapped my shoulder, asked me what I was working on. I divulged everything: what I'd be willing to do for the right information to prevent 9/11 or to save us from the next homeland invasion. I got graphic. I'd remove fingernails, then hack off fingers, one by one. My friend, the gentle son of migrant workers, a pacifist to the point of being vegan, patiently absorbed this account while his eyes widened.

Calmly, he said, "Wow, Anu, that's fucked up."

I loved his candor. I loved it so much.

"Yeah, Raul. I guess it is."

I let his words soak in. There was no pride in this moment. Just a sick realization of what and who I had become. There was safety in telling him this, a kind human being who hadn't aggressively declared his ambition in the white man's power game. Even through the shame, I felt relief in hearing his response. I still wanted to be punished. And punishment from him seemed appropriate, even though it was probably not what he intended.

I needed to understand what all of this meant, to commit violence for the sake of politics, which I privately sensed was just another version of ideology. My mind was drawn deeply toward the grotesque, to what was utterly, obviously real, and yet masked from the sugarcoated world of American reality.

I had never killed anyone. I didn't know if I wanted to. But I wasn't sure that I didn't. And god knows I certainly could have, and would have. Bristol had shown me my bloodlust, and shown me how to use it. There were fewer lines I wouldn't cross. There were fewer lines.

As a Brown person, I knew it was risky to be too curious on the Internet. It wasn't difficult to find a website where I could flesh out these questions, test my moral waters, press my own buttons, and discover what kind of lost soul I really was. It was too easy to find what I was looking for. Some poor white dude had wandered into the worst place at the worst time in some godforsaken mountain pass in Af-Pak, and now he was looking into my eyes. He was scruffy, filthy, exhausted. Wide-eyed and dazed at the same time, he knelt before a camera, surrounded by thugs.

Beheadings are primal. Beheadings in foreign languages and far-off lands predictably more so in an us vs. them world, with the guttural glottals and the Soviet-era rifles brandished against the chest. Executions seem infinite, the knife is dull, and, as it turns out, for all that gooey, warm pulsing blood pumping to and from the brain, the human neck is remarkably thick and stubborn. Still, after all of that sawing, the head just falls to the side and tumbles to the ground.

Part of me wanted to watch my first beheading again. But I couldn't. I slammed my laptop screen down to the keyboard. There was no unseeing now. The shame of watching was all mine to bear.

. . .

It was about this time that I took a tally of the violence in my life. The anger was palpable, bursting through my skin, leaving me feeling wrecked in its wake. My body did not feel like my own. My relationship to living things began to change. My relationship to those who were vulnerable filled me with pain.

My body was repulsed by bloody things. I wanted no part in harming others. Now, in this hell, I refused to eat meat. I couldn't bring myself to inflict pain on another being. I was trying to save some part of myself that I wasn't sure existed anymore. I no longer knew if I was a good person.

I could not bear the weight of my relationship with my dogs, these bundles of unconditional love. All I could bring myself to do was find ways of punishing myself for not having loved them as well as they loved me when I was in the Marines. Memories from North Carolina surged to the surface, when I had punished them for disobeying me, hollered like a crazy woman, slapped their noses or sprayed water in their faces for having accidents while I was at work. The guilt of taking my fury—at the Corps, at myself—out on these creatures who wanted nothing more than my attention just about killed me. Uma and Shiva had shuddered and made themselves tiny in these moments, while I stood over them, twisted with emotions that had little to do with them and everything to do with a life I could not control. I was racked with guilt, and self-hatred was the only thing I felt I deserved.

Greg insisted that these animals loved me. That they forgave me. But I didn't believe him. How could they forgive, and love me on top of that, when I didn't love myself? Denying that I could or should be loved felt agonizing. In truth, it also felt sublime. I was not ready to understand what this might mean.

I wanted to exorcise this monster out of me, that thing that needed to be violent in order to be heard. But it did not seem safe for me to do this. It meant becoming invisible. In this world where women—and Brown women especially—were not seen or heard or wanted, my anger was keeping me engaged, reminding me never to disappear into the background, and never to let them silence me.

I had to keep resisting. But I was exhausted. This was no way to live.

· · ·

It should come as no surprise that I tried to go back in. It was some kind of perverse irony that the thought came to me—I can be a Marine again, but better this time—as I was listening to Bob Dylan's "Shelter from the Storm." Love and violence were inseparable draws in my life, one never manifesting without the other.

I wept, listening to his lyrics as I was driving down the highway in Boston, realizing I didn't feel at home anywhere, especially not within myself, where it might matter most. I had never finished what I started in the Corps, and it was driving me nuts. The place I wanted most to be accepted had not accepted me. But I played some part in this. I never went to Iraq. I never went to Afghanistan. I still wasn't a real Marine.

My closest friends from the Corps had left active duty around the same time as I had, but then deployed to the Middle East as reservists. Jules had gone to war even when she risked being outed as a lesbian. I was too busy feeling sorry for myself to realize I wanted to experience a combat deployment. Surely I could survive. I had sucked up so much in so many years. What was one more year of suppressing joy if it meant a permanent sense of service and accomplishment?

Five years after I'd fled the School of Infantry, I called up a Marine recruiter, some emotionless staff sergeant who couldn't have cared less about my hopes and dreams about reupping and deploying to Afghanistan. He said he'd make some calls and get back to me. I started training hard again, because if I was going to do this, I needed to be indestructible. The Marines might still hate me, but at least I'd be able to keep up.

In Brooklyn, where I now lived with Greg and the dogs, I started lifting weights again in earnest. I gave up swimming and resumed running, the activity my orthopedists and physical therapists told me never to do again because of my knee injuries. A couple of months into my new regimen, on the loop around Prospect Park, I felt a sharp twang in my left knee. I paused. I tried to get going again, but the pain was piercing. I half walked, half limped two miles back to my apartment and got the ice packs from the freezer. I knew this routine too well.

I was so pissed. A doctor told me I'd torn my meniscus. No big deal if you were an amateur ground pounder, but this was my third knee injury on two knees and I was ten years older now than when I first started out to prove everyone wrong. The Marine Corps had no patience for steady physical disintegration. Neither did I.

I was desperate for a solution. It occurred to me during weeks of moping and getting my ass to physical therapy that there was another option. Perhaps I could join a different branch of service. One that was less physically demanding. I could still deploy to the Middle East without wrecking my body before I even got there. Besides, I'd been told more often than I wanted to hear that I would have been much more valued in the Air Force or Navy, where intelligence wasn't seen as a weakness or liability, as it was in the Marines.

The Air Force required only a 1.5-mile run. I figured that with enough preparation and painkillers, my knees could handle that. I reached out to an Air Force recruiter. He was courteous, friendly, and respectful. And so naturally, I was suspicious. We discussed intelligence billets, that elusive assignment that the Marine Corps had refused to give me so many years ago. He hooked me up with a C-5 unit at a Massachusetts airbase and guaranteed me an intelligence slot. I could even keep the rank of captain.

I visited my prospective unit and was greeted by the intelligence officer, a major who sat me down as though I was interviewing for a civilian office job. There were no threatening stare downs, no jabs at the contours of my body or my relative smallness. He wanted me, remarkably, to feel comfortable, to settle in, to be myself. We talked about the culture of the place, the work, the intelligence field, his time overseas. He was civilized. Smart. Unpretentious.

He walked me into an enormous hangar, where I gawked at a C-5, the biggest damn airplane I'd ever seen. This hulking piece of machinery was responsible for transporting every piece of warfighting equipment imaginable, including tanks and very, very big guns.

As I stood there in awe, the major decided it was time to meet the bosses. He brought me into a room where three colonels rose to greet me. I was completely disarmed. In the world I knew, the colonels should have remained seated. I should have been reporting to them, standing rigidly, ready to take orders, with enough fear and respect to make them feel the power they had over me in their blood. This was not how it was. These airmen were broad chested, enormous, clothed in cushy flight suits, and stood with a true ease and confidence that I was unfamiliar with.

"So, why does a Marine want to become one of *us*?" the senior colonel asked, embracing my tiny fist in his bear paw. His eyes were oozing warmth.

I was instantly in love with these guys, and not in that creepy I'll-never-be-good-enough-for-Kurtz sort of way. There was no guile, no ego, no bullshit.

"We would love to have you join us, Anuradha." I was Sir'ing up a storm to make up for this godawful state of everything being A-okay and informal, which was making them crack up. Even when they were laughing, it was not at my expense. They were clearly familiar with Marines, and they knew I'd work my ass off, perhaps too much. They insisted I'd get used to how different things were here.

Greg had taken the day off to drive me to the base, and was nodding his head vigorously when I reported to him that these officers seemed like decent dudes.

"That's how the Air Force is." I was stunned that such a thing existed. Back home, I began to process. I could ship out this year, fly out to Air Force intelligence school, get this deferred dream back on track, but with people who weren't hijacking my chances of success and peace of mind at every turn. I'd be out in Afghanistan within a year or two, serving my country, doing things the way they were supposed to be done this time around.

But something was eating away at me, and I wasn't sure what, till it occurred to me that this whole nice-guy routine, which was utterly authentic, and probably very damn good for my psyche and morale, wasn't Marine enough for me. I got on the phone with the Air Force major again, asking him how often I'd be outside the wire, with boots on the ground. It sounded to me like I'd spend most of my time overseas protected indoors, in air-conditioned spaces. The stories I'd heard from countless Marines about how spoiled and bougie the Air Force was came flooding back to me. In the Corps, we used to take pride in how few resources we had, and how rough things were. Looking down upon the other services, which were far better funded and equipped, was what got us through the day sometimes. They were sissies. We were warriors.

The irony that the Air Force might be too good for me, too safe and comfortable, or the notion that I might deserve to be treated better than I was in the Corps and that there was something wrong with being treated well, was not lost on me. The Marines had instilled all sorts of dysfunction in me, so that when a healthy alternative presented itself, I had trouble embracing it. Somehow the Corps had still managed to convince me that even if I would never be good enough for the Marines, nothing else would ever be good enough for me. Not these Air Force flyboys, that's for sure, with their laid-back banter and winning smiles.

It didn't matter if this was illogical, or even objectively disturbing. On the inside, I was still a Marine. I declined the Air Force offer. It was Marines, or nothing.

CHAPTER 10

Unraveling

In 2007, three years out of the Marines, I was in the mental health wing at the Manhattan VA Medical Center, crying in an empty room on the second floor. I was on the phone with Eli Painted Crow, a retired soldier in California whom I met through a network of veterans opposed to the US war in Iraq. She and I bonded instantly, cussing up a storm and howling over everything from our mutual suspicion of institutions to the mistreatment of everyone without enough rank or testicles to matter.

As a cried into my cell phone, Eli played the part of Battle Buddy. She was the only reason I was here today in the first place, in this Mordor-like building with stark white walls and hundreds of dudes who look like battered remnants of human beings.

I would come to know Eli as the woman who saved my life. She survived Iraq, barely. I survived, well, I still didn't know what. But she knew pain, whether it was the pain of her own tribal peoples or the pain of women who had been stomped on or cast aside. Though we came from different worlds, she didn't deny my suffering.

Twenty years of soldiering (three of them on the drill field) and rabble-rousing for powerless troops made me trust her. Three thousand miles away, she calmed me down with words about how I needed this and how it would be good for me—anything to keep me from leaving the hospital.

I returned to the waiting area, where spirits were festering. Every being was in conversation with someone here or beyond. Some men lurked before office doors, demanding an audience. Others barked at the television set, cursing idiot anchors, Al Qaeda, or the Mets. Some sat alone, reciting lengthy monologues that were interrupted only by grunts of disapproval from some invisible arbitrator.

In these situations I was relieved to be unnoticed. But I made myself smaller still. A door swung open down the hall.

"Ann-uhr . . . Ann-you . . . uh . . ."

I did not need this attention. I stood quickly. Men's voices, both real and imagined, paused. Eyes were watching all parts and angles of me, waiting for my next move. I armored, instantly, as I had learned so well to do in the Corps, and followed a woman's quick footsteps down a hall and into a small room. No words were exchanged. No introductions made. I barely knew I was there.

I sat down with a chubby fiftysomething administrative aide. She stared into a computer screen, mindlessly dishing out a government mandated survey for new veterans, a verbal back and forth about why I was here and what may have screwed with my seamless reintegration back into society. The exchange was about as warm and comforting as a military pap smear. The pace, the coldness, and the automaton-like manner of this woman were starting to mess with the fragile sense Eli had built up in me that everything was going to be all right.

I felt an impending explosion of *What the fuck, lady?* rising when her flat-line voice unevenly switched gears into the section of the survey clearly meant to draw out the female issues in the veteran population.

"Have you ever experienced unwanted sexual contact?"

"Um. Yes. I think so. I dunno."

She was throwing these questions at me like baseballs in a batting cage, with barely enough time for me to handle one before the next one was launched. Her words felt rough and dry, like sawdust.

Those tears I thought I'd fully spent on Eli started coming back, harder than before, as I fumbled through my responses. Without looking at me, she read one question after another on her desktop, checking the boxes yes and no until my crying turned into sobbing, the kind where yes-and-no responses were no longer decipherable.

Suddenly, she stopped and turned her eyes toward me. She said, "Oh. Oh dear." She was looking around in a panic, finally found a box of tissues, and shoved one into my hands.

"I'll be right back," she said, and left me there, convulsing. She returned a few minutes later and told me a doctor would be able to see me.

The attending shrink that evening was sitting behind a very large metal desk. It was past dark now and I was the only thing between him and home. I felt raw and childlike, like a small girl. I had wiped my face dry for him with my shirtsleeve, but sensing how little he wanted to be here, I started up with the waterworks again. The tears were on their own fucking program. I think this frustrated him, because he rolled his eyes like an artillery round, up and over to the other side of his head. That was enough to snap me out of my grief.

I lost it, started yelling about him, about the admin lady with the emotional intelligence of a paper clip, about me, about the state of this fucking universe and the monsters and morons I had to contend with. It was an epic, diabolical rant about my pain, much of which I imagine got lost between the heaving, the waterfall of snot, and the general shock and awe of my delivery.

Eventually my tantrum settled. He had stopped with the eye rolling. I had his attention. He offered me a spot in an in-patient psychiatric unit. This sounded extreme. And comforting.

"What would you like to do, Ms. Bhagwati?"

I got quiet. And then remembered, I had to feed and walk my dogs. Greg and I had had a fight earlier, because I wanted him to come to the hospital with me, but he needed to be out of town for work. Shiva and Uma were home alone. No shrink was going to make me leave these animals. They now seemed like all I had. I agreed instead to get a full psych eval from one of his colleagues.

At the VA a few days later, my initial consultation with a psychiatrist lasted just three minutes. Apparently that was all it took to digest the full story of my life and all the possible ways I might be hurting. After hearing my one-woman lamentation, a rapid-fire summary of the causes and symptoms of my heartache, a desperately condensed overview of my broken relationship with the Marine Corps, the doctor slowly widened her eyes, as if I posed some kind of threat to her safety, and determined I needed drugs. Little white pills, with a doozy of a pharmaceutical name no one could spell and I could barely pronounce.

This doctor didn't tell me a thing about the pills she'd given me as casually as the time of day, until it occurred to me to ask, "What is this supposed to treat?"

I sensed her hesitate, not because she was hiding anything, but because she had never been asked. She said, without a hint of emotion, "Primarily, bipolar disorder . . ."

Bi-fucking-polar disorder.

I didn't fully digest the litany of other things she said it also treated, like seizures. The sad thing was, I didn't care enough anymore to say that I was perfectly sane, and not in the least bit manic, but still hurting in one hundred ways. Pointing out the obvious to endless numbers of VA employees had become a full-time job from which there was no return. And retelling what I thought they should already know and understand was like a knife to my gut, after which the wound never healed and I was left in a puddle of sadness so deep and consuming that there was no way out but down.

I was just so tired. I would rather have these government pills numb me into oblivion, for all the wrong reasons, than give one more ounce of myself to fighting these people with their glazed-over eyes and what-on-earth-could-you-possibly-need-from-me attitudes.

Defeated, I walked down the staircase to the basement, where prescriptions were dished out. The truly hopeless among us—those of me leave these animals. They now seemed like all I had. I agreed instead to get a full psych eval from one of his colleagues.

At the VA a few days later, my initial consultation with a psychiatrist lasted just three minutes. Apparently that was all it took to digest the full story of my life and all the possible ways I might be hurting. After hearing my one-woman lamentation, a rapid-fire summary of the causes and symptoms of my heartache, a desperately condensed overview of my broken relationship with the Marine Corps, the doctor slowly widened her eyes, as if I posed some kind of threat to her safety, and determined I needed drugs. Little white pills, with a doozy of a pharmaceutical name no one could spell and I could barely pronounce.

This doctor didn't tell me a thing about the pills she'd given me as casually as the time of day, until it occurred to me to ask, "What is this supposed to treat?"

I sensed her hesitate, not because she was hiding anything, but because she had never been asked. She said, without a hint of emotion, "Primarily, bipolar disorder . . ."

Bi-fucking-polar disorder.

I didn't fully digest the litany of other things she said it also treated, like seizures. The sad thing was, I didn't care enough anymore to say that I was perfectly sane, and not in the least bit manic, but still hurting in one hundred ways. Pointing out the obvious to endless numbers of VA employees had become a full-time job from which there was no return. And retelling what I thought they should already know and understand was like a knife to my gut, after which the wound never healed and I was left in a puddle of sadness so deep and consuming that there was no way out but down.

I was just so tired. I would rather have these government pills numb me into oblivion, for all the wrong reasons, than give one more ounce of myself to fighting these people with their glazed-over eyes and what-on-earth-could-you-possibly-need-from-me attitudes.

Defeated, I walked down the staircase to the basement, where prescriptions were dished out. The truly hopeless among us—those of us in deep neurochemical shit—were lined up like sheep being iron prodded and funneled toward the slaughter chute, knowing on some level, *This is really it, this is the end of the road.* Men at this stage were too far gone to even gawk at or harass me—normally that certainty would have provided me the comfort of knowing my place and how little I mattered.

Eventually, a staff member crouched in a closet of an office who spoke barely working English processed my prescription and sent me back upstairs to a corner of the lobby, a sprawling wasteland of bodies moving in too many directions. Here in the waiting area, a herd of beaten-down old men in tribal ribboned baseball hats lingered and leaned into walls, staring hopelessly into television monitors or fuming into space, occasionally grunting in the direction of the pharmacists, who were protected behind thick glass windows and reinforced brick walls, about the length they must wait, and then inevitably, because no one ever responded, because whomever had the answers behind walls was behind walls for a reason, they settled back into the thick haze of waiting.

My survival here took on new meaning. It meant avoiding eye contact with veterans who still saw chunks of rotting flesh on winding desert roads or the thumping of helicopter blades on the way into or out of the jungle. It meant steering clear of men whose bodies were still on the move, midstride and midmission.

Their memories lay beneath the hum of fluorescent lightbulbs, sometimes lost to consciousness, provoked and shaken loose by the strange sight of me, long haired, brown skinned, tiny, dodging triggers in the hallway. To them, I was a veiled, babbling hajji mother at a checkpoint; a call girl at a Saigon bar; the ex-girlfriend who slept with his neighbor; the cunt wife who disappeared with the kids; the whore of a sergeant who shouldn't have gotten promoted; the recruit he forced underneath him in the barracks and hadn't recalled until just now. I was none and all of these things. And I was a fresh, convenient target.

I passed out at some point on an ER bed with tubes connected to my arms. The rest was a utopian blur, where I no longer had to give a damn about myself or anyone else. I was so drugged up I wouldn't have felt hurricane waters from lower Manhattan rising over the sheets and drowning me. That I had chosen to let these people take me down and put me under, when in my right mind I never would have fallen asleep in this place without armed Amazon women standing guard at the foot of my bed, must have meant I really didn't give a shit anymore.

There were hours upon hours of insecure sleep, glimpses of white coats, and the sound of feet coming and going. I prayed for some end to this, for some new reality, whether here or in the afterlife. But I got pulled back in.

I was always getting pulled back in. No amount of pharmaceutically induced oblivion could stop me from giving a shit about some poor son of a bitch to whom I would always be faithful. Even conscious, my best efforts to steer clear of these moments were useless.

I couldn't see the new patient when he arrived. But he was more real to me than I was to myself. We were separated by a thin white curtain and my heavy, aching head and the fact that I could not make my mouth move no matter how hard I tried. There were anonymous bodies standing everywhere. I saw their shoes underneath the curtain, disordered, out of formation. I was the only one who heard him.

He was a Marine. This I knew from the tenor of his voice, the edge to his rough, throaty pleas, and the way they rejected him, made him feel invisible and crazy. He was hurt. And no one was listening. I knew this.

"You need to calm down."

"I am calm. Fuck you. Get your fucking hands off me."

And the more he tried to tell them, the more their voices became detached from the rest of them. This is how experts talked when they

This would ordinarily have been enough to make me wild with fear. But today I was only timid. Withdrawn. Sinking into my cold metal chair, huddled over my chest, crossing and locking my legs shut, wondering how it would be possible to disappear more completely from being.

· · ·

Back home, I took my first pill.

The rash started too small to notice. By the afternoon it had grown, spreading across my back and legs. It reminded me of the chiggers that burrowed beneath my camouflage uniform in North Carolina swampland where, sweaty and exhausted, I was force-fed permanent lessons in loyalty about how fragile and female I really was—fragile because I was female or female because I was fragile, I didn't know—that would nest beneath my skin, bide their time, and hatch when I least expected, and no manner of scratching my skin till blood gushed over dark green socks and combat boots would stop the itching, would stop the feeling that they'd entered without permission, made a home inside my body, and claimed victory.

There was no time to get sentimental, because soon enough, the itch was in my throat, tickling at first, then going for the voice I barely knew I had. I felt some instinct rise within me that something permanent was about to happen: the end of breathing, the end of it all.

Bucking all carefully honed tools of survival—self-preservation, even common sense—to steer clear of the building I had come to know as my very own personal hell, I walked with Greg at my side into the VA emergency room.

I approached a nurse, casually. The business of my throat clamping up triggered a red flag. Even through my fog, I was impressed. I didn't know red flags existed at the VA, where I was resigned, where they were resigned, where people gave up and gave in, where people who once cleared rooms and took hills now let fate determine whether or not they would ever be someone again.

weren't just flukes, and the Military Sexual Trauma program was born.

My appointments with my MST counselor began at the Harlem Vet Center, a small, welcoming place that had the feel of a community center more than a treatment facility. As I learned early on, vet centers were created because Vietnam veterans had demanded an alternative to VA medical centers, where far too many veterans had received horrible care. Vet centers were generally considered places of refuge, where your counseling records were kept confidential, independent of big VA and its creepy attorneys, paper pushers, and public affairs hawks.

I seemed to be the only woman who walked through the doors of the Harlem Vet Center, but aside from wondering if I was in the right place, there was a palpable sense of decency here. I felt safer and more welcome with people of color, though I was only beginning to realize this. Counselors and receptionists spoke in unusually warm and civil terms as I entered and took a seat on a soft leather couch—*Good morning, Are you waiting for someone, How are you, miss*—and I felt some of my now pathological urge to resist lose its edge.

I spent months coming to the vet center for counseling, week after week, sometimes two or three times a week, just to ensure that the hours in my day didn't swallow me alive. In my first few visits, I was a one-woman ragemobile, and there was really nothing stopping me from exploding all over the world around me except Doc, who was patiently listening, taking it all in, one lightning strike at a time.

Doc was a typical Freudian head shrink, wanting to start back at the beginning, making me feel like my head was constantly turned backward. I had done my damnedest to run away from my parents' constant scrutiny, and here I was, stuck with Doc, digging up my childhood like nothing else in the world mattered. Why couldn't she focus on the here and now?

I exhausted myself trying to explain the ins and outs of the Marines to Doc. She'd been doing sexual trauma work for almost two decades, but she hadn't seen a lot of Marines. And there were so few women in the Corps that we barely left a mark on the consciousness of veterans providers. Doc was part Jewish mother and part naive audience. She had boundless patience for my outrage, but a horrible poker face. Sometimes I would tell her things about the Corps and her eyes would grow huge, her head shaking uncontrollably left to right in disbelief.

"You called one another *killers*?"

"Uh, *yeah*." Didn't everyone who worked with veterans know this stuff? The rape jokes, the porn aplenty, the sweeping assault and harassment cover-ups, and the fact that I still wanted back in the Corps despite all of it challenged her sense of logic to the core.

"You don't fear getting wounded? Dying?"

"Uh, *no*." Why would I fear losing my life? Doc's inability to relate to Marine basics made me feel more invisible. Still, I came back, again and again. It was better to come here and rage than to go nowhere at all.

Doc and I talked at some point about filing another claim for disability compensation. I had already gone through the claims process when I left the Corps. I'd applied for multiple muscular-skeletal injuries and had a gigantic medical file to support it, but despite my joints crackling daily like a Rice Krispies symphony, I was rejected on most counts. The VA was now giving me a tiny disability check each month—the smallest amount legally possible—for my right knee, a bureaucratic diagnosis that irritated me to no end because there was so much of me that hurt beyond one damaged joint. But like a good Marine, I wasn't going to complain about it—I was grateful that I didn't get my leg blown off fighting bad guys in the desert.

My friend Eli laughed off all that proud veteran talk as pure bullshit that the military drilled into us as recruits, gobbledygook that presented only the most extreme physical wounds on the battlefield as worthy of anyone's attention. The VA, according to her, was banking on our solid, guilt-ridden military training so fewer of us would ever have the gall to apply for disability compensation. She explained that I deserved support for all my injuries. My knees, my back, my shoulder. My aching heart.

"They owe you," she said. What did I have to lose? I went for it.

The nation's second largest federal bureaucracy (behind the Department of Defense), the Department of Veterans Affairs was not just a paper-pushing monstrosity with poor management and long lines. Wounded and injured veterans were subject to VA's obsolete rules, policies designed specifically to protect VA's coffers. In practice, it amounted to cruelty.

After months of dissecting my history and mind, Doc concluded I was suffering from depression, anxiety, and post-traumatic stress from facing year after year of sexual harassment in uniform. It was a story line that was blatantly obvious to any thinking, feeling person but me, as I figured I was the one to blame for how I felt. Having Doc put my pain into words was my first validation out of the Corps. Doc's words, for better or worse, gave me hope.

As I dove into the claims process, I felt as much investigative journalist as patient. Following VA instructions, I started collecting all the evidence to support my claim of harassment within the military. This included the extremely difficult task of tracking down folks who witnessed or participated in my sexual harassment investigation. Some Marines I couldn't find. They had retired, moved, or disappeared from the grid. There was no special victims support team to hold my hand while I tracked down colleagues, dredged up hostile memories, and fended off my body's emotional reactions.

After weeks of searching for the Marines who supervised my investigation in North Carolina and at Marine headquarters in Virginia, I finally found the staff sergeant who was the main point of contact on my investigation. She still remembered my case, as if it were yesterday. But she had bad news. By Marine Corps policy, my investigation had been destroyed.

I was dumbfounded. It meant there would be no official record of Lieutenant Thomas sexually harassing the women in my unit, or the Marine Corps officially recommending his censure. He was a free bird. I took the time to verify that the file had, indeed, vanished. I tracked down a senior civilian in the Department of the Navy Inspector General's office, who confirmed that the Navy and Marine Corps destroyed all equal opportunity paperwork after two years.

"Why would they do this?" I asked the guy urgently. He was wishy-washy on the phone, didn't give me a straight answer. But I wouldn't let him go.

"Is it because they're protecting the perpetrators?"

He paused.

"Yes. Most likely." Although he was on the Department of Defense payroll, even this guy couldn't summon the shame to lie to me.[*]

I went back to the staff sergeant. She wrote a two-page summary of the investigation from memory. She recalled the sordid cover-up details almost as well as I did.

My claim went through the system, with more than enough of the evidence the VA had said I needed to connect my military service to my current medical symptoms. Along with the EO account, it included a lengthy personal testimonial that I'd labored over for weeks; statements from personal friends and colleagues who witnessed the incident and changes in my behavior and mood over time, like Greg and Eli; my own private journals from the Corps; my official DOD medical records; and an official letter on VA letterhead from Doc.

While I waited for a response from VA, life went on.

· · ·

I was sitting in a small room on the mental health floor of the Manhattan VA hospital, with nine other women veterans of all ages and races.

---

[*] Later on, with the help of pro bono attorneys and colleagues, I learned more: the military also destroyed rape kits.

"Did you ever think that maybe the Marines don't *want* you back?" Sharon, a social worker who led our weekly women's group, answered as much as asked the question. A former Army drill sergeant, she had more tools to work with than most VA employees. The women were silent, listening, waiting for me to respond.

I had become a full-time veteran. I was in too much pain to do much else. I dragged myself to VA regularly now to attend to an assortment of health issues, emotional and physical. It required subjecting myself to the daily indignities of entering the hospital. Despite security measures in the lobby, nothing suggested safety.

This VA entrance was the most pathetic place I knew, where sadness festered and hovered in the air. The metal detector beeped as each of us walked through, and the routine was always the same. Every poor soul had a limp, and when he didn't have the space to limp forward, he was whining or muttering at the fool in front of him, who for the umpteenth time had forgotten to empty his pockets of keys, change, and cell phone.

The security guards beyond the metal detector had hollow, dull eyes. Some were chomping on burgers while veterans made the long, slow march through the line, crumbs nestled like white lice on their dark blue uniforms.

One morning as I walked through the machine it beeped. Combining flirtation with that particular disrespect reserved for women, the security guard said to me, "You carrying a weapon?"

I said nothing. The only woman within a mile of his comment, I spread my arms like Jesus so he could run a security paddle alongside my flanks and beneath my armpits, no doubt an instrument that worked as well as the metal detector itself. My face was blank, but my fighting instincts were on high alert.

The machine beeped. It beeped again. He smirked from a place where there was no shortage of smirks, figuring I couldn't possibly be carrying something shiny or explosive, and waved me through. I was just on this side of unhinged and would have relished the opportunity to show him what I could do with a weapon. A pocketknife. A handgun. Or even my bare hands.

Sharon wasn't trying to hurt my feelings, even though all I felt was a slap in the face. She was probably right. Why the hell would the Corps want me? Right now all I wanted to do was make the Marines love me, change my history, and make the pain go away. But pain had its own timeline, which made control freaks like me feel absolutely helpless.

The problem with Sharon's theory was that even if the Corps no longer wanted me, there was no escaping the Corps. My *Oorah* tattoo was seared into my left shoulder like a branding: *USMC: U Signed a Motherfucking Contract.* Once a Marine, always a Marine. It felt like a curse. *Semper fidelis.* Why must I still, after all this, be faithful? And yet even now I was dreaming about the Corps, in three dimensions, with my senses on fire.

The ivory tower and an advanced degree didn't save me, just like it didn't save my mother. Concealing my wounds in busyness and plans for the future hadn't gotten me anywhere. The future had no patience for unresolved trauma. And back in New York City, there were no new beginnings. My memories and nightmares revived themselves, as though the second phase of torment had just begun.

Sometimes, it was too much to take, like the afternoon I'd had shitty back-to-back encounters with VA's chair warmers, rough-throated women who would not give me an appointment for weeks even though my body was falling apart. The jock orthopedic resident who admitted to me he'd rather be working on hard-core dudes with serious injuries than patients with whatever I had. Being told, *We need you to fill out this form,* one too many times. All of these words penetrating my tough exterior like piercing armor bullets, sending me over the brink, out the double doors and into the hallway, sinking against the wall and letting gravity and heavy sobs take me down to the hospital floor.

As I sat, folks walked by my huddled mass and said little. It was best that way. I was safer collapsed in my own mute world. An employee finally approached and asked me if I was okay. I shooed her off, hand waving, muttering something like yes.

There was no love here. There was only contempt. I might as well be on the same level as rats and roaches. Depression will do this. I was in that primordial place before speech, before reason.

If you asked me how I was, I would have looked past you from somewhere beyond language. Words hurt. Words would never be enough. Words only failed me here, where I never said the right thing, in the right way, at the right time.

My body caused me nothing but pain and suffering, embarrassment and shame. Walking hurt. My knees buckled and popped. My shoulder crackled. My neck was hollering. It was better to lie down and remain still. Let the feet go by.

In this safe fugue state, the tape loop that had begun long before the Corps started up again. This body of mine, with female parts that announced themselves before I could present myself, cursed and betrayed me in the end, made men question my worth, made them resent me, made them cast me out.

I didn't know who I was without their acceptance. Without Dad's acceptance. But I didn't need them to make me feel small. I felt small all on my own.

Depression was like this, too. Self-hatred working itself thought by thought and cell by cell through my body, shutting down any impulses to move forward or move at all, impulses to feel good or make others feel good. Joy had no home inside me.

My body was numb. Shut off and locked up. It was safe that way. I couldn't remember the last time I had sex, or even thought about it. I fiercely avoided the topic for months. Doc was concerned that until I talked about sexual intimacy, I wouldn't be able to move through any of my pain. Didn't she understand that was the point?

I was detached from my body the way sociopaths were detached from their feelings. I hovered above it. Beyond it.

Occupying a broken skeleton was humbling and humiliating. I couldn't move well, or fast. I tiptoed on sidewalks and limped up and down subway stairs. And when I ate now, food was no longer fuel for physical feats. Food sat inside me, sticking to my sides, storing up for nothing in particular except more reason for me to pick on myself.

For the first time in my life, I was aware that I had hips. Womanly, baby-birthing hips. And breasts that had ballooned without warning. Rolling layers of blubber in my belly that had appeared for the first time since adolescence, since Dad had called me fat and refused to look at me. My body was out of control. Nasty. Hanging out there for all the world to ogle or demean. I could no longer hide. The Marine Corps would be laughing at my state of disgrace. Unable to hang with the men, my worth had plummeted.

I handled immobility without grace. Disconnected from the vehicle that moved me through my life—first one knee, then the other, then a shoulder, then the rest—unable to run from or pound through the anxiety and disappointment that life was throwing my way, I was forced to sit still, with my mind and all the hell of my thoughts, within my crumbling body.

My mind was a beast. My father's words from childhood had come full circle. *You're ugly. It's disgusting.* It was the kind of brutality that would make me throw a grown man to the floor before he dared say that to a child. But hatred turned on myself felt right. *I will never be good enough.* I believed and deserved every word of it. And damn you if you tried to convince me otherwise.

Time slowed. With dark sacks under my eyes, salty cheeks, and a shallow breath, I scraped myself off the hospital floor and headed back through the city to my apartment.

• • •

Home was where my dogs were. Greg, the committed partner and patient cheerleader, stayed by my side through this dark decade, watching me self-destruct, and try, and self-destruct again, one month after the next, witnessing my dangerous dance with the Marine Corps, my attempts to change them, to heal myself and move on.

I feel like I can't make you happy, he said.

It's not your job to make me happy.

He didn't know what to do. Nothing he said helped. He didn't know why therapy hadn't fixed me. Supporting every effort I'd made in the early years to try to go back into uniform, he now sensed a shift in me. Maybe a shift toward real darkness, or worse, stagnation. He shifted as well, not in the direction I expected.

These days I dreamed about being shipped off to Afghanistan. I was in the tightest quarters. An inch between my face and the rack above me. There was hardly any air and I didn't know where I was going or who I was with. I woke up sweating and terrified but feeling a strong pull to find out more.

I want back in, I said.

He usually talked about next steps. Encouraged me to follow my dreams.

If you put on that uniform again, I'm leaving. I'm serious. I'm done.

We barely touched each other anymore. He had been keeping track of time like a record keeper. Days had turned into months, and then into years. My sloppy attempts at sexual connection only happened when my guilt about his sadness made me try to touch him, try to get past my horror of feeling vulnerable while witnessing his sexual needs, but it never worked. I couldn't contain my disgust, my lack of trust. It was him, it was the Marines, it was me, it was everyone.

I didn't know if I would ever have sex again. Celibacy gave me some sense of control in a world where I had no control over how people treated me and how I felt.

His memory of the history of our sex lives was a cruel reminder of our changing circumstances. Apparently, I used to love sex. I had only vague memories of this. Flashes in my mind of wanting. This was before the ugly end of my career. He remembered every moment.

Every embrace. I just remembered shame, and hiding, and fearing everyone around me.

Are you gay?

No.

Then why won't you touch me?

I just can't.

Greg finally gave up. One day I borrowed his laptop and discovered he'd been surfing the Web for porn. I became hysterical. Self-righteous. Furious. He became furious, too, yelled at me that it was none of my damn business. Doc told me it was none of my business, too. I didn't get why she was taking his side.

We didn't talk about why he needed pornography. Or alcohol.

Greg was a large, unwieldy man with big hands and a barrel chest. He needed a lot of booze to feel booze working at all, which meant that when everyone else had called it a night, he was still warming up. I didn't know any dry Marines. Half were alcoholics; the rest appeared to be in training.

Sometimes he drank so much that his words became weapons and he'd begin raging about nothing in particular. He got louder and louder, till I got so scared I'd hide in the bedroom with the dogs. I held their warm furry bodies and cried. They loved him, their big burly dad, and they were scared, too, because I was scared and he was out of control.

On this particular night, while I was hiding in my room, he was yelling about the Corps and me, the young children he'd lost to his ex-wife, and memories that he still hadn't faced about pulling triggers in faraway places like Liberia. He released it all that night, vomiting all over our apartment, yelling throughout, till there were no more words left to say, and no more alcohol left to throw up. I rocked myself to bed with my girls.

I considered leaving him after this. We had an awful conversation, about not having anything in common. Which was absurd. We had too much in common. We had the Marines in common, and that was more than enough, and also part of the problem. Some part of me detested him for having been one of them, even if he was the only human being to protect me from being swallowed up by their devices. As I withdrew further into my own body, he became more and more like all the others. No amount of distance would separate him in my mind from the Corps. His hands were like their hands, enormous and groping. His words were loud, intrusive, and present without invitation. Alcohol magnified this, making him grotesque and me invisible. His physical presence loomed, and nothing in me could fathom how I ever felt safe enough to be vulnerable with him, naked, and open to love.

It was Greg's third all-out drunken episode in three years. It made me wonder if I was crazy to love him. Doc kept on telling me he needed counseling, as if it were as simple as that. I looked at her furiously. Why did she think this was something within my power to control? The last time I broached this with him he turned on me like wildfire. It was not my job to convince him he needed help. Eli, who'd been sober for years now, told me alcoholics came in many forms. You did not need to drink every night to destabilize the ones you loved.

I stuffed my doubts deep down in my bones so I would never talk to him about it, and he would never yell at me again. Somehow, this détente worked. We managed. We coexisted. I didn't have any real idea of how to begin to leave him. I wasn't missing courage as much as the notion that something different was possible.

And then there was this ugly suspicion that felt about as real as anything ever would: that part of the reason I couldn't leave Greg was because he was my best and last real connection to the Marines. That I needed his approval, because without it, I wouldn't know that I'd done anything right. Without his approval, I'd never have theirs, either.

In moments of private truth telling, I admitted this relationship might be doomed. Only, if I wasn't with him, I thought I would die.

He, Shiva, and Uma were the only beings who knew how much I hurt. They had stood by me during the worst of everything. Greg had forgiven me years ago for sleeping with another man when I felt like nothing mattered anymore. Surely I could forgive him for drowning his pain in alcohol, even if it felt like I was drowning with him. I no longer wanted to be a quitter. I felt like I owed him. Greg had, after all, saved me from Lowell, Fox, Thomas, and all the rest.

For all his size and bravado, Greg was a quiet, gentle man at heart. His drunken, combat-colored rants terrified me, but I felt I had no other path forward but through his suffering and mine. We contained our hurt within a giant, safe bubble. It bonded us, something no one else back home would ever understand.

He eventually stopped trying to touch me. I eventually stopped trying to make him feel better. We pushed our feelings so far down I couldn't remember what anything erotic felt like anymore. Our relationship became strictly platonic. He finally pronounced that he didn't need sex. He loved me. He would never leave me. It was a grandiose, foolish thing to say. But we both embraced the idea. The Desi part of me that had been raised to believe a partnership was simply an arrangement between two adults rose to the occasion. It felt like my duty. If this was some sad excuse for not having any say in the direction my life was taking, I was not ready to face that possibility.

We were fiercely loyal. I would have his back, as he had always had mine, even if I couldn't share all parts of myself with him or with anyone else. I would make up for all my mistakes with other men by ensuring I never disappointed this man. He would be my family. I would make sure of it, my doubts be damned.

CHAPTER 11

Rising Up

Four years out of the Marines, I sat down with my parents over dinner and announced to them that I was going to become a yoga teacher. In the Corps, I had discovered that yoga was a vehicle for healing, and I wanted to experience more.

"You want to do this as a *career*?" my mother asked, horrified.

"No, Mom, not everything has to be a career."

My mother was still frustrated that she could not explain to our Indian relatives what I did for a living. The military had been hard enough to sell to them. While Mom wrestled with the cost-benefit analysis of my decision, my father muttered to himself, with a scowl across his jaw and deep lines of judgment on his forehead.

My parents may have been Indian, but yoga was not on their list of approved activities. Spirituality was the realm of charlatans and quacks. My parents were not impressed with the white hippies who'd been taken in over the last century by enterprising Indian men in orange robes. Still, everything was relative, and Mom and Dad did the math. I wouldn't be firing any weapons standing on my head.

I had selected Integral Yoga teacher training in part because it seemed to be everything the Marine Corps was not: gentle and ego-free. Its founder, Swami Satchidananda, was one of the first Indian gurus to bring yoga to the West, even opening the Woodstock festival. The training took place in Bacalar, a tiny town in southern Mexico. I met my head yoga instructor, Ramananda, a midwestern swami in his fifties, as I was getting out of the lake one morning and he was getting in. Standing on the dock with a beach ball in his hands, he wore orange shorts, orange flip-flops, and an orange towel. He was all white skin and bones, with twinkling blue eyes.

This was not the time or place for me to meet a monk. I was sopping wet, desperately trying to hide my boobs in my bathing suit and make my body small. Hyperconscious of my Indian upbringing, I think I called him Sir, or swami-ji, might have half bowed, clumsily put my palms together in respect while clutching a towel to my torso. I was horrified to meet Ramananda in my Speedo, but he was about as interested in my curves as I was in his protruding ribs. He was too busy splashing around in the water.

For one month, I rose at dawn with a bunch of strangers, a cast of twenty- to fifty-year-old white folks, a young woman from Singapore, and an older man from Iran. We meditated, did deep breathing, learned a bunch of asanas,* and ate healthy, nutritious vegetarian food. Our yoga training had the disciplined feel of Marine Corps training, with none of the abuse. Renouncing meat, alcohol, sex, privacy, and sleeping in were lessons in honing the mind and purifying the heart. Kindness was rooted in the philosophy of not harming oneself or others.† And compassion seemed to be the focus, not just some random side effect.

The bags under my eyes started to disappear. The feeling of wanting to tear people down for looking at me the wrong way was still there, but seemed less potent. People actually cared whether or not I

---

* Yoga postures, or poses, typically associated with contemporary yoga practice, particularly in the West.

† *Ahimsa* is the yogic concept of not doing harm; it is sometimes translated as nonviolence.

was in pain. And the pain, sensing that it finally had a place to express itself and would no longer be stuffed down, was everywhere. On some days I needed to lie down, because my back couldn't handle sitting upright on the floor for so many hours. My instructors let me, while I let the ground soak up my hurt. I cursed my Marine injuries for holding me back. I did not realize I was actually being encouraged forward.

My roommate, Jen, was a curly haired triathlete and former police officer who was struggling with a debilitating autoimmune disorder. Ever the optimist, she approached the disease like a benevolent storm trooper, transforming herself from hard-core carnivore into a raw vegan enthusiast and training for an Ironman race during breaks in our rigorous yoga schedule. She reminded me of an overzealous Marine, and in the beginning her presence was a constant reminder of everything I was trying to leave behind.

As my clenched fists softened, I came to consider that Jen was my mirror. There were many moments when she would sense me struggle, watch me suffer in my own body, with my broken knees and heavy heart, and accept me, with irritating cheerfulness.

The swami and his surf-the-waves sensibility regularly intercepted my self-hating habits. Eventually I stopped thinking of him as a white guy in an orange robe. One day, as I was steeped in negative thinking, he looked at me with kind, laughing eyes.

"You know, you are not your thoughts."

Dude, you have got to be nuts, I heard myself thinking. If I wasn't my thoughts, then who the heck was I?

One evening, my physical pain was more than I could take, so I booked a massage with Melina, the woman who ran our facility. Allowing a stranger to put her hands on me was a big deal. As she pulled the towel down slightly below my shoulders, she saw the Marine tattoo I'd gotten after 9/11.

"That's impressive."

Here it was. A conversation I didn't want to have.

"Thanks."

She dug into my thighs, where two decades' worth of protective instincts had found a home.

"I kind of wish it weren't there sometimes. It's not me anymore."

Melina paused, then asked, "Have you ever thought about integrating the experience instead of trying to get rid of it?"

I could feel myself resisting but had no desire to argue. Why would I integrate sadness and shame into my life? I could barely tolerate even remembering.

As we approached graduation day, our yoga instructors had arranged a sweat lodge for us with Melina and her shaman husband. They were both indigenous to Mexico, which gave the sweat lodge a feeling of authenticity. Up north, sweat lodges were often conducted by white folks who had no real connection to tribal peoples or practices, and it made my head spin. I was not feeling settled about a bunch of gringos engaging in Native spiritual practices. But in the end, I joined. If I had opened my mouth at every culturally appropriated moment, I would never have left home.

It was my first sweat lodge. We were packed in tight, the roof inches from our skulls, crouched and huddled together on the dirt floor like too many Marines on a five-ton truck. Once we stepped inside, there was nowhere else to go.

Melina took us through several rounds of ceremony while her husband, the shaman, tended to the fire outside, chanting in some local tongue, occasionally opening the curtain to add more coals and then sealing us off again.

It was hotter than hell. We were a mess of sweat and earth, and each time I took a hand from the floor of the hut to wipe my face, I left grit like messy camo paint on my brow and cheeks. The last time I was this hot I was locked in a tiny sauna in a camouflage uniform, combat boots, and flak jacket, dog tags searing my breasts, sweat dripping down the crack in my rear end, as Bristol prepped me and my squad for close-combat drills in desert-like conditions. Back then I sucked it up like a proud champion. But here, after three rounds of sweating, I was starting to feel trapped. Discomfort was fast turning into panic.

Hugging my knees close to my chest, I shifted my butt in the three inches of wiggle room I had to either side. Hadn't we learned to breathe deeply? I tried. Nothing was helping. I hated being a nuisance. I hated being weak.

"I can't breathe." I'm not sure anyone heard me.

Minutes later, my breaths had transformed into gasps.

"I. Can't. Breathe."

I heard feet shifting, clothing rustling. Melina wove her way through clumps of bodies around the coals, making her way to me.

"Lie down," she said firmly.

There was no room to spread out. I surrendered on the ground, sideways, fetal. Something was starting to happen to my body, some mystical thing in which it was quite possible I was no longer in control, because I had started crying like an infant, and the crying was becoming hysterical. My friends sitting around the glowing coals were starting to worry. I knew this because there were murmurs of concern echoing from familiar voices within the walls of the lodge.

As my body regressed into a state of helplessness, I was aware of something happening in my brain. I knew I was here, but there were images coming to mind, a black-and-white film reel of my senseless battalion commander and the predatory lieutenant. I thought what the *hell* are they doing here, two fucking gringo military men, in this hut that was now coming down on top of me.

And then, with my face awash in wetness and my throat expelling sounds and sobs, I had the sense of my body softening. I felt it below the gasps and the tears, a small opening, forgiving them for what they should have known, forgiving them for not knowing at all. And this wave of forgiveness, the relief it brought not only that there was somewhere in the world I could let go of this hurt but that there must be something redeemable and possibly lovable in me after all, sent me into convulsions.

I thought this was it. I was going to die. Death seemed okay to me. I was no longer afraid. This didn't last long.

Words came, between sobs.

"I see shadows." My voice wasn't even mine. It was an echo in the darkness. Something from long ago.

Melina was mumbling at me. In English. In Spanish. In something before them both. I could no longer hear her.

"They're *here*. They're going to *hurt* me." Silhouettes, sharp-toothed and sharp-clawed, surrounded me. This could not be happening, and yet it was. If I ever needed a special-operations rescue, a high-speed extraction, it was now.

"They're here! They're here!"

Melina had rooted her legs deep into the ground, one on either side of me, and, squatting low like a fantastic four-legged warrior beast preparing for birth, let go a terrifying shriek channeled from someplace that was not of this earth or dimension. I had no choice but to submit. I let go completely, clutching the earth.

· · ·

Hours later, time had stopped.

I was curled into a muddy ball on the floor, weeping softly. Two older women from my class, both mothers, were holding me. The rest of the group had left the lodge. The coals were no longer glowing. My shadows were gone. I felt spent. Lighter. Safe.

"Thank you." Melina was talking to me. According to her, this ceremony was my rebirth, and through my journey I had helped release generations of people from their suffering. I was a stubborn agnostic, but if it meant leaving behind those scary-as-fuck demons, I was okay with Melina's explanation. I avoided looking at mirrors for several days after that. I wasn't sure what I would see.

My group and I didn't speak about the event. Whatever happened south of the border remained there in the dirt.

· · ·

In 2008, I was back in Brooklyn and deep in my yoga practice. I had started teaching yoga, first to men living with HIV and AIDS, and then to veterans. One afternoon, I received a thin envelope from the Department of Veterans Affairs. I made Greg open it.

VA had denied my disability claim, citing insufficient evidence.

VA's *no* felt a lot like a betrayal. I took a few weeks to think about whether I had what it took to move forward. It turns out I had plenty to say. If a person like me, a former officer with all the resources I had access to, couldn't get VA to work for me, how could I expect VA to work for folks too isolated, traumatized, broken, or broke to fight back?

This choice of mine to engage in activism became a matter of dharma, a kind of sacred duty. It was something I owed myself and others. Once I realized this, I stepped out of the shadows.

Eli and I were talking one day at my apartment about community while Shiva and Uma slept in sunbeams at our feet. There was no place for women veterans like us. Veteran dudes took up all the space, and could not imagine a world in which women played a leading role in organizing. We started brainstorming about gathering women veterans together and creating a safe and accepting environment for women of color, women of two spirits,* and others who'd been marginalized after coming home.

A few months later, while I was plowing through my VA claim and taking time to heal, Eli brought this gathering to fruition in California. Hosted by the Women of Color Resource Center, a diverse group of women veterans from around the country attended. The women conceived the acronym Service Women's Action Network, SWAN, a word loaded with symbolism about second lives, including the marginalized duckling who in time came to discover his true identity and strength. It seemed like an apt metaphor for the experience of many women veterans.

---

* "Two spirited" in Native American traditions refers to embodying the spirit of both genders in one body. It is an older, more encompassing, and less literal term than LGBTQ.

When VA rejected my claim, I was raring to get involved, and with Eli's blessing to do what I saw fit, took charge of the organization and ten thousand dollars in seed funding.

No one with my background—cultural, educational, political—had ever headed up a veterans' organization, for men or women. The equality issues I wanted to bring to a national platform—opening combat assignments to women, ending sexual and domestic violence, improving women veterans health care (including reproductive health care) and benefits—were typically the domain of the political left. But the left wasn't as experienced with the military, and when they attempted to support women in uniform, many of us who had served cringed at their misuse of military acronyms, phrases, and terminology.

I knew the left intimately. I had been immersed in leftist politics growing up; I'd lived with Zapatistas before joining the Marines, protested police brutality as a teenager, and voted more than once for Ralph Nader (much to the amusement of folks in uniform). Sure, the Marines had ignited my contempt for bigotry and my thirst for racial and gender justice. Brown, female, and queer, I was fundamentally different in a way that made powerful people uncomfortable. But as a Marine I'd also built bridges with people who were nothing like me, because I had to in order to assimilate and survive. The Marine Corps opened me to a world of people I'd never have otherwise known, many of them flag-waving, gun-toting, Bible-loving folks with genuine hearts of gold. I was a better person for it, and prepared to be a better activist because of it.

From its inception, I was concerned that SWAN was being influenced by civilian activists who had plenty of good intentions but didn't understand the unique experiences of women in the military. Throughout my life, I'd seen people with less power have their gifts, narratives, and voices appropriated and exploited by more powerful people. Like many Brown folks from the global south, I could smell colonial attitudes a mile away. I had a firm belief about the power of people to speak for themselves. And veterans sure as hell did not need to be spoken for.

Civilian activists in a post-9/11 world often came to us with mixed agendas that started with opposition to the wars in Iraq and Afghanistan. They painted women in the military in overly simplistic terms—as victims of a corrupt system that was responsible for massive war crimes. The military was all bad; men were toxic and uncontrollably violent. For most service women who'd experienced discrimination, assault, or harassment, the narrative was usually not so simple. How on earth was a civilian activist supposed to relate to a woman who had been abused by a fellow service member but was also loyal to the uniform? For activists who had never saluted a flag, or executed an order they disagreed with, the shared experience with service women was minimal. The problem was often one of authenticity.

There were also some practical issues to consider. Writing off the military in broad brushstrokes was doing nothing to win over mainstream flag-waving Americans, whom we needed on our side in order to reduce sexual violence in the ranks. And imposing antimilitary ideology on a relatively conservative group of women would alienate veterans who needed a supportive place to heal.

I avoided antiwar partnerships. I was clear about SWAN's organizational intentions: to provide a safe space for all women veterans, and not to divide our community by party politics; who had served where, how, or when; or the foreign policy leanings of any particular administration. With few folks guiding me, and no road map for the issues we would be taking on, I was learning on the job, making mistakes, recalibrating, and moving forward.

*   *   *

Meanwhile, with the help of an attorney who provided free legal services to veterans, I decided to appeal my VA claim. The lawyer read through my stack of VA paperwork and declared, "It's as if they didn't even look at your file!"

I was relieved to find out VA's rejection had nothing to do with the merits of my case. The issue, then, seemed to be VA's incompetence. As my attorney prepared my appeal, I settled into my role as a start-up executive director.

Urban Justice Center gave me and one of SWAN's cofounders, Alison—a Harley-riding Army veteran, lesbian, and no-nonsense lawyer-in-training—a free desk to use while I scrounged around for start-up funding. I hustled my ass off, trying to find foundations that would support our unique brand: edgy, feminist, no-holds-barred, and led by women of color and queer women. We filed paperwork for incorporation, set up a website, and drafted issue papers on key topics related to women veterans, including military sexual trauma. Phone calls from service women in crisis started coming in. I was wearing several hats: crisis counselor, sister, mentor, pissed-off ally.

In 2009, we had received our first sizable grant from a major social justice foundation and were invited to testify before Congress. That summer, seven of us, all veterans, headed to Washington with our legal adviser in tow. Jules, Eli, and a couple of others who had helped create SWAN flew all the way from California to join us. It was possibly the most diverse group of women the national security world had ever seen: Brown and Black, white, straight and queer, buzz cuts and ponytails, some in pantsuits and others in traditional indigenous garb. We walked through the halls of Congress, and folks stared, thunderstruck, unable to place us in any box.

I had been invited to speak at a roundtable devoted to the needs of women veterans. Some of the older women there represented the nation's largest veterans service organizations (VSOs). They wore the old-school military hats Marines referred to as piss cutters that, from above, looked like the tip of a penis. Some of these women were *auxiliary members*, a disturbing title for a subordinate class of women veterans inside the world of VSOs. Their leaders—all men—had literally transplanted the military's segregation of women into a civilian environment.

The chairman of the House Committee on Veterans Affairs was warm and inviting, like a favorite uncle who always had your back. Democrat Bob Filner was no stranger to women's issues. The news that he was a serial predator wouldn't break for another three years after a slew of women, veterans included, came forward and accused him of sexual harassment, ending his career in politics. All I knew then was that Congressman Filner was the gracious gentleman from California.

No one said anything all that memorable until a recently discharged Army officer spoke. Dawn Halfaker was a West Point graduate who had lost an arm while serving in Iraq. She shared how some folks at VA assumed she'd lost her arm in a civilian accident rather than in combat. Several of us gasped. Dawn was highlighting what many women knew as an average day at the VA: employees there still assumed most of us were merely wives or caretakers of male veterans.

When it was my turn to give testimony, I shared our clients' horror stories about navigating the VA: one woman veteran was subjected to a peeping tom during an inpatient psychiatric stay, and another who survived military rape had to endure a gynecological exam by a male doctor without the presence of a female staff member. I shared my own painful experiences using the Manhattan VA Medical Center. I talked about the vast shortage of doctors and counselors, and the broken VA claims system. I painted a dire picture of women veterans' health care and benefits. When I was done talking, I felt hot and I was shaking.

Congressman Filner paused. Something had shifted in the room. He looked at me with what appeared to be genuine concern.

"Ms. Bhagwati, we have a lot of work to do, don't we?"

"Yes, Sir, you do."

My exchange with Filner was my first interaction with a sophisticated performer—and professional misogynist—in Washington. I had no idea just how much performances by powerful folks like him would shape my next few years of activism.

• • •

One afternoon in 2009, I remember flipping on cable news and watching the president of the National Organization for Women (NOW), Terry O'Neill, debate a decorated Army general about pregnancy regulations for service women deployed overseas. The general had issued a radical new order criminalizing pregnancy during deployments in Iraq. Four outraged female senators fired off letters to Army leadership, leading to a prompt revocation of the order.

O'Neill was a person of enormous influence in the world of women's rights, but she could not relate to the personnel issues here. Threatening to send pregnant women to jail was all kinds of wrong. Still, becoming pregnant in a war zone was no small matter. Beneath all of this kerfuffle was sexism in the military—far too many men believed that women got pregnant just to avoid difficult assignments, including deployments. Pitting the general against NOW meant that these underlying matters would never be discussed in a constructive way. Neither spoke the other's language.

During these times, cable news sorely needed experts to present a feminist military perspective. SWAN carefully strategized talking points and put out press releases to the media. Within weeks, our phone was ringing off the hook.

• • •

Ten years before Tarana Burke's #MeToo was picked up by dozens of Hollywood's leading white women, we had our work cut out for us. Americans didn't understand that harassment and assault were pervasive in the military. We had to change the narrative.

Public education was an uphill battle. There was so little coverage on service women to begin with. Women simply hadn't been included in mainstream media discussions about the military. When we were included, the press tended to infantilize women, or typecast us as victims.

In 2011, I spent a long, frustrating morning with a leading national security reporter, giving him detailed background about how and why sexual assault was occurring in the military.

He took the DOD's platitudes about having "zero tolerance" for sexual violence as fact, even though the DOD itself could not explain what it was doing, if anything, to stop sexual assault. When I pushed back, he responded by victim blaming—one soldier got raped because she put her weapon down, or another woman's case wasn't prosecuted because she was in a relationship with a superior, and so on. The man knew nothing about how power and gender functioned in the military. His tepid piece ended up being one of the first big national stories on military sexual assault in ages.

Stories on women in combat were no better. Reporters tended to portray deployed women as children or sidekicks. Why was it so difficult to simply treat service women as soldiers? Nothing irritated me quite as much as the *New York Times*' headline "For Female Marines, Tea Comes with Bullets." It featured doe-eyed Marines barely fitting into their uniforms, patrolling in Helmand Province. Much was made of their ability to have tea with their Afghan female counterparts. Less was made of their ability to pull triggers and kill bad guys.

At times, it seemed that we were rewriting the entire American perspective on military service. Hero narratives in the press were typical. Civilian reporters covering military issues—most of them men, but not all—often reminded me of unpopular teens trying to get attention from the jocks. I sometimes sensed their hero worship was an unconscious way for them to get over their guilt or regret for not having worn the uniform themselves. It was rare to find reporters who created narratives that challenged the archetype of soldier as hero, or allowed soldiers to be as complicated as they were in real life. Service members were, after all, ultimately human, and therefore fallible. For journalists not to treat them as such was not helpful to anyone.

In the worst moments in the office, SWAN felt like Central Casting for the press. I spent ages wrestling with reporters, encouraging them to broaden their warped casting criteria for various stories, appealing to their better angels. They wanted drama that was so artificial they should have made most of their calls to Hollywood.

War porn and victim porn were everything. Combat veterans had to be straight off the battlefield, so their turmoil would be graphic enough for the camera. And survivors of sexual violence had to have been assaulted *brutally* (as if there were any other way). Television news producers dug into the details of a woman's assault like surgeons without anesthesia, often rejecting the veteran's interview for the final piece in the end, leaving her feeling betrayed for the umpteenth time.

Homelessness was a hot topic. Older veterans had no chance in hell of being cast. Younger veterans had to look like models. And race mattered. (Didn't race always matter?) The press wanted white princesses, like Jessica Lynch. And the Jessica Lynches of the world—young, white, and blond—were either sexually objectified or treated as the downtrodden darlings of America instead of as human beings with unique and multilayered experiences.

I quickly became a mama bear around our veterans. If a woman wanted to speak to the press, we would support her. But we wouldn't pass her on to a reporter without ample preparation for what to expect. Often that wasn't enough.

The nonprofit organizing landscape was similarly fraught with gender land mines. Early on in SWAN's life, we organized a roundtable of homeless women veterans in New York City. Many veterans faced obstacles in attending like transportation costs and child care, so we had taken care of MetroCards, lunch, and babysitting. Word got out to the larger community about our project. One morning we received a mysterious care package from an organization that gave gifts to soldiers. My assistant, Brittany, opened it up eagerly. She called me over. I approached the large box and peered inside.

"You've got to be kidding me."

Below a stack of child-size paper and polyester American flags, I found an endless supply of lipstick, eye goop, makeup remover, and many sticks and powders I simply could not identify. I was neck deep in judgment, and I had my reasons. It was generous of these folks to send the care package, but this stuff was about as helpful to homeless veterans as teddy bears were to soldiers patrolling the streets of Baghdad. If someone showed me the science that proved that eye shadow cured post-traumatic stress or that lip gloss would get a homeless woman and her kid into permanent housing, I would be willing to change my tune. (The women appreciated the makeup. Their kids loved the tiny flags. But none of them were under any illusions. When our meeting was over, they still went back to shelters.)

Most Americans had very little idea what women veterans faced when returning home from service. One day I received an odd invitation to attend New York City Fashion Week, the annual event that summoned the world's glitterati. "Fatigues to Fabulous" was meant to honor women veterans. The title of the show made me grimace, but I was curious, so I attended with a colleague.

Before a boozed-up crowd of fashion reporters and fans, three service women made dramatic stage entrances, each with a powerful story about deploying to the Middle East or surviving sexual assault. They'd been given that infamous American television treatment: the makeover. Stomping in power heels and magazine-cover hairdos, they looked ready for the Oscars, inspiring *oohs* and *aahs*. And then, just like that, it was over. My colleague wondered if the women got to keep their dresses and heels. I sure as hell hoped so.

I later read a blog post about the event by the designer Donna Karan entitled "A Woman's Greatest Strength." She wrote, "While I can't pretend to fully understand [a returning woman veteran's] psyche, I would think she needs to return to what made her strong in the first place—her womanhood. She needs to re-engage the feminine. Dress like a woman, feel like a woman, express herself as a woman." I shuddered while I read this aloud to our helpline caseworker back at the office. She'd seen more of her fair share of destruction as an explosive ordnance disposal technician in Afghanistan. She rolled her eyes while I busted out laughing, asking her, "You mean when you got home from war the first thing you needed wasn't your femininity?"

. . .

If there was one enormous gift of doing this work, it was organizing with brilliant, passionate women who did not take no for an answer. Those of us who created SWAN had a sense early on that what we were doing was uncharted territory. While other veterans organizations tiptoed around the rights of queer Americans to serve, or the wide prevalence of sexual violence in uniform, SWAN was outspoken and unapologetic. The women who were drawn to work with us were fierce feminists—both uniformed women who did not find support in the veterans organizations that dotted the DC landscape and civilian women who thought what we were doing was cutting-edge and game-changing. Building a team that would not take misogyny lying down was the antidote to the daily sexism we faced from the veterans community.

The veterans organizing landscape was mostly male and white, and fiercely uninviting to women. Our activism challenged bro-ish culture to the core. Men resisted change at all ranks and generations of service. At veterans gatherings, their handshakes with women like me were limp, their eye contact either nonexistent or filled with condescension. Some of these bros had become celebrity veterans, concerned with branding their images and increasing their followers on social media.

In offering these guys regular spots on cable news, the media did not help in creating space for a diverse array of veteran voices.

Dan Choi was the first veteran SWAN held to task for sexism. It was not an easy decision, holding your brother-in-arms publicly accountable for some stupid thing he said about women, especially when he was a gay veteran of color. Dan was a West Point grad, Arabic linguist, and infantryman. He was articulate, authentic, and charismatic, and quickly became the LGBTQ movement's poster boy for repealing "don't ask, don't tell" (DADT). In 2010, Dan was on the cover of the *Village Voice* in a story titled (in pink) "Bad Lieutenant." Dan was portrayed as a sexually liberated, narcissistic playboy and political provocateur. In one moment, infuriated that Senate Majority Leader Harry Reid had failed to move the DADT repeal amendment forward, he lashed out: "Harry Reid is a pussy," he said, "and he'll be bleeding once a month."

Back at the office, our staff and board were incensed. I was mostly disappointed; Dan was of Korean descent, and so few of us with Asian backgrounds were doing this kind of work. SWAN's conundrum was hardly new to so-called progressive movement making. Women were often thrown under the bus in the fight for men's advancement, as women of color were for white women's. Most of the queer advocates we knew (they were almost exclusively male and white) wanted to give Dan a pass for his sexist comments. They weren't even willing to call him out on it privately, or try to get him to issue a genuine apology. Disrespecting women was not their concern.

After much discussion and reflection, SWAN wrote an open letter to Dan cosigned by three other national LGBTQ social justice organizations:

Dear Dan,

Comments denigrating women's bodies, or suggesting that simply being a woman is abhorrent, are unacceptable . . . As a direct result

*of misogynistic language, a hostile work environment for service
women—both heterosexual and lesbian—is allowed to thrive. Hate
crimes, sexual harassment, lesbian baiting, gay bashing, and sexual
assault have flourished. Adopting and promulgating hate-filled
speech against women only serves to increase the danger that service
women and LGBTQ service members face on a daily basis.*

Dan was furious with us, but he eventually acknowledged his mistake and, years later, apologized profusely. Even more to his credit, it seemed he was on the verge of acknowledging deep wounds from his military service. Substance abuse was one way Dan coped with his pain, and eventually he had to leave the limelight to take care of himself. All of this took enormous guts and grace.

• • •

In lots of ways, it was easier to take on the head of Iraq and Afghanistan Veterans of America for mistreating women. IAVA was the nation's largest and most savvy nonprofit representing Iraq- and Afghanistan-era veterans. For better or worse, it had influence on every corner of the veterans world, thanks to its ambitious young leader, Paul Rieckhoff, a former Army officer, banker, and football coach who had turned his interest in helping veterans into what appeared to be a media and fund-raising empire. Most veterans grumbled privately about Paul's infamous ego and tendency to hang out with Hollywood celebrities, but few challenged him on anything, because of his far-reaching influence over politicians, news networks, and funders.

When Paul had signed a contract with Miller beer, the org got a lot of pushback from outraged veterans who had struggled with substance abuse. But even I was caught off-guard when IAVA decided to host an outreach event in the city at Hooters, the big-boobs, beer-and-wings chain restaurant that entertained its customers with "female sex appeal."[*]

---

[*] www.thesmokinggun.com/documents/crime/so-you-wanna-be-hooters-girl.

"Wait. There's a Hooters in Manhattan?" I spurted when my colleague Alison first told me the news. As a courtesy to Paul, I decided to reach out over email.

Just saw that IAVA is hosting an event at Hooters in NYC. What gives? There are other venues to host a veterans gathering, no? Decisions like this serve to isolate, harass, and further traumatize women veterans. Please tell me this is a mistake.

His response was disappointing.

No, there is no other choice of venue for this event. Hooters has a history of supporting a number of vets groups . . . [and it's] a chance for us to reach more vets (of both genders).

I chuckled at his parentheticals and sighed at the rest, leaving him with this, and an opportunity to reverse course:

A relationship with Hooters means you're promoting sexism and disrespecting women, particularly those who serve. Lots of extremely sexist people and organizations support veterans charities, but it doesn't mean veterans orgs should support them. Women make up 15% of the military. Our PTSD disproportionately stems from sexual harassment and sexual assault while serving. You're not helping any women by promoting Hooters. You're not helping any men, either, for that matter.

Preparing for the worst, I spoke to our staff to get everyone's input, and consulted with some legendary feminist mentors. IAVA was far too big an influencer for us to stay silent. We started making phone calls. Second-wave feminists and millennial bloggers stood by, ready to launch a multipronged social media campaign.

At the eleventh hour, Paul canceled the Hooters event, and I called off the cavalry, though not before Paul made it clear over the phone that we were being overly sensitive. He told me, "You know, not all women agree with you that this is an issue."

Where the fuck do I begin with this guy? I thought. I schooled him about the disturbing group dynamics that occurred in male-dominated institutions; the fact that one woman could freely support something that was clearly not in another woman's best interest; the fact that service women tolerated so much sexism to begin with that we sometimes forgot a world could even exist where we wouldn't have to put up with men's groping hands or salacious comments. Still, he didn't seem to understand that the most obvious reason to never host an organizational event at Hooters was the fact that this infamous establishment objectified women.

Much to his annoyance, SWAN continued to challenge Paul over the years. When Paul's ego got too big for his britches, or his sexism too much to swallow, I was more than happy to tweet at him about how far from grace he was: *#Hooters.*

. . .

If I was conscious of the negative influence of men veterans on the health and welfare of women veterans, I was extremely cautious when Greg approached me at home one day, asking if it would be okay to volunteer with SWAN. He'd observed me for a couple of years in my activist role. I was reenergized and inspired about life again. Meanwhile, he was working a corporate management job in New York City that was making him miserable. I thought hard about the idea of working together again. I didn't know what it would be like to have a man working in a women's organization, particularly with his Marine infantry background.

I consulted my board. They were huge fans of bringing him on. Greg had a knack for language, valuable military experience, and a sharp mind that would be perfect for policy work. They were only concerned that all that time with Greg would be hard on me, and maybe put a strain on our relationship. It was compassionate for them to consider this. I naively figured I could handle it.

Greg ended up being so good at policy analysis that when we finally had enough money to hire someone to be SWAN's policy liaison with our Washington counterparts, SWAN hired Greg. Whether or not I liked it, the conservative dudes and good-old-boy veterans in DC didn't say no to him the way they felt free saying no to women veterans. Nor could they dismiss his personal analysis of the mistreatment of service women, or his belief that women should have full access to combat assignments. It was hard to hire talent with this combination of military knowledge and experience. And Greg was willing to work for half what his counterparts were asking for.

· · ·

SWAN was uniquely positioned to influence sexual assault policy. The Pentagon had never dealt with organized resistance from veterans on this issue. It's not that individual women hadn't tried, but victims were up against a tidal wave of Pentagon pushback and civilian refusal to believe how bad things really were.

A few years earlier, in the wake of an assault scandal at the Air Force Academy, Defense Secretary Donald Rumsfeld had established the Sexual Assault Prevention and Response Office. SAPRO was now a strange beast, headed up by a civilian woman, Kaye Whitley, whose overly casual, relaxed temperament was completely unsuited to dealing with serious crimes, institutional negligence, and mass trauma.

Our relationship with SAPRO was tenuous from the start. When we realized SAPRO's public awareness campaigns included classics from rape mythology, we spoke out. One day, while sifting through their website, we came across an official poster broadcasting the message "Ask Her When She's Sober," implying that a sexual predator was just a misunderstood guy who'd harmlessly slept with a drunk woman. What people needed to know was that predators often deliberately used alcohol as a tool to undermine the wits, memory, and trustworthiness of their victims. This poster insulted the idea of consent.

There were other disturbing examples of how uninformed the

Pentagon was about sexual violence, such as the distribution of rape whistles to women serving overseas. The *women are frail* rescue narrative was bad enough, but we also didn't understand the logistics of this solution. The whole scenario, particularly in a war zone, seemed preposterous.

And yet we were intrigued. We called one of the contractors supplying the military with said whistles. The company happily sent us a free shipment. We tore into a box filled with pink plastic whistles, with logos from each of the service branches.

"I feel safer already, don't you?" someone chuckled.

I attached my pink Marine Corps whistle to my key chain to remind me of what we were up against. We were, after all, whistleblowers to the bone.

CHAPTER 12

The Civilian Invasion

I was a relentless activist, but the truth was, I was sometimes a reluctant veteran. Combining the two roles felt awkward at best. Something in my body felt off when I was among military people. I was extremely comfortable in front of cameras and crowds, thanks to months of commanding Marines in the open air, without a microphone or script. If I had any timidity left, I knew how to mask it effectively. But finding courage was not the point. This was not impostor syndrome. I knew I could do this, if I really wanted to. But something in me felt misplaced.

I wanted to be a veteran, but my fight-flight-freeze instincts were on high alert, and it was impossible to feel safe. It seemed I belonged nowhere in this community, least of all the places where combat veterans were drinking alcohol or chest thumping so hard that they rarely quieted down enough to see what I had in common with them, or they with me. Sometimes women who'd served in combat were more vicious with me than with their male counterparts. That always hurt the most.

Doing the work of helping veterans required showing up in some places I didn't want to be. In 2010, SWAN decided to march in the

NYC Veterans Day parade. I had a good reason to show up. A young Marine whom I had guided over our help line through a harrowing sexual assault investigation came with her mother to march with us. Deb's presence was incentive enough for me to face my fears about the event.

SWAN designed a banner on behalf of sexual trauma survivors. I wondered how it would be received by the crowd. We also created a banner for LaVena Johnson, a young Black private first class whom the Army had officially declared a victim of suicide. Her father believed LaVena had been murdered by a fellow service member, and was spending most of his time and resources to prove this. It was hard not to think racism played a part in the way the Army was treating his daughter's case.

Our new office was right off the parade route in Manhattan. I headed down early to get a preview of the crowd. Tanks were parked on one side of the street. Beyond the armored vehicles, I saw a bunch of young women laughing as they spun around on their heels and modeled for men taking photos on the sidewalk.

This seemed odd, so I looked closer. The women wore tight red sequined shirts and white miniskirts. They were all legs and cleavage, blow-dried hair, and crimson lips. Above them on an enormous parade float I saw the three-lettered logo that I'd seen at dozens of airports around the world: USO. They'd been hired to entertain the troops. As I let this sink in, it occurred to me that barely a single woman veteran was in the crowds lining up on the parade route. And yet here were enough USO showgirls to man the turrets on every Humvee on Fifth Avenue.

In the crisp morning air we passed out glazed doughnuts and steaming cups of coffee and chatted with neighbors. We had reluctantly decided to march alongside another women veterans organization, run by Genevieve Chase, a career Army reservist and Purple Heart recipient. I was still getting over SWAN's first meeting with Genevieve when she looked straight into the eyes of rape survivors in our group and announced that military sexual trauma wasn't as bad as we said it was. Her assertion was all bluster, passed on to her from generations of military voices.

I would discover after years of advocacy that this I'm-no-victim attitude was extremely common among women veterans. I recognized it because the Marines had tried it on me, too. But it wasn't right. Instead of confronting the men who held us down—a solution to discrimination that was risky or doomed from the start—many women lashed out at one another, particularly those whom the system considered weak, hoping to gain a stronger foothold for climbing up the ladder.

Undermining the work of your fellow women veterans was rooted in self-hatred and jealousy, typical of every marginalized population. I acknowledged my own deep envy of Genevieve's combat creds. I hadn't served in a war zone, and it was still eating away at me. I spent a lot of energy worrying about what I hadn't done instead of remembering what I had done and was actually doing now. I had to face my insecurity head-on and talk it down. The self-hating Marine in me was like a child who never felt good enough. I had to remind myself of my inherent worth, and that service to one's nation was not restricted to the battlefield. That there were, in fact, different kinds of battlefields. Different kinds of bravery. And plenty of honorable ways to serve.

Women like Genevieve felt uncomfortable and resentful of our work, the way it allegedly highlighted them as victims, rather than warriors. No service woman wanted to look weak in uniform. Genevieve didn't, and neither did I. SWAN was trying to create a new narrative, that one could be both a warrior and a victim of abuse at the same time. One did not negate the other. In the military, this was a radical notion.

I detested the world of infighting and pettiness among women that was created over limited media space and funding for our work. So even if she didn't value SWAN's work, we agreed to walk with Genevieve. It was no small compromise on my part. She'd rallied together a contingent of color-coordinated, red-scarved women carrying guidons so large and patriotic I felt besieged and slightly nauseous. I badly wanted to get this parade over with.

I'd worn my black leather combat boots from OCS with a baseball hat, jeans, and a vegan leather jacket. The boots were as thin and worn as a chapati, but I'd polished them to Baughman's standards the night before, and somehow they made me feel safer in this mess of posturing, loud noises, and throngs of thousands squeezed together on the avenue. As I stood on the sidewalk among uniforms, getting ready for the parade to start, my client's mother appeared out of nowhere, with flushed cheeks and anxious curly hair.

"Anu, Deb needs you. She saw a group of Marines and she's freaking out."

Oh fuck, I thought, imagining Deb curled up on some street corner, triggered by memories of her rape. A platoon of manly Marines in their dress blues looking all handsome and intimidating was the last thing she needed to see. I found Deb on the sidewalk, all twenty years of her, crying in power heels that were going to destroy her feet on this long parade route. Uniformed Marines stood behind her under the traffic light, yukking it up and waiting for their platoon sergeant to call them to attention. Hell, even I was triggered looking at those devil dogs. I pulled Deb closer to the storefronts lining Fifth Avenue, so we could get shelter from the crowds on the street.

"Deb, talk to me."

She was a mess of tears, memories, and sentences that started but didn't finish. Poor kid. This parade may have been too much for her, and too soon.

"You don't have to do this. Wanna go upstairs to the office? I'll go upstairs with you."

Deb was a tough cookie. She was playing Marine. She looked at me and tried like hell to convince me she was good to march.

"I'm okay, Anu. I wanna do this. I need to do this." Tears were dripping down her cheeks. She was still shaking.

"Okay, Deb, okay. I'll support whatever you want to do."

There was no time to discuss Deb's options. Before she could catch her breath, or I could say much else, I noticed a camera and two male bodies erupting from the crowd behind Deb. A gigantic lens was suddenly focused on our faces. I looked more closely at Deb and saw a microphone glued to one of her ears. I had no idea she was being recorded. When had she consented to that?

We had agreed to let Kirby Dick, an award-winning filmmaker, follow us around that day. Dick had exposed sexual abuse in the Catholic Church, earning an Oscar nomination, and examined the homophobia of closeted gay politicians, still a favorite among LGBTQ activists. Military sexual assault was his next target, and since we were deep into exposing the issue, we'd become his go-to resource early on. If I had known the tactics he would use on this day, I never would have agreed to work with him.

I stood on Fifth Avenue, inches from Deb, with Dick's camera in our faces, as things got quiet in my head. I was outraged, and felt my heart pounding. Were these people serious? In what world was this the right time for a close-up, when a young woman was having post-traumatic flashbacks in front of tens of thousands of people? This may be how award-winning filmmakers got their awards, but this was not how decent people behaved. This was also not how human beings healed.

I was having a hard time recognizing Deb's agency here. She was barely out of her teens, and her Marine career had been violently cut short. She was on shaky ground back home, and I didn't think the public eye was the best place for her to recover. She had told me with unnerving enthusiasm that Kirby's movie would make her a reality star. She had notions about sharing her story so that other women wouldn't go through the hell she went through as a rape survivor. It was noble of her. It was kind and courageous. And still, I sensed that this public staging of a traumatic episode was not helping her, or anyone. But I had no right to tell her not to do this—it wasn't my choice. It was hers.

I felt ashamed to be standing there. I resisted the overwhelming urge to smack Dick's camera to the ground and stick a Marine Corps boot up his ass. I got in close and tried to whisper to Deb. I didn't want any part of this right now. *I* certainly did not consent to this circus. And I did not know how to stop it, much like I did not know how to stop the men I'd met in the Marines. I did not know what to say. I did not know if I had a right to say anything at all.

Thankfully, the parade was about to start. Thinking about Deb's welfare took my mind off the terror I felt walking uptown. As the parade began, onlookers cheered for the enormous floats, the armored vehicles, large formations of dress-blued Marines and soldiers in desert camouflage uniforms marching in unison. As we passed behind them all—Genevieve's red scarves and SWAN's somber banners, a few dozen women and supporters putting on smiles and managing nerves—the raucous crowd grew quiet.

It was a long walk up Fifth Avenue. We pressed on. I had so much anxiety from taking in the silent onlookers on both sides of the street that my jaw hurt. Five hours later, it was over. Deb's feet had survived. And I had avoided a panic attack. I took her to Applebee's in midtown for a free Veterans Day meal, trying to play it cool the whole time.

It was the last time I spoke with Deb. She did not become a reality television star. While crowd footage from the parade was included in Dick's film, all Deb's scenes were cut from *The Invisible War*, the documentary that would eventually be nominated for an Academy Award. Deb was devastated. Her mother wrote to me later that year, telling me they never should have trusted those filmmakers.

• • •

I do not share these stories to tear people down. And I would like to believe that anyone is capable of learning. Dick and other activists like him are not my intended audience, although if they wish to understand and repair their approach to working with vulnerable or exploited populations, I hope that humility guides them. My primary motivation in sharing my experiences is in making sure women, and future movement makers, know about the dynamics that are present when our lives become interesting to people who have some combination of power, access, money, or impressive résumés, particularly those not from our communities.

We need to protect ourselves, and each other, from making choices that do not benefit us. We must be patient and more discriminating in whom we choose to work with. Better yet, we must organize ourselves rather than allowing ourselves to be organized by outside parties. When people tell our stories for us, we often lose control of the narrative, and too often, we never get it back. Many veterans are still recovering from the harm done by various outsiders who have exploited their stories or intruded upon their lives. I write for their healing as much as for my own.

In 2011, when Dick was wrapping up his film, most civilians didn't understand our world. With only 1 percent of Americans serving in the military, this was no surprise. The work to build that bridge with funders, reporters, and fellow activists was taxing. It was easy to become disillusioned. Some folks took the time to learn about us. The ones who became allies we could trust and rely on were humble. They elevated veteran voices and let us steer policy. They asked a lot of questions. They didn't rush to conclusions. They didn't pretend they understood. We had the final word on what to say and how to say it.

The folks whom we had issues with wanted our time, our trauma, and credit for the organizing we did. Authenticity had no bearing on their choices. They tended to have prizes or reelections on their minds. It's painful to write about—in some ways, more painful than any experiences I had in the Marines or with my family. I think part of the reason it hit me so hard is because I had partially bought the hype about the nation caring for our veterans. With slogans like Support Your Troops; corporate red, white, and blue advertisements on every television channel; and a couple of national holidays that come with three- or four-day barbecue weekends, it's hard not to get swept up in the notion that America cares. But on the ground, reality looks different, and often ugly.

The story of how we made national change is new only in that service women had never been the focal point of national attention. It would be simpler to tell a story about how easy it was—it happened relatively quickly, and on the surface, I'm told I looked like an unfazed, smooth operator. But the dynamics that developed among those of us who carried service women's issues to the national forefront were not only toxic but often traumatizing. Because our work was so new, I did not have the benefit of guidance from previous generations. All movement building is gut-wrenching, for sure. But our work didn't need to be quite as difficult as it was. I've decided to tell these stories, despite the pushback I surely will get, because there is still so much work to be done. And we must get to the bottom of these toxic organizing dynamics for women in and out of uniform to succeed.

A few of SWAN's founders and staff, including me, had been interviewed by Helen Benedict, a professor at the Columbia University School of Journalism, for a book on service women's experiences. She was one of the first civilians to bring attention to military sexual assault. Eli, who'd lovingly steered me out of my deepest depressions, ended up on the cover of Benedict's book, *The Lonely Soldier: The Private War of Women Serving in Iraq*. Within months of its publication, things got sticky.

Some amount of controversy is inevitable when a white woman from the ivory tower writes a book on the experiences of women of color and working-class white women. Extreme controversy is inevitable when that journalist is also new to military culture, and not much a fan of the military. Benedict had oodles of credibility writing on sexual assault generally. But she came not only with too much unchallenged privilege but also with heavy leftist baggage, including a resistance to militarization that she did not honestly own up to when writing *Lonely Soldier*. An antiwar and antimilitary perspective colored the way she presented service women's experiences to the public.

Like several civilian activists I would subsequently meet, Benedict also assumed a knowledge and a familiarity with military culture that made me question her authenticity and motivations—as if she knew the system even better than women who'd served and who'd suffered while serving.

Benedict's ignorance led to inevitable criticism from veterans who'd given testimony for her book. She'd oversimplified their lives. Many women appeared like agentless victims of a war that shouldn't have happened. It was a narrative that just screamed exploitation.

Eli ended up going head to head with Benedict, demanding an explanation for the way in which she and others were portrayed. I had Eli's back and then some. Benedict did what most privileged white women do when women of color demand accountability: she got defensive and started talking paperwork. She insisted she'd gotten the veterans' permission. She insisted they'd all signed contracts. She even insisted that she was a true ally, and that her secondary trauma from digesting veterans' traumatic experiences was proof of this. That just about left Eli speechless. It reminded her of the generations of white people who'd come to Native lands, taking and exploiting Native traditions and narratives for profit, and leaving nothing in return. I couldn't argue with that. Sadly, Benedict considered herself heroic. More heroic, even, than her subjects.

When the Columbia University School of Social Work made Eli's life the subject of the students' final project, based on Benedict's portrayal of her, hell broke loose all over again. This moment conjured up a nasty history of white supremacy in the medical world—including experimentations on Black bodies, eugenics, and a history of white folks exploiting the resources and lives of poor and Brown people for personal gain. When the social work students, many of them students of color, found out that Eli was not only upset but retraumatized by the school's decision to use her "story" as a case study, several of them boycotted the assignment. It was an impressive and moving show of solidarity that demonstrated that sacrificing their privilege—and possibly their Ivy League degrees—was worth it in order to defend the agency of an exploited veteran.

These harmful experiences in which veterans were mistreated by people insisting they were innocent made me very cautious about engaging in the future with civilian activists. One of the things I needed to learn most, and that I had not yet grasped, was that as veterans, we did not need to work with everyone who came to us, and that if we did, we could set the terms for our relationships. We could say no. Or we could say yes. That most of these dynamics mirror conversations on sexual consent is not lost on me. That most civilian activists who touted their gender expertise did not bother to consider this parallel is troubling.

Even though I'd seen the press corps' horrendously insensitive treatment of traumatized veterans, I still wanted to believe it was possible to report on women in the military without harming them. I didn't say no to Dick, not at the Veterans Day parade or in subsequent conversations. Dick made me feel like he was on our side from the beginning—and hell, when hardly anyone was on service women's side, this felt rich. It felt validating. Like we weren't crazy or alone.

Kirby hinted at just enough to make us excited about the project. The Sundance Film Festival. The Academy Awards. I'd seen his films. An eternal optimist with my heart on my sleeve, I opened up. I let my guard down. I offered him our resources and technical expertise. My staff trained him in Military Culture 101. Then in Military Justice 101. We suggested talking points. Gave him a list of dozens of experts and policymakers. Discussed the pros and cons of various organizations and congressional offices. We made ourselves available, week after week, month after month, guiding him toward something that would be a legitimate analysis of the military's failures on sexual violence. I felt like we were planning the invasion of Normandy. We could all feel the excitement of working on a major project.

I ended up a key character in the film, underslept, hair frazzled, bags under my eyes, looking exhausted. In its review, the *New York Times* called me a "fierce victims advocate." But by the time I saw the film, I felt furious and victimized. I also felt like a fraud. How could my testimony and activism be used to support a narrative that was not entirely legitimate? I had never felt so out of place or far from the work of helping people as I had working on that film, or with the attorney whose litigation it featured. Our careful contribution had been sucked into a whirlwind publicity storm that often seemed to have more to do with fame and little to do with healing, or even with actual military reform. Dick seemed to have made a lot of promises to a lot of people, or perhaps not enough promises to the right people. Either way, a whole lot of veterans were pissed off. And all of a sudden, some of them wanted my head.

It seems hard to fathom, but when all of this was going on, I may have been the only former Marine speaking out and organizing against misogyny in the military, and without the kind of cautious deference with which most veterans engaged the powers that be. But I was deeply uncomfortable being looked to for all answers or being expected to be all things to all people. Folks didn't like being disappointed, especially when they'd pinned all their hopes on you. I'd heard that this type of thing happened in organizing—that becoming a lightning rod was part of the job—but I didn't realize this was inevitable. We were starting something that had never been attempted before. As the only folks on the block, we were all things, good and bad, depending on your perspective.

Early on in our work, we'd been approached by a rabble-rousing trial attorney, Susan Burke, who had taken on the now defamed Blackwater Corporation. She seemed to thrive on taking down powerful opponents. Burke wanted to enlist my personal testimony and SWAN's organizational support for a case she was putting together against the Pentagon on military sexual violence. Burke had been inspired by Helen Benedict's book, which gave me pause. However, being an attorney, and having sued the military on behalf of burn-pit victims in Iraq, she knew military law and policy. Working with her was an opportunity to hold the Pentagon legally responsible for widespread sexual violence. We jumped at the offer to partner.

Anxious but excited, I gave her a full day of testimony about my experiences with sexual violence in the Marines. It was triggering, but a relief to be able to share my experiences with a smart attorney who blamed me for nothing I'd gone through and validated the institutional misogyny I'd been forced to endure. I remember feeling lighter that day. I agreed to be an individual plaintiff in her case.

Fierce in her convictions and unforgiving in her pace, Susan was part attorney, part pit bull. During the week of the lawsuit filing, I met the plaintiffs, my fellow veterans, in Washington, DC. A group of mostly young white women—Regina Vasquez was the sole woman of color—who'd served as enlisted service members in the various branches of the military and Coast Guard, they had flown into Washington from around the country. Sitting in a white-walled conference room, they looked shell-shocked and worn out. They were clutching water bottles and coffee cups, making small talk.

I was already uncomfortable.

I wondered about my fellow vets. I saw no social workers. No counselors. No media trainers. I don't remember seeing a spouse, a relative, or a supportive loved one, the backbone of any human being's ability to survive a political shitstorm.

I had dealt with individual national security reporters for a while now, and I knew the kind of support that was necessary to get myself through a typical day of facing them—Doc, yoga, my dogs, and Greg were just a starting point. I also had media training, and a growing community of feminist activists who validated my contributions and recognized the chutzpah it took to show up and speak about this stuff. Even with all that support, I was still triggered and raw with the average reporter. These plaintiffs were about to face the national press corps over the most intimate details of their lives. How exactly was this going to work?

Susan had decided at the last minute that I would not be a plaintiff, and that I would support her case as a subject matter expert. Apparently, my harassment was not as bad as her other plaintiffs' rapes. *No shit*, I wanted to say. But what kind of a woman would actually say this to another woman, and in this way? And how were we going to change a culture of everyday sexism in the military by thinking just like the patriarchy, by creating a narrative about a few of the worst cases, rather than recognizing that the full spectrum of wholesale sexual violence should be under the microscope, from rape to harassment? I was interested in cultural transformation: daily discrimination against service women allowed sexual assault to thrive, and also explained officers' unwillingness to prosecute it. Talk only about so-called brutal rapes and that's all the public would pay attention to, and all the generals would be forced to respond to on camera. The truth was so much deeper and more pervasive than that.

Susan needed someone to speak to the American public, and she knew that a civilian attorney doing all of this media would not come across as sincere. Whoever ordinary Americans were, they seemed not to trust lawyers, reporters, and politicians. I became the media's go-to person for explaining the issues the lawsuit raised to a national audience.

The media may have considered me an expert, but behind closed doors in Washington, I was not always granted respect, and I often had to fight to be heard. I was always surrounded by a sea of white folks wondering who I was and what I was doing there. The day before the lawsuit was filed, I joined Susan on a series of high-profile congressional visits. My relative youth and race confused this group of powerful white women. Susan neglected to introduce me to the members of Congress, and they must have assumed I was Susan's "help," because they barely looked at me. I could not afford to take a backseat in these meetings where you could practically taste and smell the power. None of these people were veterans. And white women had no qualms about running over women of color. I wasn't going to let it happen again.

All the while, I was learning what it took to manage real people behind the scenes, all of whom wanted justice, particularly when so many of us were reeling from hurt. Some of the civilian power brokers who surrounded us—attorneys, heads of women's organizations, news producers, and politicians—had cast us in distinct roles. A lot of hoopla was made in public to call the women who were plaintiffs "survivors," but behind closed doors, I witnessed how cruel people could be toward my fellow veterans. Biases about those of us who had served stung me deeply. I overheard disturbing conversations among so-called allies about the plaintiffs. They were the kinds of conversations I was used to when white folks would talk smack about Black folks and oddly assume I would take their side. What about me would make these powerful people think I had more in common with them than with my fellow veterans?

There was perverse talk among these civilians about the validity of each plaintiff's case, which I took to mean, *Could you really trust these women?* The elitism was palpable. I wondered how many women and men hadn't made the cut for this lawsuit. I wondered why a male plaintiff in the case, an infantry guy who'd been raped by fellow infantrymen, wasn't more prominently featured in news accounts. If more men were being assaulted in the military than women, why was this band of civilians not talking about it? I wondered how many veterans had shared the intimate details of some corporal or lieutenant's betrayal only to be told years later, *It's not good enough for the nightly news, because you were drunk. It was your fault. You're not white enough. You're a man. You're not likable on television. No one will believe you.* My heart broke.

And I was angry, too. Defensive of veterans. There were the jokes these activists told about the military, a kind of sick leftist arrogance about America's continued losses in wars from Iraq back to Vietnam. If the Pentagon couldn't get its shit together on warfighting, they said, laughing, how could anyone expect them to get sexual assault right? I cringed inside. These civilians sounded like monsters. Jesus, had they no respect for the dead? For the wounded? For all those kids?

They painted me as the organizer and reformer, and the plaintiffs as victims. Dick and Burke told me one day, *You're the only one who can do it.* By that they meant, I was the only one among all of us who could be an expert. I looked at them, skeptical about their motivations. It was an artificial division that I did not agree with. The truth was, all the veterans Susan had brought together, me included, were both victims and experts. She and I had very different views on optics.

That week, Burke offered me an insight that I will never forget: the public saw you as either a victim or an expert. You could not be both. If you were a victim, the public doubted your credibility, even unconsciously. It wasn't fair, she insisted. But that's the way it was. In this scenario, I would be the expert, not the victim. Susan warned me that some of her plaintiffs would be upset and jealous that she was not extending airtime to all of them. It was all part of a big strategy to select the right plaintiffs for a narrative the public would relate to. Not surprisingly, Susan's lead plaintiffs were white, female, and blond.

I took this home with me and wondered to what extent all of this crafty staging was necessary. If these were the rules of the game in Washington, I could not accept it. This is not how change was supposed to happen. I had been raised to believe that the personal was political. Feminists and women of color in particular had encouraged me not to compartmentalize my feelings. We did not need to divide our real lives from our public lives. In fact, being ourselves and sharing our heartfelt truths, including and especially how we had been hurt in the world, and how we were going to rise up in spite of it, was the whole method behind cultural and political transformation. But in Washington, I was young, Brown, and a veteran. Credentials didn't matter—they looked down upon me.

· · ·

We announced the lawsuit to the nation at the National Press Club, where photos of presidents, media pundits, and celebrity change makers plastered the walls. Susan wisely did not allow reporters to directly address the plaintiffs. It would have been carnage, a victim-blaming onslaught, which was more than any human being should be expected to handle. Meanwhile, my protective instincts were on high alert. I felt responsible for these veterans. This place seemed foreign and cold. The bright lights, rolling cameras, and stern white faces of national security reporters, many of them men, did not inspire comfort.

Susan's cases, first one and then another, ended up blasting a hole through the Pentagon's zero-tolerance bullshit. The military had no idea what hit it.*

SWAN was such a huge part of the media presence following the litigation that many folks in DC thought Susan's cases were, in fact, ours. I joined two or three of Susan's clients in a series of national interviews that set the stage for congressional interest. My most memorable was an almost forty-five-minute live interview with the conservative pundit Piers Morgan. It was a surreal experience in which, both before the show and during several commercial breaks, from across an enormous, shiny CNN news table, he genuinely asked me to explain the facts. I carefully coached him on rape culture in the military so that he would not come across as a monster when redirecting questions to the plaintiffs. I did dozens of interviews. We were all over cable news and the major papers. Lawmakers were urgently calling our offices, wanting in. The game had changed, almost overnight.

---

* Susan's strategy was all shock and awe. Her litigation did little to actually chip away at the legal barriers service members faced in challenging the military. The main one, the Feres doctrine, upheld by the Supreme Court, essentially prohibited service members from suing the government for injuries sustained during military service. But my sense was that by focusing the media's attention on how much these women had suffered, someone powerful would have to pay attention.

CHAPTER 13

Shock and Awe

These initial encounters with civilian activists informed how we organized our first major national conference. "Truth and Justice: The Summit on Military Sexual Violence" made waves in Washington. We'd moved mountains to make it happen, raising about two hundred thousand dollars to host a hundred military sexual assault survivors on full scholarship to the nation's capital—housing, travel, the works. My staff worked tirelessly. Meanwhile, we'd made such a ruckus over sexual violence in the news that politicians were clamoring to meet with our veterans.

Our guest of honor and keynote speaker was Mary Lauterbach, a Marine mother from Ohio. Mary's daughter, twenty-year-old Lance Corporal Maria Lauterbach, was killed in 2007 while serving in the Marines. Maria's murder was widely considered a revenge killing by Cesar Laurean, the man she'd accused of raping her. She was seven months pregnant when he killed her (Laurean was not the father), buried her in his backyard, and fled to Mexico. In 2010, he was found guilty of first-degree murder.

Mary was everyone's mother this week. Wherever she went, hugs followed.

SWAN was presenting the Lauterbach Award for Truth and Justice to Senators John Kerry and Susan Collins, and Representatives Nikki Tsongas and Mike Turner.* Tsongas and Turner were the best example of bipartisanship I'd seen so far on this issue. They founded the Military Sexual Assault Caucus, and with our regular input, legislated literally dozens of military reforms, all designed to improve a survivor's chances of accessing justice in a grossly unjust system. One of these was the ability of a victim to swiftly transfer units in which her or his perpetrator also served. If Maria's request to transfer out of her unit had been approved, she might have escaped Laurean.

Kerry towered over us with silver hair, lanky limbs, warm eyes, and a long face. When I walked him through the room, my skull a foot below his chin, it felt as though the seas had parted. Veterans rose to greet him and I was in no rush to get him to the stage. This was no ordinary official, and we all knew it.

Kerry stopped by a table where some of our older survivors, several of them male, stood up to greet him. Like Kerry, they were Vietnam veterans. Some of them had been trapped beneath the weight of invisible wounds for forty years. This was possibly the first time their pain was being publicly recognized, by a man of Kerry's stature no less. I think Kerry knew this. How could he not? This formidable man was bearing witness now to the tremendous suffering of his community. Many of us were in tears.

I was balancing about a hundred things on very little sleep that day, including media appearances and congressional visits, while my staff was balancing several hundred more details supporting the veterans who were attending. We had brought a few social workers to the summit for extra emotional support. We had required a letter of recommendation from a counselor or other similar person to vouch for each veteran before

---

*In 2018, when Collins chose to cast her vote in favor of Supreme Court nominee Brett Kavanaugh, I was outraged. It felt like she had dishonored Maria's memory and disrespected all veterans who'd had the courage to speak out about their assaults.

we provided a scholarship—we knew that traveling hundreds of miles from home and spending forty-eight hours with a bunch of strangers wasn't necessarily in every veteran's best interest.

There were so many unknown factors, which meant a minefield of potential emotional and psychological triggers for our participants. One of our attendees hadn't been out of her apartment in years because of her trauma. And visiting Congress was often enough of a horror show to send anyone packing. Two years ago, I'd had a particularly infuriating meeting with a senior congressional aide—a tall, white, conservative Marine infantry officer. He refused to look me in the eye, instead just addressing Greg. Filled with so much anger that I was barely able to speak, I canceled my remaining meetings and hopped on an Amtrak out of Washington, DC.

We were carefully trying to minimize any chance of our survivors having traumatic experiences at the summit. But some things could not be controlled.

We had put together a series of panels for our attendees. Our board president, Kalima deSuze, an Army veteran and social worker who continually blew me away with her ability to ensure that all people felt validated and welcome, had just finished moderating a discussion with a diverse panel of survivors. They had echoed experiences from the crowd itself, and many veterans were feeling seen and heard for the first time in a long time.

Touched by what I'd heard, I walked out into the hall to get some water while the next panel started. My assistant, Olivia, suddenly appeared, pulling me aside. "You need to get in there, Anu."

I opened the door to the ballroom and anxiously chugged my water as I took in the scene.

Our next panel looked as if it were about to self-destruct. We'd gathered a group of experts on military law and policy to lay out the obstacles to making change to the justice system. A retired military judge was digging himself into a grave. An older white grandfather, he was a liberal advocate for reforming the Uniform Code of Military Justice (UCMJ) and had contributed behind the scenes to major changes in legislative reform for victims. But the judge had misjudged his audience.

He was deep into a history lecture about how the UCMJ came to be.

"Military law isn't half bad. This is why it works."

One veteran was standing, teetering on her legs, her voice cracking.

"No way!"

"Are you fucking . . ."

Feet shuffled beneath hotel tablecloths and a wave of murmurs and panicked looks passed from one end of the room to the other. His blasé legal oversimplification was coming across as a slap in the face to a room maxed out in human suffering. Hadn't we briefed him on what kind of an event this was?

Much to my relief, his presentation quickly wound down, and another panelist—a civil rights attorney and a young woman of color from the ACLU—took over. I followed a small group of veterans out of the hall and walked into the bathroom, desperate to splash cold water on my face. A dozen women stood, leaning against sinks and walls, deep in anxious conversation. They stirred when I entered.

"Oh my god," I muttered. "I can't believe what just happened. He isn't like this usually. I'm so sorry." Several sets of eyes opened wide.

"Oh thank god, Anu."

"Are you kidding? I'm so mad I could hit something."

They all looked at me. I must have seemed beside myself, because they gave me warm smiles. I pulled myself together.

"Hey, will you come back inside? I'm gonna say something to the whole room."

They agreed, and we walked back in. One of our other civil rights attorneys was, thankfully, giving the final remarks on the panel, sounding thoroughly compassionate, despite his lawyering, and wrapping up loose ends that had derailed many of our participants.

I waited till he finished. Kalima had taken the mic, and other social workers were already working individual tables, calming nerves, listening to cries and complaints. I walked to the podium.

"Hi, everyone. I want to say something."

Some folks looked up. Others continued to look shell-shocked.

"Our panelists have spent decades carving out expertise in different ways the justice system does and does not work for sex crimes victims. They are all our allies in fixing a broken system. But the point of this is not for you to agree with everything they say. I've heard a couple of things today that make me want to bang my head against the wall. But we can make up our own minds about what we choose to listen to.

"Take what you want that's useful. Leave the rest. Remember, you're the only expert on your lives, on what happened to you. So take whatever frustration you have, and ideas you have, and rage that you have, and use it for change.

"You're fired up? Good. Stay fired up. We're visiting Capitol Hill this afternoon. Channel all of this and unleash it on your elected officials. *They're* the ones who have the power to change the system. Tell them your stories. And if they don't listen, remember, you have the last word. You don't like how they respond? Then vote them out of office."

Veterans were hooting and hollering, getting out of their seats. Congressman Mike Turner, who'd witnessed my speech from the back of the hall, was less than thrilled—I got a talking-to the way a senior officer might have counseled me back in the day—but his fear of being voted out of office by angry veterans was a small price to pay for getting the group focused and back together. I was flushed, exhausted, and exhilarated—but still very, very concerned.

• • •

It was like something out of *House of Cards*. If you'd told me I would be in a one-on-one battle with a sitting member of Congress, with an entire community's sanity hanging in the balance, I would have thought you were nuts.

On the second day of the summit, my staff received an emergency call from one of our participants. A veteran had thrown herself down a large set of stairs in the Cannon House Office Building after leaving a party hosted by Representative Jackie Speier. The woman had not been drinking and had not slipped on the floor, nor was she suicidal. All of that would have been understandable, forgivable. Instead, her fall was a stunt orchestrated purely for attention. A hundred veterans wandering around Capitol Hill with cell phones meant news traveled fast. When we got the call, I thought only one thing: *Fucking politicians.*

Jackie Speier, a Democrat from California, was royally pissed off that SWAN had not given her a role to play in our conference. We'd been careful to recognize hard-fought victories on both sides of the aisle and train our veterans to know the policy issues on the Hill. Most importantly, we'd given them the platform to tell their personal stories to elected officials who by this time were desperate to be included in our House and Senate visits. Speier wasn't interested in all of this organizing. Her impromptu party for our summit veterans appeared to be a way to get back at us, throwing a wrench in our plans to get a hundred trauma survivors safely and efficiently around the halls of Congress and back home in one piece.

In retrospect, we should have probably just let her speak and called it a day. But by then she'd gotten too unpredictable. A tiny but vocal band of her supporters had surfaced as well, occasionally unstable, hurling vicious, sometimes threatening comments left and right on social media at anyone they felt was a traitor to the cause. The cause itself was often unclear, and the list of traitors included many activists, including me. This had nothing to do with their character, or mine, and everything to do with unresolved trauma. Speier had little idea how to manage a traumatized population. She was a politician, not a therapist, and yet she often acted like she was the only one in the world who cared about people who were hurting. I'm not sure what she was trying to prove.

Speier had hooked dozens of summit survivors away from our carefully scheduled activities on the Hill with a fancy reception. She had coordinated nothing with our staff. Not even a request, or a heads-up. Our veterans left Speier's party late, missing planes, trains, and automobiles back home. My staff, overworked and under-rested from eight months of planning and supervising one hundred trauma survivors and twice as many congressional offices, was ready to leave Washington. But that wasn't possible now. My staff paid out of pocket to remedy the congresswoman's move and get our veterans home safely. And just when we thought things couldn't have gotten worse, we got the call about the jumper.

Speier's background was legendary. As a young congressional aide, she'd survived the massacre at Jonestown, where Jim Jones ordered his henchmen to assassinate Speier's boss, Congressman Leo Ryan, and then persuaded his followers to kill themselves. Speier almost bled out on the tarmac in Guyana. I have no idea how this trauma shaped her, for better or worse. We were told it was an experience that she rarely talked about.

Speier was a bundle of empathy and raw emotion. She burst onto the scene after Susan Burke's first sexual assault case was filed against the Pentagon. She wanted to unscrew the military's broken judicial system overnight.* She had fewer boundaries than any other member I'd met. Speier was a hugger. She tried to be your favorite aunt. At our first meeting, she'd laid out enough fruit and cookies to feed a starving village. She didn't know the military and was out of place in the defense world, but she was determined to get involved. She grilled us for an hour or two about everything that would need to be fixed in

---

* Jackie Speier and Bruce Braley, also a Democrat, were the first members of Congress in this era to take on military sexual assault comprehensively. They didn't need extra convincing about the merits of sticking up for survivors or daring to speak out against military generals. Braley's legislation, the Holley Lynn James Act, named after an Army second lieutenant who was murdered by her husband, was far more radical than anything that came out of Congress in the last decade. He was challenging the military's power over survivors at the core: he was taking on the Feres doctrine, which protected the military from being sued by uniformed victims. Without this critical reform, rape, assault, and harassment survivors, in addition to victims of medical malpractice, domestic violence, and discrimination, would be told that their injuries were "incident to service." In other words, they were harmed during the course of their job, and therefore the military could not be held responsible. It was insane, and enough to make survivors feel insane once they found out about Feres. No one aside from Braley was ballsy enough to go there.

order for survivors to get justice, as her staff furiously took notes. She wanted us to hold nothing back. On the spot, she asked us to write a bill to repair the military justice system. And we did.

This was no small effort. The military justice system was as old as George Washington, and its vehicle, the UCMJ, was deeply entrenched in the way the military conducted its day-to-day affairs. The military justice system was as ingrained as Marine Corps customs and courtesies. It was as sacred as the American flag. It was a stinking artifact that had survived the Civil War, both World Wars, and the transformation of modern warfare. It was going nowhere. Nonetheless, we pressed forward, because we were idealists and dreamers, and with the system as broken as it was for victims of sexual violence, we had nothing to lose by attempting to transform it.

We worked with our attorney colleagues to lay out legislative language that would eventually become Representative Speier's signature bill. At its core, it would remove commanders from overseeing judicial proceedings. This needed to happen if any change was possible in the military. Commanders would all too often try to avoid scandals from breaking, rather than repair them at their root. I had seen this firsthand, and so had most of the victims I'd met. Commanders were not impartial arbitrators of justice. How could they be, when both the victim and the accused worked for them?

Years after our fallout with Speier, I still recognize her contribution to keeping the heat on the military. In recent years, she took on the Marines when no one else would, aside from SWAN and a couple of reporters. Do I wish that someone like Tammy Duckworth, Tulsi Gabbard, or Seth Moulton, with military backgrounds and the language and temperament to engage the Pentagon, had taken on the Marines instead? Hell yes. But they didn't. And in not taking the lead, veterans who were members of Congress left the work of military reform in the hands of colleagues without any military experience, like Speier.

Speier seems to have finally found her political stride in the

#MeToo era. But back when I was working with her, she was a mess of histrionics, misplaced blame, and grudge holding. I'd much rather tell this story without including her, because there are few things worse for me than calling out a fellow woman in a patriarchal institution. But I can't tell this story authentically otherwise. For better or worse, Speier was as close to our issue as a member of Congress got.

I'm concerned with the things that should and should not happen in the name of making change for service members and veterans. Jackie Speier didn't know how the military operated, and she was too impatient to understand why customs and traditions were the way they were. When we pushed back on basic facts, she took this to mean we weren't on her side. Her colleagues in both parties were so frustrated with her emotional tantrums that some quietly attempted to train her in military basics, while others flat-out ignored her.

Within months, fishy things began to happen. The congress-woman quoted our staff's talking points verbatim, in conferences, on television, and in House chambers. But she had also created a huge platform for her close friend Nancy Parrish, a wealthy older white woman from Florida who was a Democratic fund-raiser. Out of thin air, Parrish created what appeared to be an "AstroTurf organization," a nonprofit designed solely to support a member's legislation. Just as badly, the organization, Protect Our Defenders, was neither founded, led, nor staffed at the time by people with any experience on the issues. Therefore Speier could use it to push forward her agenda without resistance. It was as creepy as anything I'd seen in Washington.

It's one thing for an author, moviemaker, or go-get-'em attorney to exploit the experiences of military veterans. It's another thing altogether for elected officials to do this. Service members, at the end of the day, risk their lives to execute political goals. Most elected officials—even the downright rotten ones—knew there were lines that could never be crossed with our community. Speier couldn't have cared less.

We first met Nancy Parrish in a coffee shop at the Sundance Film

Festival, where Dick's film was screening. I listened respectfully while Parrish vigorously lectured my colleague and me for an hour about what veterans needed. I remember thinking, *Jesus, this lady has no idea what she's talking about.* I felt outraged that it was this easy for someone with a whole lot of dollars to enter a community with no experience and no expertise and just grab a microphone. I was also sad. Why didn't people with money support those in the community already doing the work well? Instead, they engaged in cultural appropriation. Worse than that, this behavior was exploitation of a community that was so beaten down by military injustice and betrayal by a nation that it may have been too overwhelmed to see this woman for who she was, or worse, even care.

I pushed back hard, especially on the day she offered to merge her fledgling organization with SWAN, as if we would ever be so foolish to do such a thing when we worked so hard to build something from the ground up, with our own sweat, tears, and life experiences. Like Speier, she grabbed what she could of our talking points, although she didn't understand them, and delivered them poorly. She proved every American's concern that money and connections were the things that counted most in Washington. Not facts. And definitely not people.

As we approached the date of our first summit, Representative Speier called me, wanting me to make Parrish's brand-new organization a cosponsor of our conference. We'd worked for several months to raise funds so survivors of military sexual violence could come to Washington, DC, for free. Close allies, veterans and civil rights organizations that had served veterans for years were contributing valuable support for these scholarships. It was an impressive coalition of groups that simply wanted to help.

There was nothing friendly about Speier's request. Being strong-armed by an elected official for personal ends has a particularly eerie feel. Being a veteran made it feel almost unreal. I told her a word she was not interested in hearing.

"No."

Speier was pissed off and huffy, and responded with a line that became legendary on the Hill.

"I'm *shocked*." I was relieved that my staff witnessed the conversation. In the days that followed, her attempt to influence our organization morphed into an ultimatum. She and her staff made it clear that SWAN had to let Parrish in. *Or what?* I thought. They were speaking like mobsters. The idea of Jackie Speier throwing down with a bunch of Marines and soldiers was almost laughable if it weren't so sinister. Her treatment of us reminded me of my experiences being threatened by senior Marine officers. The only difference now was that I was no longer forced to tolerate those threats. I don't know what exactly triggered Speier's menacing behavior. Politicians disagreed with constituents and advocates all the time. But they didn't often cross these kinds of lines. (This was before Donald Trump's unhinged behavior became the new normal.) They usually backed off and went on their way.

Speier, as a colleague put it to me, had just decided to "shit all over SWAN and move on." She refused to play nice with folks who disagreed with her. After a House hearing one day, she walked away from me and another veterans leader in the middle of a conversation. He too was *shocked*. Soon after, she just flat-out stopped saying hello to me in the halls of Congress.

In the meantime, Speier pressed forward with a revised version of the bill we'd worked up for her. We agreed with the intent to remove commander influence over sexual assault trials, but we were concerned about the actual content of the bill. There was at least one section that violated the constitutional rights of defendants, and a couple of others that made no logistical sense. How were we supposed to back an unconstitutional bill? It was blatantly wrong. We couldn't support a bill that wouldn't work, even if we'd laid the ground for it.

Meanwhile, Speier was shocked with everyone, and her recklessness was multiplying. On the floor of the House, she accused colleagues who didn't sign onto her bill of being complicit in military sexual assault. Human beings did not want to be compared to a bunch of sexual predators. It was below the belt. The members Speier considered enemies came from all stripes: Democrats who were caring, experienced, and far better equipped to interact with the military, but not passionate enough for Speier's taste, as well as Republicans who were genuinely interested in reform. She treated them all like they were traitors.

Speier became the symbol of survivor outrage. She gladly played the part of messiah, a role that was cursed from the start. (One didn't heal trauma by projecting hopes and dreams onto powerful people with questionable motives.) But this was politics. She was angry, and for many survivors, that was, understandably, all that mattered. Being pissed off meant you were on the right side—forget the law or governance. It didn't matter if she knew the issues, or was misrepresenting facts to survivors, whose last hopes were pinned to a bill that had no shot at making it through Congress, in part because of the messenger. Over the years, folks signed on, but the bill was mostly symbolic. The kind that if you didn't put your name to, the average constituent might accuse you of being pro-rape. But most folks knew the bill would never fly.

The jumper, unfortunately, was put on SWAN's watch as our staff, exhausted and ready to go home to New York, wrestled with who was going to monitor the veteran in the hospital. One of our board members, a Marine Corps veteran and also a social worker, took over, working overtime to monitor the veteran for several days. After some investigation, it appeared that the veteran was totally unhinged and hallucinating. I called Speier's aide, furious, telling him that after all the trouble they'd put our organization through, perhaps the congresswoman would like to take the time to visit her Californian constituent in the hospital. This was one of those moments that makes or breaks an elected official's career. His boss was lucky I called him and not the press, and he knew it. Speier visited the veteran, acting the innocent angel. It was the last time I ever engaged with her staff.

Working with trauma is messy at best. However, powerful folks playing savior to traumatized people is beyond the pale. It was unfair and psychologically damaging for Speier to promise legislative miracles to veterans—victims, no less—especially when taking on a system as deeply entrenched and problematic as military justice. That she had obviously survived something just as awful may have had nothing or everything to do with her bullying, her desire to be a political hero, or her tendency to vilify the whole world. But plenty of members of Congress on both sides of the aisle had survived trauma—domestic violence, sexual assault, combat wounds, and imprisonment by enemy soldiers. It hadn't held them back. In fact, it often elevated them.

Speier's behavior may have been some indication of how unresolved trauma can manifest at the highest levels of power. Meanwhile, several rungs below, unresolved trauma was spilling out across an entire community of military survivors. And I had no idea how to manage it.

CHAPTER 14

Bleeding Hearts

SWAN's high profile meant that we were a target for everyone's discontent. Being from the community that was on the attack, it hurt like hell. SWAN's multiple advocacy initiatives and regular presence in the media and on Capitol Hill pissed off some survivors who had been featured in *The Invisible War*. It seemed I was always being accused of doing too much, or never enough. A couple of veterans were seething with jealousy and rage, toward me and toward each other.

Fights were breaking out on social media. Survivors were trolling one another. There were threats, one survivor against another, and talk about law enforcement getting involved. I was alarmed reading the back-and-forth. The pain was palpable, with untreated post-traumatic stress dominating social media threads and causing enormous rifts in the community. No qualified person was providing guidance to this group of women, including the best directive of all: get off social media.

One day, I opened my Facebook account and read a post by one of Susan's original plaintiffs, accusing me of making money off the backs of rape survivors. I read this in my closet-size office, almost laughing. I made hardly any income doing this work over the years. I had refused a salary so I could make sure my staff was paid and had benefits before I did. And there were many months I was hustling just to keep our office doors open.

Thinking I would explain things and set the record straight, I responded to the veteran. I should have kept my mouth shut. She lashed out and attempted to shame me publicly. Despite a sea of civilian activists now using survivors from the military—trial attorneys, members of the media, politicians—I was the biggest villain.

More than one trauma expert, including a trauma psychiatrist on our board, described these group dynamics as completely normal. They said some folks would be consumed with anger and jealousy toward me because I seemed to be unfazed by trauma or hardship. They described the betrayal trauma caused by the military's negligence toward their welfare and the impact of my public profile. They were speaking in clinical terms, and it was scary stuff. These veterans essentially wanted me dead while also wanting what they thought I had. I was grappling with my own mental and emotional demons the entire time I was being attacked, and clung to these explanations just to get by.

Animosity and, at times, personal threats continued to mark my relationship with a handful of extremely loud sexual trauma survivors. I was enemy number one, and I quickly learned the best way to engage with these voices was not to engage at all. It ate me up that I was forced to do this for my own safety. It went against my nature. I wanted to connect with people. This work was forcing me to put up huge boundaries between me and members of the community, women whom I'd gone to bat for, just like I would have if they were my Marines. Detaching didn't feel right. But it was absolutely necessary, both for my health and for the work.

This small but vocal group had no compunction telling lies about me and, as the work developed, other veterans who had become key voices or faces of the movement. Slowly, any advocate on these issues would be idolized briefly—no matter what their level of expertise or integrity—and then cast aside as some sort of traitor to the cause. None of the hostility I faced from male misogynists could ever compare to the sting of hatred from a fellow woman in the military, who, like me, had been hurt while serving.

While turmoil over SWAN's success was brewing outside our offices, I was also faced with the challenges of managing a diverse staff that was part civilian and part ex-military. Hiring was often difficult. Civilians were idealistic about service women's rights, but took time to adjust to the realities of veteran experiences and learn about military culture. Civilians were sometimes slower to act, and at times seemed more entitled or naive about everything from their personal welfare to notions about politics.

In a perfect world, I'd have hired an army of shit-hot women veterans. But not all women veterans were willing or interested in putting themselves out there in what was obviously a radical way in order to change policy for service women. And lots of veterans were dealing with personal reintegration issues—everything from learning all over again how to live free of orders and regulations to more urgent challenges involving health, emotional well-being, or trauma. At SWAN, where gender and sexuality were the focus of our work, the challenges of reintegration appeared in unique ways.

One weekend I'd flown to Las Vegas to speak at a veterans conference. I got a phone call from Greg on a Sunday. He sounded anxious. And still, somehow, reserved.

"Things happened over the weekend. You're going to hear about them."

My stomach began to rumble.

"What do you mean?" I asked.

"The staff went out to a bar. I said something to Olivia that offended her. I apologized, but she's upset." Olivia was smart. Sensitive. Young. Greg was at least fifteen years older, a lumbering giant who had seen and done things in uniform that folks like Olivia would never be able to process.

"What did you *say*?" I insisted.

"She brought a boyfriend. He said he was taking her home. I told him, 'You're in there like swimwear.' She overheard me."

My mind was reeling. It was my first time hearing this odd phrase, but any reference to sure things and bathing suits could not be innocent. In the end, if Olivia was offended, then I was too. I could barely contain my anger. There was this matter with Olivia, and then there was this:

"Why were you drinking with the staff?" I was alarmed.

He struggled to answer, and then did, quietly.

"We were just letting off steam."

I could have hit him.

Greg had no business hanging out at bars with our staff. With *my* staff. It was a question of judgment. He was never right with alcohol. Only bad things happened. You didn't drink with your troops. And you didn't drink with your subordinates. One drink, maybe. Then you left, before everyone got too drunk to care what was right and what was wrong. Hadn't we both learned this the hard way?

I sent Olivia a concerned email and met with her in my office first thing on Monday morning. Olivia was an invaluable assistant. She'd gone to some fancy-pants liberal arts college and was a theater geek. When I'd heard her sing for the first time (she grabbed the mic at our "don't ask, don't tell" repeal party), it brought me to tears. She was on top of my frenzied schedule and had never let me down. And she'd almost single-handedly organized the logistics for our first summit.

I let her know despite my relationship with Greg she could come to me with anything.

I know. I trust you.

That comment pierced me. If I was so trustworthy, how could something like this happen in my organization?

Was this all about Greg? Apparently not. Alison had made some dumb comment about Olivia's short hair, telling her she'd gotten a dyke haircut. Alison had meant it as a compliment. A millennial who'd moved well beyond the gender binary, Olivia didn't take it that way.

While I listened to Olivia, I was reminded of a female Army veteran on staff, whose in-your-face style and frequent use of the word *bitch* had my head spinning. So many self-proclaimed feminists insisted on using the word *bitch*—I thought, who was I to argue with her? And yet the word stung. I felt its misogyny. Why hadn't I said anything to her? Jesus. Was there a culture of sexual harassment blossoming in my own women's rights organization?

I asked Olivia what she wanted to be done. Did she want to file a harassment complaint? Did she want Greg fired? Did she want a formal sit-down with Alison?

She wanted none of that. It seemed she wanted Greg and Alison to understand what they'd done wrong, and for it never to happen again.

With Olivia's consent, I brought Greg in. Olivia spoke to him while I witnessed. He didn't say much. I can't remember if he apologized. I wondered if clamming up completely was his way of avoiding sticking his foot farther down his throat. But I wasn't sure.

And then I spilled my guts.

"What you said was a betrayal. It was like what Thomas did with Katz and Hamby. It was like that."

Olivia didn't have a clue what I was talking about, but the tenor of my voice was probably enough. Greg had fucked up royally. He had let me down. And I wouldn't get over the disappointment anytime soon.

As best I can tell, Greg heard me loud and clear. He never apologized to me, or brought this moment up again. I don't think he had any idea what pressures I was under as a female executive, of color no less. I'm guessing his silence was about shame as much as anything. Over the months and years that followed, he was more and more vocal about decrying the basic indignities that women faced. Still,

I wondered what soul-searching he was doing internally. Had he fully processed the misogyny the Marines had instilled in him? He wasn't just one of the good guys. He was quite possibly the best. He'd thrown his career into the toilet to stop sexual assault and harassment in his unit. He was no average Marine.

None of us who've worn the uniform are untouched by misogyny. It takes time to process it, and I'm not sure most veterans even get to a place where that's a priority. Hatred of women has never not been a priority for me, because, as a target, I don't have the privilege of ignoring it. It's painful work, and people like Olivia get hurt as we learn to replace the military's othering of women with kindness and respect.

One doesn't emerge unscathed from ten years of infantry experience. In this way, Greg is like many Marines. And he is also exceptional. Greg ended up being responsible for ushering in more legislative changes to military sexual assault policy in the last decade than any other human being that I'm aware of. His expertise was unparalleled. He was a workhorse, and there wasn't a congressional office or member of the media for the seven years he worked these issues in Washington who did not benefit from his analysis, writing, and passion for change. I still sit with this, recognizing how much good can follow so much immersion in violence and discrimination. We are all capable of transformation.

· · ·

One weekend in 2013, the *New York Times* quoted me in a piece on Dick's film called "This War Is No Longer Invisible." I had said the Department of Defense was "definitely taking [sexual assault] seriously. After Afghanistan, combating sexual assault is probably its highest priority." I was not exaggerating—DOD was running around defensively, often helplessly, trying to keep up with the arrows we were throwing at them. I'd never seen so many senior officials being called before Congress and the press to answer for their inaction. We had finally gotten the Pentagon to pay attention, and the quote was meant to acknowledge our work in lighting a fire under their asses, not to congratulate it for a job well done.

After the article was printed, a discussion forum had been started over social media with one person saying SWAN was no longer serving the community's interests. I was a Pentagon sympathizer. Hate mail was coming in, including one call by a veteran to pound me in the throat. I quickly called my communications director.

"Robin, Facebook is on fire. Survivors are asking for my head."

Robin was perplexed. I did not need perplexed. I needed a solution.

"Why don't you just talk to them?" she proposed.

Robin was not a veteran, nor did she have experience in crisis communications. She was unprepared to deal with sexual violence on such a massive scale. Between a stressed-out boss and hysterical veterans crying mutiny, she had shut down.

SWAN was doing work that happened so fast, and with such intensity, that my staff was completely unprepared to handle the impact and keep up with the pace of change. If I'd been wiser, I might have been able to defend us from impending implosion. I might have refused to do half of the work we did. But it felt like we were making history. And some part of me didn't know how not to embrace every good opportunity that came our way. I was a workaholic and perfectionist with more stamina than was healthy, who was racing against each day to make up for the humiliating time I'd had in the Corps.

Meanwhile, a few staff members were fast approaching burnout. Being a Marine did not help me navigate this well. I was used to supervising folks who conquered every challenge that was thrown at them. I forgot that the real world didn't run by the same rules to suck it up, or sacrifice yourself for the greater good. The veterans on my staff were used to dealing with everything life threw at us, all the while taking orders from assholes and sucking up a dozen other different headaches. Our civilian counterparts never had to play by these rules, at this relentless pace, with these kinds of pressures. I had no patience for my staff's fragility, because I had no patience for my own. I was focused on changing the world. I didn't realize that I couldn't do it without taking care of myself first. And I couldn't do it on my own.

Trauma has a way of multiplying. When vicarious trauma happens on a staff, it is something that requires complete attention. I chose to press forward, for the cause. My staff was handling legislation influenced by relentless congressional timelines and media dictated by breaking news. Some of them were ready for this onslaught. Many were not. Had trauma not been the air that we were breathing, the substance of our work, and the thing that connected all of us, this might have been doable. But that's not how trauma operates. The growing pains were excruciating. Fissures that exist in every young organization became gaping holes. I was learning, fast.

In one moment of despair, after handing in her resignation, one staff member asked me how and why I would ever choose to do this job. Several of my staff had lost faith in why we were doing the work anymore. Moreover, they felt a palpable sense of frustration with me. I couldn't protect them from the emotional onslaught in the community. I couldn't protect them from my own pain. And I couldn't help the women and men out there who were spitting venom every which way, mostly because they were hurting. I felt like I had failed everyone.

The *Times* column was a turning point. Our organization had little to no experience handling security threats. The civilians on our staff were freaking out. By the time our second summit happened, a couple of folks had simply broken down.

· · ·

At our second summit on military sexual violence, with our staff burned out and overwhelmed, we hired undercover security. It had come to that. We rescinded or denied invitations from people we thought threatened the safety of the event. The staff was concerned I might be attacked. I was worried that a veteran might attack a member of Congress. Indeed, a fight between two veterans had to be broken up at the second summit.

I was tired of feeling upset and scared of the women who tried to tear me apart. It was important for my sanity to see these veterans as whole human beings, and not as enemies. These were supposed to be my sisters. We were all supposed to be supporting one another, weren't we? This was hard to remember when we were mired in individual she-said, she-said dynamics.

One day, a veteran compared me to Jesus. Even, unbelievably, offered to walk my dogs. Three months later, she hated my guts and all I stood for, and tried to get everyone she knew to hate me, too. I suppose in retrospect it was a method of asserting control in her life, particularly given that she must have figured I had so much control over mine. I'd used this method myself when I'd felt lost, battered, or unsupported by unjust circumstances way beyond my control. I barely knew another woman who hadn't. But knocking another woman down only made me feel more miserable and less in control.

In the world of meditation halls and yoga studios, where I was spending increasing amounts of time, I practiced being joyful for other people, especially when I felt jealous. I practiced forgiveness when I felt hurt. I practiced generosity, even when I wanted to withhold kindness. This was no Pollyanna, can't-we-all-get-along bullshit. It was often harder than hating everyone. But it felt so much better than living in fear and resentment. And it was working. I couldn't control how these women felt about me. But I could control how I responded to them.

I largely kept it together in front of the cameras and in high-stakes meetings because of this personal work. I tried to see people as fully human, capable of good and bad, kindness and cruelty. At the same time, my healing was being threatened on a daily basis because I was handling hostile people, with very little support, while still in the limelight.

Reliving the worst parts of our lives for our work while also keeping some semblance of wellness was a delicate balance and a risky proposition. I knew this intimately, because the more time I spent with the media or in congressional offices, the more toxic and damaged I felt. I was absorbing the community's emotions and my staff's frustrations while having little time or space to deal with my own. I was sometimes so busy and overwhelmed that I completely forgot that this work was not only difficult, it was personally triggering and retraumatizing for me. Veterans needed to take the lead in policy work if it was to have any meaning or impact, and yet few people seemed to be caring for our welfare or longevity. I needed to take my life into my own hands.

· · ·

Some of the board members who knew social justice history seemed to think I was facing the challenges every woman-of-color activist stepping into white- or male-dominated roles had ever faced. It was not lost on me that I was one of few women and usually the only person of color in the rooms I was walking into—House and Senate offices, Pentagon chambers, cable-news greenrooms. This is what power and influence looked like. In the national security world, my Brownness and my gender were so loud and obvious in a sea of white dudes that it often felt like I was screaming even when I said nothing. The Marines had prepared me well for this.

But as a Brown female activist, I was the object of unfair expectations. I was supposed to be a healer, caretaker, and savior at all hours. My body and my time were expected to be public domain. I was not even entitled to my own joy. This was the hustle, but it was no way to live. No person could be this for other people. Selflessness was a hoax, something that just exhausted us out of caring for ourselves and others. I rejected this role, and very likely offended a great many wounded veterans because of it.

Like most women, I needed to say no more often. It was my parents' lack of boundaries with me, and then men's, that made saying no a radical act in my life. The white men I knew rarely had to wrestle with saying no. They were never expected to be all things to all people.

Boundaries were their gift. But saying no was causing some kind of existential rift among survivors who expected me to be therapist, friend, fixer, and changemaker. It was an unfair and impossible situation for me to be in. And still I was a hopeless empath, incapable of truly shutting veterans out. Other people's pain weighed me down constantly. And what's worse, I felt the burden of guilt as old as my ancestors every time I established a personal boundary. This, too, was unfair.

I wasn't just facing hatred from women veterans, though theirs felt the most vicious. Military men wanted a piece of me, too. The hostility against me was often most visceral after a media hit. After one television appearance on MSNBC, I found myself glued to my laptop, neck deep in a Twitter backlash. I had more enemies than I knew how to deal with. Sometimes they were individual hell-raisers. Other times, they were well-organized groups. Military men were particularly aggressive after my Fox interviews. I was *chickenshit. Stupid.* And the worst insult of all: *ugly.* I really missed just being someone's *disrespectful little terd.*

I believed in civil conversations. I was convinced that despite the abyss of technology between me and hate-spewing veterans on the Internet, that we could find common ground in the basic humanity that we shared. I even wished attackers well before signing off. I was so naive.

Three hours after one Twitter storm, I was sitting on a therapist's couch, shaking, hugging a pillow, crossing my legs so hard I was cutting off circulation. He asked me as I clutched the pillow, "Do you feel safe?" He wanted to know if I needed to call the cops, or the feds. These were legitimate questions. Some of my feminist colleagues had had to move out of their homes after trolls had threatened them online. The only difference here was that my trolls were members of my own community. The truth was, in the military, "I got your six" was usually employed only for the straight white men among us.

I felt like trauma was ricocheting around in my body on repeat. "Sure. Yeah."

Three minutes later, sinking into the couch, I had changed my mind.

"No, I don't."

I was not equipped to defend myself on social media against gangs of older, conservative military men, most of them desperately, hatefully holding on to the last vestiges of the military they once knew. Nor was I prepared to defend myself against hordes of traumatized women who had turned me into their favorite punching bag.

I was an ex-Marine. I was one of Bristol's protégées. But nothing the Marines taught me prepared me for the onslaught of hatred spewed by veterans. I was terrified of my own community.

· · ·

My gentleness had been a subject of some debate in the years I was back home, fighting the good fight with my organization. Many folks found me *fierce*. This was generally intended as a compliment, but I found it harsh, and out of sync with who I remember being, and who I wanted to become again.

I remembered a me before all of this Marine madness happened. I was kind and loving, and yes, even gentle. But I no longer knew what or who I was.

In 2014, I decided to leave SWAN. Later that year, I decided to leave Greg. It was a lot to leave at once. For ten days, I was practicing mindfulness meditation and compassion at a silent meditation retreat in Barre, Massachusetts. I paid close attention to everything I was doing and feeling: physical sensations ranging from the minor itch on my elbow to the merciless throbbing in my upper back; a head-banging narrative of emotions, thoughts, and extremely convincing monologues. My breathing. My boredom. My bitter, protesting knees. The endless supply of unwelcome people from back home—some uppity woman in my building, a jerk member of Congress.

The heartache, doubt, and emptiness were overwhelming. I'd ended a twelve-year relationship with Greg so I could find out once and for all who I was in the world and if I could actually survive on my own without the Marines, without Greg—heck, without anyone but me. I was desperately unsure.

We may have been in silence on these retreats, but there was nothing remotely quiet about it. My thoughts were often paralyzing. I was relieved no one could read my mind. *You're not good enough. You're never good enough. You're wasting your time.*

Insights came in meditation without warning, like an ambush, or maybe a blessing.

We were encouraged to avert our gaze from other practitioners, in order to focus more on the inner world of our minds and bodies. I looked up at some point and noticed a white guy on my left, walking at his own pace. With otherworldly speed I took in the length of his toes, the wrinkles in his shirt and stubble on his cheeks, how his head drooped forward and his hair stood on end. I looked to my right. Another young man, tall, shuffling along, with a different stride and pace and set of peculiar sounds. Beyond him, another man. And another. And another.

I was the only woman in the room. Lost in my own universe, I'd been walking parallel to these dudes, all of them white, all of them, like me, absorbed in an effort to focus on the now of simply walking, back and forth, and back again. And I found myself suddenly overwhelmed, my belly warm, tears on my face, and now the sound of me crying softly mixed with the sound of me picking my feet up and placing them on the wooden floor again.

In their careful, quiet stepping, none of these men even remotely posed a threat to me, to themselves, to each other. Their harmlessness, and more than that, their deliberate effort to take ten days away from booze, bottom lines, Tinder, jerking off, and god knows what else to tune into the realities inside them, and maybe to even make themselves kinder, gentler people, suddenly blew me away. It *was* possible for men to value things other than violence, killing, and the manipulation of women. Wasn't it?

When did I start scanning the rooms of my life for danger? When did every man in my path become a potential threat to my safety and sanity? Surrounded by white men, I was completely outnumbered. But I was okay.

I was okay.

When I checked in with my senior teacher hours later, she sat facing me in a chair, her reddish-brown hair loose and wild across her shoulders and back, her feet firmly on the ground, hips and legs comfortably wide, exuding such a solid power that I wanted to stay there for hours, witnessing her strength. This power I sensed was coming entirely from her tuning into me—my pain and sorrow, my capacity for joy. We barely talked. We didn't need to flesh out the details of my history, because she was listening more deeply than that. This was no magical hocus-pocus. She'd practiced this kind of listening, with full attention, with complete compassion, without talking back, without judgment, for decades. I realized this is what it felt like to be truly seen for the first time. And I realized I wanted to do that for other people.

. . .

It was inevitable that Greg and I wouldn't last. Working together at SWAN was hardly the reason I let him go, but it was a catalyst. I needed to fully recover from the Marines, and doing this without him seemed necessary. I broke his heart when I left him. My own heart shattered into pieces as well. No one had ever been that loyal to me. He was now family, but I couldn't depend on him if I wanted to heal completely. I was not a whole person. I needed to put myself back together, on my own.

Letting go of the weight of fear and releasing the desire to fight others meant that even in the saddest moments, I was now looking for joy. If you'd asked me what I did for fun a decade ago, I would have said *Nothing*. Now I sought and embraced meaningful activities that I would not confuse with self-harm or ego. I discovered the healing power of open-water swimming in the waterways of New York City. I threw myself into flying trapeze. Joy returned to my life, slowly.

I returned to dating, announcing to my parents in an elaborately constructed email—a second coming out—that I was open to exploring relationships with women as well as men. But in my early forties, out of practice, and navigating a creepy online landscape, dating was hard as hell. When a firefighter dumped me a week after Uma died, a year after Shiva had died, I spiraled in a downward depression so fast and hard I figured I might never get up again. I felt like I'd lost everything. I didn't know what my purpose in life was anymore. Beating myself up became my new mission.

The despair felt existential. In Indian terms, laid out by patriarchs and mothers-in-law throughout time, being forty, single, and childless meant my life was worth nothing. It seems the independent life I'd chosen to live had gotten me nowhere, because *somewhere* existed only if you had a husband and children. On some level I knew this was garbage. But the cultural indoctrination was deep. I could feel a herd of Indian elders screaming, *I told you so.* I was grieving so much I could barely see straight. I felt like I had no reason to live.

I called Eli one day, crying my brains out, and she flew out from California for an intervention. Eli told me that I needed to like what I saw in the mirror. I needed to practice liking myself, the way I was already practicing feeling the emotions and sensations in my body and witnessing my thoughts. Petrified, I stood in front of my bathroom mirror, unable to look up. *Damn,* I thought. *This is how little I think of myself.*

I lifted my chin upward and dared to look.

"I like my eyes." Yes, but that was easy. I had Furby eyes, after all.

"I like . . . my nose." Who was I kidding? I hated my nose, the nose that connected me to my father. I went on. It was agonizing. But when I was done, I was still breathing. I continued.

"You're beautiful." I could hear Baughman saying, *I can't hear you, Bhagwati!*

With some oomph, I said, "You're *beau*-ti-ful.

"I'm beautiful. I love myself. I. *Love* myself. I love you. I love my-self." Goddamn, this was exhausting. And it was less than 100 percent authentic. But some of the terror and weight of staring at my face in the mirror had shifted. So I made this a daily routine that followed my meditation practice. I wouldn't leave the apartment in the morning until I'd recited my self-love schtick. I was slowly believing my own hype.

• • •

There's a controversial treatment in trauma psychology called exposure therapy. Rape and combat survivors report mixed results. Some women veterans I know vehemently discourage it. Essentially, you're asked to retell—and, therefore, relive—your most traumatic experiences under supervision of a mental health expert. Sometimes trauma symptoms can multiply, making life feel horribly worse.

My entire time serving in the Marines and advocating for service women felt like this. I rarely felt safe enough to let my guard down in front of military personnel or veterans. Many thought I was fearless. As if. I was just extremely high functioning under stress. There was only one place where I felt safe exploring my issues with men in the military: teaching yoga to veterans.

In 2008, before I'd started SWAN, founding a yoga class for veterans in NYC felt like a calling. My classes were packed with men. I was not so sure about this. Exposing the softer side of myself to veterans after doing so much personal work to heal from my interactions with them was a risk, for sure. I was terrified they would reject me, as the Marines had done. Despite this, I felt it was important to try.

Sure enough, in my first few classes, testosterone was thick in the room, and I felt myself withdrawing into a familiar shell. But ego wasn't an asset in yoga, and I think most guys discovered that muscling through class got them nowhere. As the teacher, and often the only woman there, I was able to control boundaries for the first time with military men. It seemed that most were willing to trust me, and were there to heal whatever needed healing. This was unique for me, and for the first time in a long time, allowed me to see men in uniform as capable of deep reflection, even transformation.

Most guys were totally new to yoga, and I witnessed the posturing that took place before class started. It never lasted long. In my first class, a few minutes into a deep breathing exercise, an older veteran started shifting in his seat. Seconds later, he stood up.

"Can I leave? I . . ."

He didn't know what to say.

"It's okay." He seemed terrified to move, and terrified to stay. He was alarmed. Wild-eyed. I tried to exude warmth. He ran out of there, like I had years before.

It would be the first of many times over the next decade I experienced veterans wondering why they were having traumatic responses to relaxation techniques. Few would be ready to ask me why. Occasionally, someone dared to be vulnerable, and I would do my best to explain that what they were experiencing was normal. But it was up to them to choose to dive deeper. There was no way to fast-forward healing.

Because most of my students were men, I was extra conscious when a woman came to my class. The yoga classroom was my new laboratory for examining the dynamics of gender, power, and trauma.

The younger guys barely blinked at the presence of other women. They'd acclimated, perhaps, to my authority in the room. But some of the middle-aged and older veterans occasionally acted as though they were witnessing the arrival of a new species. The older veterans' gazes were informed by generational norms, and I had no patience for it. I realized the thing I wanted to develop most as a teacher, and as a person, was the confidence and presence in my body to ensure that all people felt safe. I did not realize that I was developing a new voice.

I took extra precautions I rarely saw teachers take in normal yoga classes to make sure that each person would feel protected and comfortable. My queer students, particularly men, were often in the closet with their military peers, and I could feel them compartmentalizing their lives as they walked among the other veterans and settled down to their mats. In the work of embracing vulnerability, some of us wore more layers than others.

I ensured women, regardless of their experience with sexual objectification or trauma, would not have to suffer the extra burdens of daily harassment if I could help it. The tough-guy persona that many women had adopted in the military was impressive, as far as feats of survival went, but I wanted to ensure that no woman had to wear this armor in my classroom.

When I taught poses that looked or felt extra vulnerable—ones in which butts were raised in the air, or inner thighs and hips were opened outward—I made sure that veterans weren't facing one another. This way, they could practice yoga without needing to keep on high alert. I was intimately aware of when this dynamic was present. I hoped I would have enough authority to stop anyone from objectifying or otherwise harming a fellow student.

With most of my attention on my students' welfare, I didn't expect that I would be a target of student harassment as well, but military culture sometimes desperately lingered. Phil, a middle-aged veteran, simply could not resist subversive behavior with me in front of other students. Like Fox, Thomas, and Franco, he was unruly. Wouldn't take suggestions from the teacher. Would interrupt and challenge me. Flirted. He'd offer to help me set up the classroom with a slippery voice that made my skin crawl. Ten years out of the Corps, and it seemed I still couldn't handle sexual advances and personal humiliation from a man without boundaries.

I could picture Gunny Cain telling me to just manhandle the punk, but force was not something I wanted to reinforce in this setting. I did the best I could at the time. I cut off his remarks and went straight back to teaching the group. I gave him a very exasperated, *enough-is-enough* look. I flat-out ignored him. I was trying to cultivate equanimity in myself and my students, all the while wrestling with wanting to kick Phil in the nuts. I didn't want to disrupt the flow or feel of the class. I just didn't know what to do with him. He eventually stopped coming, much to my relief.

Over time I learned that my instincts about boundaries were very good, and that I needed to believe in myself. The Corps didn't have boundaries, and I couldn't help enough women inside the Corps because of that, but I sure as hell could protect the veterans in my own classroom. Learning to say no was my first step. Learning to say no without feeling that I was doing something wrong was the next. Doing this while completely grounded in my feet, and aware of my breath, and conscious of my emotions was real power, the kind that harmed no one and helped everyone.

Yoga seemed to be the key to bridging two remarkably different parts of myself: the part that was still Bristol's minion and the part that was devoted entirely to kindness and nonviolence. During SWAN's hardest months, my staff can tell you that when I had to skip yoga classes to be in Washington or fund-raise around the country, that bridge was lost. The commander in me came out and consumed whatever kindness I'd cultivated toward myself and others. This wasn't sustainable. I wanted to stop hurting. And that meant I also wanted to stop hurting other people.

I had faith in the veterans to whom I taught mindfulness, and therefore I could retain some sense of humanity for the veterans and Pentagon officials I encountered in my activist life. I genuinely saw them as capable of change, all evidence on C-SPAN to the contrary, because the guys I worked with in the yoga classroom were entirely devoted to examining their worst demons. I suspect my being female, a Marine, and a former officer had something to do with this. I think it allowed my students to find the place where they, too, were bridging aggressiveness with humanity. It was a place men could get real with their softer side, something that absolutely needed to happen if any of us who had served were going to heal from the harm we'd committed or received.

Teaching veterans was only partly responsible for keeping me together through these years. The rest was all thanks to the hodgepodge of dudes who showed up, week after week. The more compassionate I was with them, the kinder I was to myself. And, there was Jimmie.

A seventysomething African American Navy veteran from North

Carolina, Jimmie came to my first class in 2008 and has barely missed a class since. I have never needed to try to be strong around him. He has never needed to thump his chest around me or the other guys. Jimmie walks gently, the way he speaks. He is slender and has a still, curious face. He reminds me of the softest and most merciful among us. This is not to say Jimmie is without impact. He says only a few words, smiling each time I enter the room and thanking me when he leaves at the end of class. This seems important to him.

One year early on, Jimmie told me his VA doctors asked him what he was up to. His blood work had never looked this good. He told them *yoga*. They seemed fascinated and maybe a bit unconvinced. Over the years, though, they become more interested.

Jimmie was the reason I kept coming back to teach. I knew he'd be there, twenty minutes early, lying on his back on top of bolsters and blankets, in his favorite restorative yoga pose. On those hard evenings when I'd given up on the Pentagon, on my parents, on myself, there was still Jimmie. When I didn't feel like teaching, because I was too hurt or exhausted, I remembered that he would be there, waiting to practice. He always helped restore me.

A year back, Jimmie attended a teacher training in therapeutic yoga. He now assistant-teaches weekly restorative classes and loves it. He stands with great presence these days. I call him Benjamin Button, because he looks younger every year.

A decade after our first class, Jimmie speaks to me more frequently, often to remind me of my goodness. I sense in his quiet insistence that he wants me to believe it. I settle back and try to accept his offerings, as uncertain as I am about their implication. When I miss class now, it isn't to rail against bad guys in the military. I'm usually off to a meditation retreat, where I will tune into my breath and my body, and practice compassion for all people, especially those who hurt me. Especially myself.

He tells me, "That's good. You always come back a different person." Jimmie is not a tall man, but he stands tall when he says this. "Go enjoy it. You deserve it." Sometimes I forget who is teaching whom.

CHAPTER 15

Handling the Truth

SWAN's work was grueling, but also more rewarding than anything I'd experienced in my life. When organizing for service women's welfare worked well, it was because good people put their best intentions forward, and mutual respect was unquestionable. One of my favorite moments arrived in 2012 when we joined a couple of dozen retired general officers to end one of the military's most unjust policies: service women who became pregnant as a result of rape were required to pay out of pocket for their abortions.

Abortion was an unspeakable thing for veterans groups. Not surprisingly, SWAN was the only organization that supported this reform. Iraq and Afghanistan Veterans of America called the issue a "political football," and refused to support us. I wouldn't even get started with their staff on what kind of nonsense it was to treat violence against service women with a sports metaphor.

Our ragtag group of former officers was led by a tireless attorney from the ACLU, Vania Leveille, not a veteran but the only other woman of color I knew at the center of military reform conversations. I was the youngest member of this team, and being a former captain and about thirty years younger than most, I often felt in awe of these retired officers. Vania had even managed to pull in Carol Mutter, the first woman to be a three-star general in the Marines.

Our contingent hit every corner of the Hill and the White House, pleading with wavering members of Congress to have a heart. Federal employees and incarcerated women were granted government-paid abortions after being raped. But service women weren't?

I'd never been part of such a well-organized policy overhaul. It was as covert as any military operation. It needed to be; we were talking abortion, and we had to be careful with how we played this issue in order to get Republican votes. In the end, enough Republicans came to our side, and Congress repealed the policy. I had my first shot of whiskey after that victory, shared with an Army colonel on my left and an ACLU feminist on my right. After getting pro-choice legislation through a Republican Congress, it seemed literally anything was possible.

When organizing by and for service women succeeded, awards, reelections, and fame were not part of the picture. Veterans led the way, and their voices and vision for justice were bolstered by civilian expertise, not the other way around. This was the way movements created hope and minimized damage to people already in pain. This was the way to create lasting change.

• • •

Early in 2011, SWAN received a phone call from Yale Law School. A professor there had recently established a pro bono clinic for veterans, and he was interested in supporting our work. A few days later, Mike Wishnie visited our office in New York City. As we sat down, he handed me his card. His contact info was written in Spanish on the back. *¿En español?* Was this guy for real?

I had no idea I was meeting with a living legend in the legal community.*

---

* Mike's influence on civil rights law and policy is extensive and far-reaching, but his most well-known case to date is his students' federal case challenging President Trump's executive

Mike wanted his legal clinic to serve veterans who had been left aside or forgotten, and women were at the top of his list. I was now used to feeling colonized or used by manipulative personalities. But Mike didn't stir up the smell and feel of exploitation. I'm not sure how a white man in his ivory tower position had learned to sit back and listen, but my instincts told me to trust him.

Mike and I homed in on one issue area that I knew all too well: Veterans Affairs' disproportionate rejection of women veterans' PTSD claims. Based on word of mouth and the experiences of numerous clients, we believed that VA needed to overhaul its PTSD regulations.

VA was incompetent at best in dealing with most claims. But women faced an extra layer of institutional incompetence. VA hadn't caught up with the fact that tens of thousands of women were serving in combat. On paper, the combat exclusion policy, a twenty-year-old Clinton-era policy, was designed to keep women out of direct ground combat. It denied women assignments to male-only specialties like infantry, armor, and special operations. However, due to warfighting needs in Iraq and Afghanistan, women now served in frontline roles never seen in previous American wars.

Today's campaigns blurred the distinction between forward and rear areas—support units where women traditionally served were now vulnerable to enemy fire. Soldiers in combat support roles were traversing roads in Iraq and Afghanistan that had been laden with improvised explosive devices (IEDs), meaning women were coming home with traumatic brain injury, PTSD, and many other combat-related injuries.

Military awards were being denied to women who had served alongside men in combat, and VA was adding insult to injury by denying combat-related disability claims filed by women. Eventually,

---

order banning Muslims from entering the United States (https://law.yale.edu/system/files/documents/pdf/Clinics/1-_complaint.pdf).

the government could not argue with flag-draped coffins of female soldiers on the nightly news. But VA would not budge when it came to PTSD stemming from military sexual violence.

VA had institutionalized rape culture in its own policies, making it agonizingly difficult for a PTSD claim based on sexual harassment or assault to be approved. On top of institutional hurdles, there were reasons we needed to pay extra attention to wounds stemming from sexual trauma. Unlike harassment and assault, combat injuries were largely experienced among military peers, with witnesses, and officially recognized by markers like combat awards and badges, like a Purple Heart. From the military's perspective, there was no shame in being wounded in combat. Injuries that stemmed from the battlefield were considered legitimate. However, those that stemmed from military sexual violence were not.

One of my colleagues who had experienced both combat injuries and military sexual assault—what women veterans had named in typically sinister military parlance "the double whammy"—told me VA wasn't going to believe she was raped. She focused her entire PTSD claim on her combat experience, even though she was clearly still suffering from the impact of sexual trauma.

Wishnie's clinic filed multiple Freedom of Information Act (FOIA) requests for SWAN so we could get the VA's records on MST claims rejection. Unsurprisingly, VA could or would not give us the material in a timely manner. So we sued. Twice.

When VA finally gave us the FOIA'd data, it blew our minds: PTSD claims based on sexual trauma were being denied at twice the rate of total PTSD claims. We had uncovered the VA's institutional bias and released our findings to the public. The press had a field day.

While VA was rounding up its lawyers, we hit Capitol Hill hard. In 2012, I testified before Congress about MST claims alongside Ruth Moore, a Navy veteran and rape survivor who had spent twenty-one years fighting with VA to get her PTSD claim accepted. Ruth spent a quiet life on a farm in Maine with her husband, daughter, and a group of baby goats. She gave hugs freely, even to members of Congress.

I took Ruth aside after the hearing and invited her to join our MST claims campaign. She agreed. A few months later, we'd crafted the legislative language and the Ruth Moore Act was introduced to Congress with Representative Chellie Pingree and Senator Jon Tester as its main sponsors. Pingree was one of our earliest champions. A former farmer and small business owner, she brought her folksy, honest brand to this incredibly emotional issue. Her staff oozed empathy and patience, and we all spent countless hours over this bill, haggling with VA leadership, wrestling members of Congress, and massaging the media over to our side.

I traveled to Washington for the press conference a few days after abdominal surgery removed a cyst in my ovary. I was laid out on the floor of my Amtrak train, and almost passed out on my walk over and through the Capitol building for the press conference. But there was no way I was going to miss this. Ruth's historic bill represented my own journey with VA as well.

Reporters listened. And they quoted us liberally. All of this activity and attention caused a sea change at VA, where attorneys, public affairs reps, and leading administrators had failed to defend a broken, unjust policy. In an attempt to ward off our bill—we were demanding that Congress rewrite VA's PTSD regulations to allow sexual trauma survivors to provide no more evidence than that required of combat veterans—VA finally decided to play nice. They retrained all their claims officers and began to apply a much more liberal approach to MST claims.

I know this intimately, because while we were taking the Hill, I was also still a patient. After four years, and the combined efforts of six pro bono lawyers, one senator, and one member of Congress, my claim for conditions related to military sexual trauma was approved. I received a 40 percent disability rating. Years later, my colleagues and veteran friends finally convinced me to appeal for a higher rating, but at the time, I was just grateful that someone in VA was finally listening.

In 2014, the VA awarded Ruth more than four hundred thousand dollars in back pay for PTSD. It was one of the sweetest victories I'd ever witnessed.

. . .

Changing the culture of the VA involved a lot of press, and would not have happened without litigation. Veterans service organizations (VSOs) were always a factor, though, even when most of them avoided us. Vietnam Veterans of America (VVA) was one of the few VSOs that regularly had our backs, signing onto our litigation to change VA's PTSD regulations for sexual trauma, and supporting sweeping sexual assault reforms. It wasn't surprising that they did and so many others didn't. At the time, VVA was the only VSO that had elected a woman president, and currently had a female vice president. When I spoke to the men who led the organization, it was apparent they recognized that women who served during the Vietnam era had made a difference in the organizing efforts of the larger community. Women weren't just window dressing. Lots of the other organizations were having issues just hiring women or dealing with extreme day-to-day sexism among staff members still steeped in military culture.

Representation always mattered. When the Phoenix VA Medical Center was in the crosshairs of congressional attention after veterans had died waiting for appointments, binders full of men (and no women) were invited to testify to the Senate about the failing VA system. The chair of the Armed Services Committee, Bernie Sanders, didn't seem to mind this glaring misrepresentation of the veterans world, proving that Democrats often had as little interest in service women's empowerment as Republicans.

In 2014, VA secretary Eric Shinseki resigned in the midst of the scandal, making way for new leadership. A few months later, Bob McDonald invited SWAN to his first meeting of veterans organizations. It had taken five long years for SWAN to get a meeting with a VA secretary. The large VSOs, chartered by Congress, held a closely guarded monopoly on the ears of power brokers. Despite SWAN's exposing VA's discriminatory practices toward veterans suffering from the health consequences of sexual assault and harassment, General Shinseki had never fully understood the impact of sexual trauma on veterans. I was hoping Secretary McDonald would be more open than his predecessor.

Before heading into the meeting, I paused outside VA headquarters to get a long look at VA's motto. Uttered by Abraham Lincoln, the quote was sacrosanct:

To care for him who shall have borne the battle and for his widow, and his orphan.

I sensed that at VA, where shutting up and waiting was a rule, and badly behaved women were in short supply, few had questioned the meaning and impact of this phrase. VA clearly was not only *not* caring for him who had borne the last century of battles, it most definitely was not caring for *her* who had borne twice the battles.

I snapped a photo of the plaque and posted it on Twitter, with a defiant tweet that inspired a variety of aggressive responses from white male veterans who didn't understand what the big deal was.*

My intro to VA headquarters didn't begin well. After passing Lincoln's obsolete quote, I headed through the metal detector in the lobby and attempted to pick up my name tag. I finally found it. It said "Ann." Several years ago, in a conversation with a media adviser, I made the unfortunate decision to shorten my name to Anu to spare myself the misery of constantly feeling othered and marginalized in public.

Ann was a name I'd come to despise in Washington. Nancy Pelosi called me Ann. I'd experienced nothing quite as odd as publicly

---

*In 2017 a bipartisan group of senators finally introduced legislation to change this VA motto to be more inclusive of women. We have yet to see if such a law will pass in the current political climate.

correcting that living legend of the left that I was not, in fact, Ann, only to have her call me Ann again. My full name had practically put a stop to congressional business during a House hearing. Republican congressman Jon Runyan, a former NFL tackle and by all accounts one of the few nice guys in Washington, was completely flummoxed by "Anuradha" when introducing me at the hearing. He stuttered for what seemed like minutes, staring into his prepared notes, sounding out the letters, again and again, trying to piece together the syllables. I felt awful for the man.

My nickname was a merciful sacrifice, a compromise I made for the American people. It didn't get much simpler than A-N-U. (Feeling the full brunt of selling out my heritage wouldn't come until the 2016 presidential election, when I would go back to my full name, with fervor.) But today I was either Ann or no one at all. I slapped the sticker on to my chest and forced a friendly smile at the administrative aide.

The room upstairs was like most that I entered in Washington. It had that peculiar feel of male-only spaces: bodies were sized up, chests were thick with inflation. Men who entered were greeted with frat boy handshakes. In loud voices, they engaged in power banter. The few women who entered were looked over, and then overlooked. These guys practiced a risky game, as some of these women were occasionally lesser-known members of Congress or power staffers who moved mountains in Washington.

The few women who were invited to these top-level VSO meetings rarely brokered in power. They were safe bets, their soft suggestions to "serve our veterans" so nonthreatening that they were immediately forgotten. I rarely met a woman veteran. If I did, she was usually the only one in the organization.

I settled into my seat next to a friendly senior from Jewish War Veterans, who seemed to have little ego and little need to invent one.

It was obvious when the secretary entered, because silence fell over the men, and a nauseating obsequiousness replaced the chest thumping. Veterans could play the roles of servant and sycophant with disturbing ease, as both skills were perfected in the military. There was a rush to be identified and known, to *Sir* the secretary into some kind of trance.

The new guy circled the room, shaking hands, patting backs.

Call me Bob.

Yes, Sir.

No, please, call me Bob.

Trying to charm veterans with this schtick was a hell of a bet. I found it much easier telling folks what they needed to hear when I addressed them by their titles. I wasn't here to make friends with a man whose agency we'd sued several times over for sex discrimination. Mr. Secretary would do just fine for me.

Bob, the former CEO of Procter & Gamble, launched into an epic speech. He was showing off his business creds, the billions of people on the planet who used Procter & Gamble products every day, his relentless focus on customer service and innovation. He started showing off about VA employees, many of whom I'd known to be lazy, incompetent, or downright mean. It was refreshing when he started telling the old guys at the table, some of whose joints had been creaking and popping since Vietnam, that one of the best orthopedic surgeons in the country was working at a VA hospital out in California. She was a West Point graduate. I perked up. The fellas around the table joined in, insisting they'd see her for knee and hip replacements. We were all rooting for the surgeon.

Then Bob stepped in it, deep.

It's unbelievable! She's about this short. Just unbelievable!

The secretary held his hand at his waist, suggesting a surgeon of hobbit size. He shook his head in amazement and laughed. An uneasy silence ensued, but no one said a thing. I wondered if the VA's best orthopedic surgeon knew her boss was reducing her to a tiny, cute girl doctor.

Bob wanted our feedback on a new VA promotional ad, so he

played it and asked for our reactions. I was never afraid to give one, but it took him ages to call on me. He called on one guy at the other end of the table three times before his assistant, an overworked, enthusiastic ex-Marine, told him to take my question.

The secretary approached, and the room grew silent. The first female voice all day, I introduced myself, firmly and formally. Bob's well-oiled smooth-guy banter, which had gone on now at a quick, uninterrupted clip for two hours, stopped suddenly. He squinted at my sticker.

"Ann?"

"No. Uh-nu." He squinted again at my chest. *Here we go*, I thought.

"They got it wrong, Sir."

"What's it supposed to say?"

I told him again.

You could feel billion-dollar corporate wheels turning in Bob's head. There was no movement in the room. Bob had made me hypervisible. Whether it was my strange name, the unruliness of my hair, the brownness of my skin, or the fact of my having been a Marine, I had disrupted the rhythm inside this room within seconds.

Bob walked over to me. Came in close. Too close. I could hear myself breathing.

Bob reached his hand over to my chest, touched the lapel over my left breast.

Removed my sticker. Placed it on the table.

Bob took out his pen and squeezed himself between my body and the old Jewish war veteran next to me. Bent over the table on the right side of my body, Bob crossed out the second "n" in Ann and wrote a "u."

I managed somehow to look up at the veterans across the table from me. I could not read their detached, deadpan expressions, but somehow with a straight face I formed the words, "Valuable use of his time, huh."

It was a useless thing to say, joking around about how Secretary

Bob was playing Bob the secretary, to buy time while my body re-assessed its options to fight, flee, or freeze. The strange thing about shock is the way it interrupts time and space, slowing all one's senses.

He peeled the sticker up off the table. Bob shifted back and then slightly forward, telegraphing his next move, as he prepared to slap the edited sticker back on my chest. Bristol's training kicked in, hard.

My arm was up, fending off his hand. I took the sticker from him, saying, "I've *got* this, *Sir*." I put it back on the lapel of my suit. I don't even know why I bothered to wear it. I felt naked.

The silence from the men surrounding us was so loud it felt like I was screaming inside my head. Later, my colleague from Vietnam Veterans of America would tell me he thought I was going to punch the secretary. I wondered why I didn't. I wondered, why didn't *he?*

I felt myself slowly disappearing, floating above my body and theirs. Despite years of doing this, honing my advocacy skills, shaming brass giants into admitting their weaknesses and taking hits from powerful enemies, it still happened sometimes, and it had happened here and now.

The lines between safety and security had been blurred long ago by this experience of offering my body and life as a battleground for political posturing. In that moment, Bob and I had an audience, but no one intervened to save him from me or me from him.

When the meeting ended, I stayed an extra hour to speak to the secretary's assistant. I was back in my body and was speaking calmly. This conversation was a courtesy to him, a fellow Marine and a decent guy. And it was a heads-up to Bob. Because clearly Bob had not been prepped to meet a veteran like me, or an organization like SWAN.

I did what no one else in that room was going to do: I briefed him on the inappropriateness of the VA secretary touching me. And I reminded him that the secretary was a named plaintiff in my organization's lawsuit accusing VA of sex discrimination.

His assistant nodded vigorously. His face was already pale, but it was now ghostlike as this information sank in. He insisted he'd set up a private meeting for me with Bob. I even believe that he tried. It was our last invitation to VA headquarters.

．．．

Changing VA's approach to military sexual trauma was deeply satisfying, but I was desperate to attack sexism and sexual violence at its source.

It had always been clear to me that the root of the military's hostile work environment and high rates of sexual assault was the ban on women in combat. For several years we'd been in discussion with veterans and attorneys about how best to go about repealing the combat exclusion policy. In 2012, our colleague out of the University of Virginia sued the military on behalf of an Army colonel and a first sergeant who argued that the policy had affected their career progression. The ACLU decided to up the ante, and a few months later, SWAN was an organizational plaintiff in *Hegar v. Panetta*, a groundbreaking case challenging the combat exclusion policy.

MJ Hegar was an Air Force major from Texas and a decorated helicopter pilot.* Her helicopter was shot down while she was flying a rescue mission in Afghanistan. She sustained injuries but fired back, and was awarded a Purple Heart and the Distinguished Flying Cross with Valor, one of the Air Force's highest combat distinctions. MJ was humble and unafraid to be vulnerable in person. I'd met few officers in any branch as authentic as her. Three other women joined MJ as plaintiffs: Jennifer Hunt, an Army NCO and Purple Heart recipient who kept cracking me up with jokes, and two Marine officers, Zoe Bedell and Colleen Farrell, who had been members of female engagement teams in Afghanistan.

SWAN joined the four trailblazing service women—I started

---

* Hegar ran as a Democrat for Congress in Texas in 2018.

calling them the Fantastic Four—in order to provide organizational support to back up the plaintiffs' claims of discrimination. What made the Fantastic Four particularly impressive wasn't their military résumés or brainpower, all of which was obvious to anyone who met them. It was their willingness to take on the Pentagon while they were still in uniform. Suing the DOD while you were earning a military paycheck took a particular kind of courage.

It's important to realize that service women's integration had not happened organically, or because it was the right thing to do. Service women had sued over all sorts of civil rights matters, including the right to be pilots and to deploy to the Middle East without wearing headscarves. Integration—equality—required litigation. We were following that precedent.

We argued that combat exclusion was preventing the plaintiffs from accessing prestigious assignments after returning home, and from attending follow-on schools like Army Ranger School, all of which were critical for career progression. When we launched our press conference in California early one morning, the press went nuts. One week later, I hadn't gotten more than a couple of hours of sleep, and the five of us had done so much media on so many networks that I lost my voice and got the flu. We were all high on adrenaline. The press finally had enough ammunition to take on Pentagon leadership. The generals in charge appeared utterly out of touch. Old. White. And very male. Women in the military had never looked more deserving of meritocracy. It was the most exciting time I could have imagined.

Two months later, our phones wouldn't stop ringing. The secretary of defense had decided to overturn combat exclusion. We watched tearfully, our eyes glued to every network in the stratosphere, as Leon Panetta stood alongside the chairman of the Joint Chiefs of Staff and spoke about the courageous women who had served in Iraq and Afghanistan, and the long overdue need for change.

Our lawsuit transformed the military rapidly. In 2015, I was stunned as the chief of naval operations announced he was opening the Navy SEALs to women. I couldn't believe that sixteen years after my adventures with *G.I. Jane*, I was finally seeing the military's most elite force allow women a shot at going through Basic Underwater Demolition/SEAL school (BUD/S).

When the Marine Corps opened up Infantry Training Battalion (ITB) to enlisted women volunteers, they came forward in droves. And then, in the most uncensored way possible, news broke. A photo of four of ITB's female grads-to-be was circulating around social media. PFCs Cristina Fuentes Montenegro, Julia Carroll, Katie Gorz, and Harlee "Rambo" Bradford had posted a selfie, and it had gone viral.

The Marine Corps was incensed at the women's audacity at going public, knowing Americans would eat this up as some kind of feminist milestone. The women were allowed to graduate with their male counterparts, but they were not assigned infantry jobs. Two years later, well over four hundred women had passed enlisted infantry training. It was enough to create an all-female infantry battalion, conjuring up mythological narratives about Amazon armies. But the Corps was doing all it could to prevent these women from being assigned to infantry units and hoping for an exception to the secretary of defense's announcement.

Meanwhile, the Marines had opened up Infantry Officer Course (IOC) to women officers, a far more mentally and physically grueling school than the enlisted counterpart. Thirty female officers had given the course a shot, but few were making it beyond the first tough week of training. A small debate was breaking out among women veterans advocates about whether or not IOC's curriculum was adequately measuring infantry officer potential. These voices were largely coming from the non-Marine community, and from women advocates who had no interest in single physical standards for men and women. Their frustration with IOC's training requirements sounded like they thought IOC was just too physically tough. That was code for something I refused to support: a desire to lower physical standards for women.

Lowering standards was a loaded phrase in our world. It partly represented men's paranoia with women's presence in the military. But it was also a legitimate concern that fundamentally ate away at men's confidence in women's performance and women's confidence in themselves. The fact was, women *were* capable of all sorts of physical prowess, particularly in events that required long-term physical and mental endurance. I'd personally witnessed a colleague of mine, all 130 pounds of her, swim for two hours across the Strait of Magellan in forty-degree water in nothing more than a bikini and two swim caps. I'd seen women in CrossFit competitions lift more than most infantry guys I knew. I was convinced these extreme athletes were the types who would be able to pass the Marine Corps IOC standards as well as those required by special forces.

The real question was, was the military going to make the job welcoming and hospitable enough to draw these women away from the civilian job market? Why would women like these give up legal protections and chances for career growth in the civilian sector only to face the military's hostile work environment and still deeply entrenched rape culture?

· · ·

With fully integrated basic training and far more women (18 percent of the Army was female, as opposed to 7 percent of the Marines) in the ranks, the Army was way ahead of the Marine Corps on combat arms integration. When the Army opened Ranger School to women volunteers, it changed everything.

My cadre of West Point sisters was feeding intel to me whenever possible about the progress of two young West Point graduates who were slogging through Ranger School. Eventually, I got a call. Lieutenant Shaye Haver and Captain Kristen Griest were about to graduate. Buzz-cut, rugged-faced, laser-eyed, and lean and wiry, these women had not only survived the course, they had thrived. That week, they garnered their own hashtag on twitter (#ShayeandKristen) and had unwittingly earned a legion of worshippers, both male and female, across the globe.

I celebrated over the phone with my colleague Sue Fulton, who'd graduated from the first class of women at West Point. Sue was a tour de force, standing over six feet tall with a bellowing voice that I could imagine summoning legions from the underworld. She was one of a handful of pioneers who had paved the way for women in the Army. I then called Donna McAleer, another West Point alum from the early eighties, who'd written a book about women at West Point years ago. Donna had given me solace over the last few years of lonely activism, listening to many of my stories, always lifting me up. I was crying, she was ecstatic, and we were both beside ourselves with hope. Anything was possible now.

I was elated, but part of me deep inside was torn. There was no way for Shaye or Kristen to know the weight or significance of their accomplishments. In finishing Ranger School, they had enabled a collective emotional catharsis for an entire community of women veterans, over several generations of sacrifice. They had done what we always knew women could do, if only given the opportunity. I wish I'd had that chance. I thought of every woman who'd survived rape, sexual harassment, and discrimination over the years. I wondered if other women's emotional landscape felt as complex and layered as mine today.

Army leadership held a major press conference to introduce Kristen and Shaye to the world. Army played every move like master political campaigners; the women, still buzz-cut and ruddy, looking every bit like GI Jane, sat alongside several of their male peers, who spoke in surprisingly genuine terms about their original skepticism over the women's presence and their changing opinions as the women proved themselves, time and time again, occasionally outperforming the men. These were no feminist icons (of course, they *were*, obviously, but how the Army spun this was of less concern to me than that these women were truly part of the team). These officers were just like the guys.

This was a far cry from the Marine Corps' efforts to hide its female infantry grads from public view. Some of the Marine Corps' most senior leaders were publicly expressing their discontent with female integration, while Army leaders were embracing it in their own branch. It was like night and day.

Army's senior leadership had ensured every step of the way that the women would be treated just like the men, without either special treatment or special abuse. Meanwhile, the Marine Corps was still fighting the Pentagon to keep boot camp segregated. There was no way Marine women were going to succeed at the same rate as Army women. They just were not being trained on the same level playing field. Doubts about their competency and potential would always exist.

In 2016, Captain Kristen Griest became the Army's first female infantry officer.

CHAPTER 16

Our Last Best Hope

I first met Senator Kirsten Gillibrand in 2010 at the New York City Lesbian Gay Bisexual and Transgender Center—"The Center" to locals. She was the guest speaker at an event to support Dan Choi and the repeal of "don't ask, don't tell." A brand-new senator who'd been appointed to replace Hillary Clinton, Gillibrand came from a progun, upstate background, and liberals wondered if she was really one of them. Gillibrand was establishing both her progressive and national security credibility by advocating for a repeal of the military's gay ban.

I attended with my colleague Alison from SWAN. Aside from Dan and the two of us, it was a mostly civilian crowd, and almost entirely gay, male, and white, as many LGBTQ political events were. I knew this crowd didn't know the ins and outs of what Dan was talking about, or what I was going to ask, but I stood up to ask Gillibrand a question.

"Senator, what are you doing to prevent sexual assault and harassment in the military?"

The room shifted and settled as the men looked to see who I was. The senator was polite, but she deferred. She suggested we reach out to a couple of her Senate colleagues who had experience working on sexual and domestic violence. Later, Alison and I approached the senator to chat in more detail. In photographs of the encounter, Gillibrand's face looks typically porcelain—composed, not a worry in the world. I, on the other hand, appear so pained that my head is tilted on its axis and my face is cracking with the look of someone extremely disappointed.

A few years later, Gillibrand ended up being our biggest congressional ally on military sexual violence. We worked closely and relentlessly, crafting a bill and talking points for her signature issue on the Hill, part of a coordinated feminist and defense platform that would prepare her to run for president someday.

People often ask what I think of Senator Gillibrand. Feminists want me to gush. But she does not do it for me. Most politicians don't. Doesn't mean I wouldn't vote for her, all the way into the White House. Unlike Speier, with her fire and brimstone, or Braley, with his legal acumen and passion, Gillibrand needed convincing to take on our issue. The woman is a politician to the bone. What makes her so damn convincing is that unlike some of her counterparts, she does not come across as calculating in person, though behind closed doors she is as cautious as they come. She is neither cold nor heartless. She is approachable and gracious. But the woman will not move until she's ready to win something. And then you better get the hell out of her way.

Gillibrand was carefully, strategically bucking the system as much as she was entrenched in it. I had every idea what it was like to be a woman in a male-dominated institution, but watching women in the Senate was never boring, because there was so much power and influence at stake. She was playing a game that had been played for ages. Surrounded by celebrity senators like John McCain, Gillibrand was one of a tiny handful of women on the Senate Armed Services Committee. Her staff was keeping an eye on areas that the senator could make her own while keeping things friendly with her male and Republican peers. She was unwilling to challenge combat exclusion. That was too radical. Might have made her seem antimilitary. In the end, after careful consideration, she took up military sexual violence with a vengeance.

We'd laid the legislative and moral groundwork for her bill. Survivors were pouring forth, and members of the media were painting a picture so dire that politicians would look like beasts for not taking action. Trying to avoid the land mines present in Speier's earlier bill, SWAN helped Gillibrand's staff write language for a Senate bill that was legally sound. Gillibrand did her homework. She was smart. And she could sell the hell out of an issue. She introduced the bill, the Military Justice Improvement Act, and hit the ground running.

In 2013, Gillibrand invited us to testify before the Senate. I hadn't seen her face-to-face in several years, since that time at The Center. The hall was filled with large men wearing dark suits. SAPRO generals, JAG leadership, and legal aides. Twenty-five-year-old staffers. And us, four veterans testifying about the horrors of military sexual violence. Two of us women of color. One of us male. More than one of us queer. SWAN had a lot to do with the makeup of that panel. We recommended people who we thought would make a real difference. And representation mattered when everyone dealing with the lives of service members seemed to be old, white, straight, and male.

Before it all went live, we were standing at the front of the room, settling in. The senator was upon me before I noticed her, shaking my hand, thanking me. I will never forget that it took me a minute to realize who she was. Gillibrand was short and unassuming. Cool as always. I'd met her before, and yet among all these large-chested men, it still seemed like she was in the wrong room. I hated that I thought that.

Gillibrand's first hearing was on the cover of every major paper the next morning. Military leadership was defensive and alarmed. Republicans didn't want to appear like they were ganging up on the military. Being in the majority, they took over, attempting to squash Gillibrand's momentum in the media. A few months later, the full Senate Armed Services Committee convened another hearing on military sexual assault. The entire Joint Chiefs of Staff, the keepers of our current wars and the president's key military advisers, were summoned before the committee with their chief legal advisers: the Army, Navy, and Air Force Judge Advocate Generals (JAGs) and the Marine Corps Staff Judge Advocate.

The Joint Chiefs and the JAGs stretching from one end of the congressional hearing room to the other was a fucking spectacle. With the exception of Navy JAG Nanette DeRenzi, every one of them was an older white man weighed down by the bling on his collar and stacks of colored ribbons on his chest. Each had served decades in the military. Their testimony, mostly the same old bluster about zero tolerance, barely made a dent. The sight of them was intimidating, the intent to bully and defend the system palpable, the audacity to suggest they were doing enough cruel. We barely needed a rebuttal.

It wasn't my first time dealing with the military's top leadership. The Lackland Air Force scandal put our calls for reform in the news big time, but the Air Force secretary and his generals treated SWAN with cautious friendliness, rather than contempt. The Marine Corps was a different institution altogether. But I already knew that.

My few limited encounters with Marine leaders shook me to the core. The Marine Corps systematically avoided SWAN, including our emails, phone calls, and good faith attempts to build bridges and find common ground. The three-star Judge Advocate Generals of the Army, Navy, and Air Force—all of whom were testifying before the Senate on this day—had graciously attended our second conference on military sexual violence. But the Marine Corps staff judge advocate hadn't even gotten a lance corporal to respond to our invitation. When I ran into him at a hearing he'd been called to attend, he told me, "You know, a lot of things have changed since you left the Corps." He had some nerve. Whatever *had* changed had changed in spite of the Corps' resistance and because of our activism. And judging from an obscene number of stories now breaking in the press every month about sexual assault cover-ups and scandals, a lot still needed changing.

I'd had one opportunity to meet with the assistant commandant of the Marine Corps and blew it royally. General Joseph Dunford had agreed to sit down with me to talk about the issues Marine women were facing in uniform. His aide cold-called me one day, putting Dunford on the phone as I sat on an Amtrak train headed to Washington.

I already knew what this conversation was about. I'd foolishly given an unscheduled interview early one Saturday morning to a rabble-rousing reporter, and it had just hit the press. I'd spoken to him about the sexual assault scandal at Lackland Air Force Base, where a dozen military training instructors had allegedly assaulted or abused over thirty recruits. We'd just had a constructive meeting with the four-star general in charge of Air Force education and training, General Rice, about how to change the culture of the military. And I'd mentioned we were about to meet with Dunford to discuss the same. It sounded as though we had the Corps in our hands. Worse than that, it sounded like I couldn't keep a secret.

Dunford got straight to the point: "I read the news clip."

"Oh?" *Oh fuck*, I thought.

"Ms. Bhagwati. What exactly do you think you're meeting with me about?" No Marine general wanted to be referred to in the press without having been briefed on it first by half a dozen subordinates.

I attempted to suppress my nerves and defuse the situation. I tried to dazzle him with what we were doing to improve women's integration and reduce sexual assault and harassment. He was unfazed.

"Well, I don't think I need to meet you. We already have enough input from Marines on these issues." I was picturing the kind of input the second most powerful Marine on earth was getting from subordinates twelve rungs beneath him about what it was like to be a woman in the Corps.

"Well, Sir, it looks like the Marine Corps could use some extra insight—we hear from Marines all the time about what they're facing inside. You're not always going to hear the full story when there's so much fear and stigma about reporting."

"Ms. Bhagwati." His tone had shifted. "Are you a Ma-*rine*, or are you just representing this organization of yours?"

I paused in disbelief. Dunford was testing my loyalty to the Corps. He wanted to know if I still bled Marine.

"Uh, Sir, I'm both." It seemed to be a better response than, "*Are you fucking serious?*"

"Mm-hmm. Well. I think we have all the information we need."

The future chairman of the Joint Chiefs of Staff had made up his mind. I never met him face-to-face. Just like that, he'd made me feel like I wasn't good enough for the Corps, and I would never be good enough for the Corps. When the Marines United Internet scandal broke four years later, exposing just how broken the Marine Corps was, I thought of Dunford. He needed guidance in those earlier years, when there was still hope of shifting course. But Marines never looked outside their box for help.

When the Joint Chiefs were done with their dog and pony show before the Senate, I pushed my way through a stack of uniformed officers to get to the commandant of the Marine Corps, James Amos. He looked at me the way I was used to being looked at by Marine officers. He didn't know who the fuck I was and couldn't have cared less. I pushed past his aide and his Staff Judge Advocate and placed a business card in his hand.

"I'm testifying on the next panel, Sir. We represent a lot of survivors. I hope you listen." Amos said nothing. Didn't even crack a smile. And then his eyes fell on my lapel, where I was wearing a shiny eagle, globe, and anchor, a sign that I'd worn the same uniform he was wearing now.

"Semper fi, Marine." He nodded at me and walked away with his entourage.

Jesus fucking Christ, I thought. *That's all anyone ever gets from these dudes, isn't it.*

It felt like I had the whole weight of the world on my shoulders in this hearing, which Republicans had essentially thrown as a bone to Senator Gillibrand after their show of force with the generals. I ignored the allotted time I was given, going over by three minutes. No senator was going to stop me. I probably would have kept on speaking even if they had. I was pissed off by all of that unholy brass. I spoke directly to the camera, just in case anyone retraumatized by the generals was still listening.

"If you are a survivor, I want you to know that I believe you."

Gillibrand did not let the Joint Chiefs circus deter her. She was a workhorse, putting together a bipartisan group of supporters for the bill that eventually included Tea Party poster boys and 2016 presidential candidates Rand Paul and Ted Cruz. No senator with a heart or sense of survival wanted to support a system that was allowing women and men to get raped and letting serial sexual predators run free. When Hillary Clinton got on record supporting the bill, we knew we were making waves. Military sexual assault was now officially a bipartisan presidential campaign issue.

SWAN joined forces with VVA and IAVA and tried to educate dozens of civilian organizations that had entered the fray in a sudden burst of enthusiasm for Gillibrand's bill, so we could keep the heat on Congress.

The core message of the Military Justice Improvement Act was that command influence undermined victims' chances of accessing justice. Ninety percent of sexual assaults were not reported. In fact, 62 percent of those who reported assault experienced retaliation. Prosecutions of sex crimes rarely occurred, let alone convictions of predators. What made the military system unique was the way in which military justice was integrated into the chain of command. Military commanders—who were not attorneys or judges, but who were given the authority of those roles—had legal discretion to determine whether or not cases were prosecuted. As I'd seen in the Corps, commanders often refused to prosecute the predators in their units, either overlooking the crimes, transferring predators to other units, or punishing the victims who reported.

Trying to remove the chain of command's authority over certain crimes was a delicate thing, because there were many offenses that we thought could still be taken care of by commanders in-house, like your average DUI or marijuana charge, cases that I remember handling myself as a junior commander. We were simply trying to shift authority in one regard—making sure commanders were not allowed to adjudicate felony offenses, like sex crimes and murder—not burn the whole military judicial system to the ground. There was inherent bias—and an enormous amount of comparative disadvantage—in a military boss, who was not an attorney, being able to determine the legal outcome in a case in which both the accused *and* the accuser belonged to his unit. It made no sense in today's world. It only made sense in a military that no longer existed, when courts-martial were literally convened on the battlefield while muskets were firing, and the functions of commander, judge, and jury had to be combined into one role for expedience.

As the winter holidays were approaching, we were five votes shy of the sixty that were going to get this bill through the Senate, onward to the House—that was another nightmare, but one that would lessen if the Senate could get behind this—and finally over to President Obama. I got a call from Senator Gillibrand one day, asking for a suggested change to the bill. She thought that if we made this purely a sex crimes bill, she might have a shot at getting a couple of senators to switch their votes. But she didn't want to move without our blessing.

We had given a lot of thought to this matter and had consulted with a handful of leading civil rights attorneys, military minds, and legal organizations. I was primarily concerned with what was in the best interest of service women.

The problem with a sex crimes–only bill was establishing a precedent for "pink courts" in the military. The term referred to the notion of gendered courts, something we were convinced would further segregate service women in an already hostile and sexist environment. Although men made up just over half of total victims, sex crimes were disproportionately affecting service women, and siphoning these cases to special (pink) courts while everything else was being adjudicated in the normal military justice system seemed absurd. It was the entire system, after all, that was broken. And commander bias was a factor in all cases, not just sexual assault.

With the winter holidays fast approaching, time was running out in the congressional calendar. Senate Majority Leader Harry Reid got his staff on the phone with us one day to talk this through. None of us budged. It suddenly got contentious.

"We're not a one-trick pony. We care about the long-term welfare of service women, not just one issue," I said vehemently, leading a senior Democratic staffer to bark back. She could holler all she wanted. The Democrats were looking for easy options and quick victories, and we weren't about to sacrifice the better bill for a short-term solution. We wanted the bill passed as it was. They listened.

On the day the bill was being voted on, we sat in the Senate chamber with colleagues from Vietnam Veterans of America, looking down on the short haircuts and bald heads of elected officials. The process was painfully slow, so I began playing a little game, identifying the senators who were Black, Brown, or female. It was a tiny group.

In the end, we could not get the five votes we needed to pass the bill. There were lots of reasons we lost. The main one seemed to be political infighting in the Democratic Party. Senator Claire McCaskill, a recipient of a SWAN Summit Award in 2013 (I'd nicknamed her Mad Dog McCaskill for taking on four-star Marine general James "Mad Dog" Mattis on sexual assault in the military), had come forth as the key opponent to Gillibrand's bill. Our best guess was that McCaskill, a lifelong champion of assault survivors, had taken the other side in an effort to stay relevant to conservative voters in her home state of Missouri. But she'd awkwardly positioned herself as the bad guy, the defender of a sexist, broken status quo.

Watching the two senators run around Capitol Hill chasing Senate votes for opposite platforms was bewildering. Weren't these two supposed to be working together? Worse than this, the conflict-obsessed press was eating it up. It irritated the heck out of me that these two impressive women were being portrayed like a couple of teenage blondes in a catfight.

One year later, I was relieved to see them working together on campus sexual violence, even sharing an umbrella in press photos. So much had changed by 2014. Campus reform had the public support of President Obama and Vice President Biden, both of whom stayed shamefully silent on military sexual violence. The Democrats had pulled their act together for civilian women, crafting the Campus Accountability and Safety Act in order to improve the way universities handled assault and harassment. But to my eyes the college campus work looked mostly like an orchestrated attempt to show unity in the party.

It was easier to rally Americans around college women than around service women, because far more American women were attending universities than enlisting in the military. Women made up only 15 percent of the military, and this was a tiny fraction of the American population. But 50 percent of the average university population was female. That was a lot of women, and a lot of parents. Numbers meant votes, and we did not have the numbers to sway a Democratic White House on military reform. We cheered the work of campus activists, but it burned inside knowing that politicians cared so much less about women who served in uniform.

Formidable women like Valerie Jarrett, Tina Tchen, and Sara Rosenthal made space for SWAN and survivors in the White House, but in the end, President Obama never publicly took our side. I remember the feeling of walking into the White House and never for a minute letting my guard down. After my experiences with the nation's two largest bureaucracies—the Pentagon and VA—and witnessing the behavior of members of Congress, I trusted no one in Washington.

I vividly remember meeting Valerie Jarrett. She sat us down in her office and told us first thing that she and the president deeply sympathized with us, because they had daughters. I wanted to tell her that this line did not work on me, on us, on anyone, really, that many of the commanders I knew who were sweeping assaults under the rug had daughters, too.

We had brought one female and one male veteran to the White House that day to share their stories about sexual assault with Jarrett and other aides. When Ayana and Rick had finished telling their stories, Jarrett wanted to know more about me. I said very little. But I told her, "The military doesn't teach moral leadership. It teaches battlefield leadership." I thought I saw a flicker of something in her eyes, but she said nothing in response. She couldn't.

The president never budged. I often wondered if Barack Obama would have changed his tune if Malia or Sasha had wanted to attend a military academy. There was no stake in this for him, or Biden, a military father who prided himself on being a champion of ending violence against women. Even today, Biden, a fierce advocate for military personnel and families, has ignored the issue of sexual assault in the military, despite recently setting up an entire foundation devoted to violence against women.

The military had far more lobbying power than we ever would. Military culture was still fundamentally harming women, the branches had yet to fully integrate their assignments, and all across America, the social tide was rapidly shifting against women's equality.

I was tired of trying to convince average Americans that service women were worth their time and money. I was tired of being a community's sacrificial lamb, the Marine Corps' pariah, and a woman whom politicians used, abused, and then tossed aside. Mostly, I was tired of seeing people treat one another so poorly. There had to be another way to make change. I knew things would shift once I left. There was no way of telling if anyone would carry the torch forward. But I needed to take care of myself. It was time for someone else to step up and figure things out. In early 2015, I bowed out, said good-bye to Washington and SWAN, and retreated inward.

CHAPTER 17

Red (White) and Blue

The #MeToo movement exploded on American consciousness like a cluster bomb in the fall of 2017. My relationships with men—my dad, my friends, and the masses on social media—were suddenly all worth reconsidering. I was constantly on edge. Cranky. Sobbing. Furious. I considered never dating men again. I did not even want to hear their voices. I wondered how one might go about banning them from public spaces. I realized I was not the only woman plotting their end. The women in my life reminded me that I was, in fact, completely normal for feeling all of these things.

I was so busy trying to keep track of which of America's celebrity darlings had been cast from grace that it didn't quite hit me that #MeToo had bypassed the military. I didn't realize this fully until I was watching clips from the Golden Globe Awards. I was thrilled that activists, several whom I knew through SWAN's work, were accompanying Hollywood stars on the red carpet. I knew that no one from the veterans community had been asked to join. It bothered me, but then came Oprah's speech.

I wept as Oprah channeled our collective rage, our memories of being harassed and assaulted in the workplace, on the streets, in subways and churches, at home. She was speaking for all of us.

And then, among victims of sexual violence, she mentioned military women. I saw Hollywood's glitterati and my fellow activists nod their heads, and I stopped in my tracks. I wanted to howl at them, "You couldn't find *one* Black Woman Veteran to invite to this shindig? Not *one*?" For all of Hollywood's sweeping overtures, the nation was still paying lip service to women in uniform. After everything we'd done to expose and reform the culture. After all the scandals that continued well into the present. #MeToo was going to talk about military women and bow down to the pressures of patriotism, but they weren't going to invite veterans to the freaking party?

Civilian advocates who knew so much better had dropped the ball. They'd forgotten us. They'd forgotten that women in the military faced more burdens than women in the civilian workplace and had fewer legal options to address assault and harassment. That without civilian oversight, service members were fending for themselves in a system that literally owned their bodies. They'd left them to fend against generals. They'd left them in Trump's hands.

• • •

In September 2016, I attended a live town hall with Secretary Clinton and Donald Trump on the USS *Intrepid*, the WWII aircraft carrier docked off the west side of Manhattan. I had every reason not to attend. I'd retired from professional advocacy for good reason. By attending an event where veterans would be posturing around powerful people, I was revisiting old wounds. Folks would be clamoring for photos, chumming it up with bros, and sizing me up, from my ethnically ambiguous features to my chest on downward.

On top of this, I was burdened by the certainty that I'd be one of few women and people of color at the forum. Even before neo-Nazis rallied in Virginia, I was sure of one thing I'd suspected before but never fully known till now. In the United States, more than I was anything else, I was Brown—more than I was female, more than I was queer, and more than I would ever be a veteran. This was never a choice, but by now I had learned to embrace my Brownness like a badge of honor. I was no longer shortening my first name.

Half of the folks in this room were voting for Trump. Some part of me knew that being there in my body and in my skin was important. I sat with Hillary's people in the front row.

Clinton's portion of the town hall was largely unremarkable, but then Trump arrived with an entourage of family members in haute couture and red-carpet hair. The glitz and glamour was starkly out of place with the feel of the room, in which the results of war were, if not the point, then at least the backdrop, with several veterans in wheelchairs or carrying canes, and most of us dealing with one thing or another.

Like we were a distant idea on the horizon, Trump called veterans "them" and "they" so many times in thirty minutes that I wanted to get up and say, "Jesus Christ, Sir, *they're* right here in front of your face!"

Matt Lauer was hosting the candidates, and eventually turned to us for Q and A. An older African American man stood and was introduced as a former Marine. As the cameras rolled, he said, "I have a daughter who is interested in joining the service. But when she researched the military, she saw the stats on sexual assault, and decided not to go."

He continued, "I have a concern, about the rape of women in our armed forces. As president, what specifically would you do to support all victims of sexual assault in the military?"

Trump was nodding, long and slow, as if to convey he understood the girl's decision, while my head spun. Was this really happening? Had our work gone so mainstream that a playboy celebrity real estate tycoon turned presidential candidate was about to formulate a response before tens of millions of people about military sexual violence?

"Your daughter is absolutely right. It is a *massive* problem."*

While my mind raced between verklempt and stunned, Lauer dove in, reminding Trump that he had tweeted the following only three years earlier: "26,000 unreported sexual assaults in the military—only 238 convictions. What did these geniuses expect when they put men & women together?"

Suddenly, service women's welfare was in the hands of a treacherous billionaire. Some of us had practically thrown ourselves on pyres to draw attention to this issue. This guy had done nothing but objectify women for most of his adult life, and he was now commanding the attention of tens of millions on the topic. I was sickened. And transfixed. God, this was great television. I wanted to vomit.

As we held our breath, Trump defended his tweet as "absolutely correct," causing a stir in the crowd that despite all our military training could not be fully repressed and provoking an explosion on Twitter.

Within five minutes, I'd witnessed Donald Trump say more about sexual violence in the military than any sitting president. Barack Obama, a darling of feminists, had said little and done next to nothing. Was Trump for real? What the hell would all of this mean for us?

I thought I'd seen it all. And then, one month later, came Pussygate.

. . .

When a secret 2005 recording was released of Donald Trump admitting to *Access Hollywood* host Billy Bush, "I'm automatically attracted to beautiful [women]—I just start kissing them . . . I don't even wait. And when you're a star they let you do it. You can do anything . . . Grab them by the pussy. You can do anything," he was still just a villain without a title. He had neither nuclear codes nor armies under his command.

Pussygate emboldened the forces of misogyny and ensured job

---

* Trump also seemed to think the military had no judicial system. But his legal ignorance was completely lost within his characteristic one-liners.

security for tens of thousands of therapists around the nation. But no one seemed interested in what it would mean for the military.

Despite Trump's predatory proclivities, in November veterans voted two to one for Donald Trump over Hillary Clinton. This betrayal was one too many for me to take.* Lines were drawn, and I saw them clearly. Military women, like their civilian women counterparts, favored Trump. Only Black service members were more likely to vote for Clinton.†

What did it mean then that most veterans voted for a man who had outed himself as a sexual predator? What would it mean to salute or serve the predator in chief?

It would be easy to cast aside this discussion, as most who voted for him have done. But not if you support the troops. It makes me wonder what lines have been drawn when generals choose to serve at the pleasure of an admitted sex offender. But then, the president's generals come with related baggage. Not nearly as heavy as the president's, but relevant nonetheless.

For starters, the president's former national security adviser, General H. R. McMaster, mishandled a sexual assault case involving two former West Point rugby players while he was commanding general of Fort Benning.‡ He had allowed the two accused lieutenants to attend Army Ranger School, even though they were still under criminal investigation. He received nothing more than a slap on the wrist by the Army vice chief of staff.

And then there's Vice President Mike Pence, who has made his views on military women well known. (His son is a Marine officer, if

---

* www.aol.com/article/news/2016/11/11/why-veterans-voted-donald-trump-swing-states/21603486.

† www.military.com/daily-news/2016/11/02/survey-career-oriented-troops-favor-trump-over-clinton.html.

‡ www.washingtonpost.com/investigations/mcmaster-rebuked-by-army-in-2015-for-his-handling-of-sexual-assault-case/2017/03/02/e8421a8e-fe8b-11e6-8ebe-6e0dbe4f2bca_story.html?utm_term=.782036468152.

that matters.) In 1999, Pence famously wrote about the Disney film *Mulan*:

> From the original "Tailhook" scandal involving scores of high-ranking Navy fighter pilots who molested subordinate women, to the latest travesty at Aberdeen Proving Grounds,* the hard truth of our experiment with gender integration is that it has been an almost complete disaster for the military and for many of the individual women involved . . . Put [men and women] together, in close quarters, for long periods of time, and things will get interesting. Just like they eventually did for young Mulan. Moral of story: women in military, bad idea.

And finally, there are the president's Marines. Defense Secretary James "Mad Dog" Mattis, a four-star general who spent over forty years in an all-male infantry environment, has legendary views on integrating (or not integrating) the Corps. At a speech he gave in 2014 at the Marines Memorial Club, he said,

> In the atavistic, primitive world of Marine infantry . . . the idea of putting women in there is not setting them up for success . . . [The point is] whether or not you want to mix Eros. Do you really want to mix love, affection, whatever you call it, in a unit where you as a twenty-year-old squad leader can point at someone else and point forward, knowing full well you've now introduced all the affections and the testosterone, and the love and everything else that goes into young people, and some of us aren't so old that we've forgotten what at times it was like heaven on earth just to hold a certain girl's hand, okay?[†]

---

* www.washingtonpost.com/wp-srv/local/longterm/library/aberdeen/caution.htm.

† www.youtube.com/watch?v=IDxU4Y4aXPg.

And, as recently as September of 2018, he told students at Virginia Military Institute that "the jury is out" on women in the infantry, calling into question once again whether he has the right character and temperament to be a secretary of defense.

Of course, pick up the news any day of the year, and it is hard not to think that Secretary Mattis, Chief of Staff John Kelly, and General Joseph Dunford, a trio of Marines as hard as nails, are the only civilized beings guarding us from the president's madness. But they are not above our scrutiny simply because their boss is madder than they will ever be. Let's hold our standards higher than this.

It boggles my mind that we are living in a nation run by Marine Corps infantry generals. How did we come to this? The answer, I suppose, is that we are in a state of emergency. In no other White House would one justify the need for a band of extreme, knuckle-dragging warfighters to keep the republic from imploding and the planet from exploding. But their influence over civilian governance comes at great cost. I do not want these men steering our nation's policy, or constructing guidelines about what men should do or what women should not dare to dream about doing. Steeped in a lifetime of the worst forms of misogyny, their old-school segregated infantry views about women are unacceptable. Until these men confront misogyny in all its forms—their president's, their own, and the military's—their views about women are a liability to average Americans and uniformed personnel alike.

· · ·

Since Pussygate, my weekly sessions with Doc are not enough to hold back my awful feeling that the world doesn't care whether women live or die. Since the 2016 presidential election, I must walk by official photos of Donald Trump on my way in and out of VA doctor's appointments. Some days, I cuss at him. It is an awful photo, even for a sexual predator. He is all scowl, with narrowing eyes and swollen lips.

"So," Doc said one day during a session. "I'm thinking of starting a support group just for women who were Marines. Are you interested?"

It still felt agonizing to let my guard down in front of other women veterans, so I didn't know who was more surprised when I told her, "Yeah. Definitely."

While Doc scrambled to hide her enthusiasm, not wanting to jinx my response, I started thinking.

"Doc, are we different? I mean, women, in the Marines, are we different from your other patients?"

How many of us has she seen? I wondered. Thousands? Each of us thinking we're the only ones who've been kicked out, rejected, or beaten down. What would we even do with ourselves if we healed and organized and, god forbid, hit back together?

She paused, then replied, "Yes. You're much harder on yourselves."

Of course we are.

* * *

In March 2017, when Marines United became breaking news like Armageddon in cyberspace, my visits to Doc's office seemed urgent. I was fending off waves of depression and fury.

Marines United was a male-only Facebook group in which over thirty thousand active and former Marines shared sexually explicit photos of US service women and female civilians without the women's consent. Revenge porn; calls to rape, assault, and harass the women; and racist and homophobic comments saturated the site. Sadly, the press regularly softened the impact of the story, calling it a "nude photo scandal" in far too many headlines to count.

Marines United was not a new phenomenon. In 2013, Representative Jackie Speier alerted the defense secretary and the Marine Corps commandant about the prevalence of similar sites, but in response, Facebook merely took the sites down. They reappeared again and again, but the Marine Corps did little to punish the men responsible for their creation. Speier herself received threats for calling attention to the issue. And yet the Marine Corps did nothing.*

---

* http://archives.sfexaminer.com/sanfrancisco/facebook-threats-to-speier-probed/Content?
  oid=2349902.

When Marine veteran and reporter Brian Jones wrote a detailed investigative piece in *Task & Purpose* about these sites in 2014, the Corps still did nothing, and few people aside from those working in women's rights paid attention.* Jones cited extraordinary postings like "Roses are red, violets are blue, be my fucking Valentine, or I'll rape you."

What made Marines United different in 2017? Two dramatic things had changed the moral landscape for the military. The first was the election of Donald Trump, a victory for sexually violent men, particularly in the military, where service members get their behavioral cues—and marching orders—from the commander in chief.

The second change was closer to home. In January 2017, the Marine Corps began integrating enlisted women who had graduated from Infantry Training Battalion into Marine Corps infantry units. The backlash from men who'd been trained since segregated boot camp to think of women as weak and undeserving of this rite of passage was vehement. Marine leadership was lost and seemed terrified of these misogynist rabble-rousers. The Marine Corps had essentially created a bunch of monsters. And now they didn't know what to do with them.

It was a sad state of affairs. And I could only hope that Marine leaders—Mattis and Dunford among them—were taking long looks in the mirror. They and men like them had created this problem every time they opened their mouths in public to resist women's integration. They had no concept of moral leadership in this regard, and they certainly had no shame.

. . .

I'd like to think our advocacy efforts were partly to thank for a new generation of veteran activists stepping up to change Marine Corps

---

* http://taskandpurpose.com/sexist-facebook-movement-marine-corps-cant-stop.

culture. If ours was the first attempt to transform military culture, the second wave looks promising, precisely because it is coming not just from new veterans but also from within the ranks. And women are not entirely alone in their outrage.

Former Marine infantryman turned investigative journalist Thomas Brennan broke the Marines United story. After Brennan spoke out against his own, his family received death and rape threats. Former intelligence Marine John Albert created a team of infiltrators, each named after knights of the Round Table, to monitor and shut down each site.* For this, he too received death threats. The gallant white male rescue narrative aside, it's pretty impressive. Young veterans are learning for the first time that in order to change military culture, men have to have a stake in the game. It means being vulnerable to the same attacks that women face as a matter of course.

These young men are a world apart from Marine Corps leadership, which has in the last five years changed its tune from pretending sexual violence isn't a problem in the Corps, to acting like it's defenseless to stop it. As for the commandant, General Robert Neller, he had no idea what was going on below him. The press largely reported Marines United as a social media story, as if the horrors of revenge porn, Internet stalking, rape and death threats, and other variations of online trolling were new to the Marine Corps, or to women, for that matter. Worse than this was that the press seemed to blame the Internet for Marines United. The Marine Corps' culture of misogyny didn't start with cyberspace, and if the Internet went dead tomorrow, hatred of women in the Corps would still be alive and kicking.

Marines United may have used the Internet to stoke the worst forms of misogyny, but women are fighting back. It is a beautiful thing to watch unfold. There is tons of chatter among uniformed

---

* www.rollingstone.com/culture/features/facebook-revenge-porn-how-two-marines-helped
   -stop-it-w478930.

people on social media. Facebook groups for women and survivors have multiplied. Women in uniform are pissed off. And they're expressing it out loud. I cannot overstress how brave these women are. One just *doesn't do* this kind of thing in uniform. But they're doing it. Because they know shit's not going to change otherwise.

This second wave of activism faces fierce cultural resistance. Ignorance about sexual assault—why it happens, what victims suffer and sacrifice, and what rarely happens to predators—suffuses the chatter. In one Facebook group that I joined, several genuine attempts by well-meaning women to change Marine culture were met with vehement challenges by other women who were automatically defending the Corps. As if the Corps ever needed defending. I stayed quiet until I realized I had no patience for victim blaming. I called out a fellow officer for enforcing rape myths, and then quietly left the group.

If activism is happening within the Marines and the military at large, it mirrors much of what is happening in the larger world of #MeToo. Some folks—both women and men—are slow to realize their own culpability in a culture that harms women with abandon and is quick to blame them for being harmed. Soul searching the causes of these abusive attitudes will take time, patience, and humility. It will require a transformation of values. It will require centering the lives of women who are most vulnerable in the military, as they are in the rest of the nation: women of color, enlisted women, and queer women. It will require elevating their voices and giving them the microphone. In a grossly hierarchical, classist system such as the military, this is a tall order. But it must happen—with enormous support from more powerful people—if we want to change military culture.

In 2017, one of these Facebook groups wrote an open letter decrying misogyny in the Corps, signed by almost a hundred senior Marines, including some I served with way back at OCS. It was a group of mostly women officers, and their letter was filled with plenty of inspirational language: "In a culture that prizes masculinity, it is easy to mistake barbarism for strength. Brutality for power." And yet it was also clear to me that the letter fell short, in characterizing the Corps as some bastion of equal opportunity: "Our leaders decided they would no longer embrace bigotry."[*]

I wondered what Lance Corporal Ameer Bourmeche would say to that. In 2015, Bourmeche's Marine drill instructors hazed him for being a "terrorist" and stuffed him into a dryer, turning it on three times. It was one of several racist incidents at Parris Island, including hazing that led another recruit, Raheel Siddiqui, to leap to his death. I wondered how many of the women who'd signed this letter had deeply reflected on their own culpability in a Corps in which racial epithets against people of color still run rampant. I wondered how many women of color had signed this letter. I wondered how these officers could be so naive as to think racism wasn't part and parcel of life in the Corps, as it was across the United States. I wondered how many had made the connection between white supremacy and racism across the country and within the Corps, where bigots had access to rank, weapons, and the luxury of an echo chamber.

•　•　•

Since I left SWAN several years ago, legislative momentum for service women's issues has slowed. Senator Kirsten Gillibrand reintroduces her bill each year, without much fanfare, and Representative Speier continues to take to task anyone with the audacity to mistreat service women.

There are still clear policy changes waiting for a champion to push them through the Pentagon. Deep in the swampland of Parris Island, South Carolina, Marine women and men continue to be trained in separate battalions. Inside the Corps, more women are resisting double standards. Many are volunteering to do pull-ups. There's even a

---

[*] www.scribd.com/document/344880282/Actionable-Change?campaign=SkimbitLtd&ad_group=1025X498259X56f51715d2214dd61f4df2e6623e6ac4&keyword=660149026&source=hp_affiliate&medium=affiliate.

jacked lieutenant colonel, Misty Posey, who's come up with her own successful pull-up training program for Marines, with an eye on getting all women to do them.*

Still, despite this evidence, pull-ups for women aren't required, because the men in charge underestimate women, and allow women to choose a way out, instead of requiring them to train to standard. And as long as women are taught that they are separate and unequal, as they are at Parris Island, it's hard to get all of them on board with the idea that they can do what the guys can do. It's a vicious, endless loop.

I thought I was the only one beating this point into the ground until I heard about Lieutenant Colonel Kate Germano. In her last stint as a Marine officer, Germano was in charge of the female recruit training battalion at Parris Island. For trying to improve women's training—for holding women to a higher standard and actually improving their fitness and marksmanship marks—she was fired. It is a story that is so absurd, and so unjust, that it almost sounds unbelievable.

When I found out about Germano's story, I was moved to tears. She was the only other Marine I knew of who put her career on the line to help women in the Corps. For the first time in fifteen years, I was not alone. I wondered what kind of world we lived in when it seemed like the right thing to do was to fire Germano and prevent thousands of women from succeeding in the Corps. I want a better world.

The Marine Corps is facing stubbornness and bigotries that are deeply entrenched, but the policy changes to remedy Marines United and all its nasty permutations are clear. The moral courage required to make these changes—to integrate boot camp, increase women's numbers, and make physical standards gender neutral—is enormous in a system where misogyny rules. Unfortunately, Secretary Mattis, an old-school infantryman to the core, does not have the broad ex-

---

* www.marines.mil/News/News-Display/Article/673308/zero-to-twenty-plus-marine
-develops-program-to-improve-pull-ups.

perience or forward vision of Leon Panetta, who integrated women into combat assignments. But I have no doubt that these changes will come with new leadership.

I'm optimistic, because as I write this, the Army has integrated hundreds of women into infantry and armor units throughout the service. And the Marine Corps has its first female infantry officer. Times are changing on the inside, and federal policy always catches up to reality. I've seen it firsthand. An enterprising defense secretary under the leadership of a forward-thinking president will see this. It's only a matter of time till they force the Marine Corps to do the right thing.

#MeToo has laid bare what countless women have lost and sacrificed simply navigating their lives. What I'm curious about is how far men are grappling with how much they've lost as well in this patriarchal mess we're all living in. For military men, the losses are rarely talked about in the open. I am speaking not just about the loss of humanity that comes from taking lives. I am speaking mostly about the mistreatment of women all around them. I am speaking, obviously, of Thailand. And Okinawa, the Philippines, South Korea, Vietnam, and so many places around the globe where American GIs have left and continue to leave a horrendous imprint of commercial sexual exploitation and sexual violence. And of course I'm speaking about the violence committed against US service women and service men. How do men take part in this system and then leave the service without a worry in the world, as if they've seen or done nothing? The truth is, most don't.

I have spent years resenting and fearing these men with whom I served, and seething in enormous contempt for the women who protect them. I no longer feel that particular burn. I know deeply now that the harm committed upon others never sits still. It eats you up inside. And when it cannot be contained, it harms the ones you love.

We must take stock of this matter.

There are few men who've spoken openly with me about the impact of military misogyny on relationships with the women and children in their lives. But every man who serves, who is wrestling with the questions of how he ought to treat women, or how he can be a better ally to women in the military, needs to consider these matters, and with a sense of urgency. It is not enough to call forth the knights of the Round Table. We women don't need saving. We need you—military men—to get your shit together.

Women already know from direct, felt experience the harm caused by segregated service and the rape culture that it fosters, even if the language to describe this experience isn't encouraged or readily available. My own incredible inferiority complex in the Marines was not my own fault, but rather by careful design. This self-hatred took ages to see through, and discard, and the language that I searched for to describe my own and others' experience not only lay dormant, it lacked the privilege of a platform that the heroic male experience was often granted.

What does it mean for a man to volunteer to join this same culture that causes so much deliberate harm to women? I have never understood why men have let themselves off the hook for this. Can the rite of passage in becoming a Marine or soldier be distinct from the rite of passage of degrading women? Can a man honestly say he is untouched by his total training, and that degrading women was not part and parcel of his right of passage? That the power of military culture to think of women as without worth has evaded him, while he has absorbed everything else that makes him a Marine? This, I think, is the harder question for men to answer truthfully. What does it really mean to stay silent as you are told by peers from every direction to look down upon women who serve, and to objectify women back home, to be immersed in slut walls, revenge porn, and constant banter about how little women deserve to wear the uniform?

Service men's conditioning to degrade women is as much of a threat to long-term individual wellness and the health of our communities as post-traumatic stress or traumatic brain injury. Most men do not walk away from the military with PTSD or TBI. But every single military man has been indoctrinated in some amount of misogyny. Why don't we consider misogyny as much of a threat to the health of our veterans as any other injury from service?

It's unfathomable that a man who has spent several years being trained to look down upon women can totally respect women. This is not *his* fault. It is the fault of the institution. It takes great work to undo misogyny, even as a woman. I know this. But most women are intimately familiar with self-hatred. It's rooted early on in our lives, in our first anorexic Barbie dolls and Photoshopped magazine covers. Do men know how misogyny affects *them*? It doesn't seem so. Even those rare men who support women's full equality in the military would have to doubt women's place at least a little bit. Segregated training by the most effective trainers in the world does this. I've seen the best men clam up and lose their ability to speak on behalf of women's dignity once indoctrinated in military training and group-think. The choice to learn to step out and speak up again is theirs.

It's hard to talk about this, but we need to. Inculcation in violence and misogyny are a deadly combination, and we need to think hard about the impact not only on human beings who serve but also on their families. Few people dare to talk about domestic violence (DV) by our service members. When I spoke about DV to members on the Hill, the rooms literally went silent. It is hard to believe that back then, sexual assault got more attention than domestic violence, when sexual assault barely got much attention to begin with.

It's easy to say DV happens everywhere. That it's not worse in the military. The powers that be used to tell us this when we were educating folks about military sexual violence. But the fact is, it is *always* different in the military.

In my experience, when it comes to matters of sexual or domestic violence, the only people who are often treated worse than service women are spouses themselves. And it's heartbreaking. Units tend to close ranks, protecting their own at the expense of wives and children. Simply wearing the uniform can protect a man from facing the law.

Which means, of course, that military spouses and children suffer unnecessarily. According to the Pentagon, in 2016 there were 13,916 reported cases of child abuse and neglect, and 15,144 reported incidents of domestic violence. We have no idea what the total numbers are, because most cases are unreported, and the DOD does not do annual surveys on domestic violence the way it does on sexual assault. Amazingly, the DOD refuses to share some of the data obtained through Centers for Disease Control research on the military with the public. There's clearly a lot more to this than the government wants the American public to know.*

In a March 2018 Senate hearing on intimate partner violence and child abuse in the military, much was said by senators about the unique hardships experienced by deploying soldiers, but little was said about the unique culture of misogyny in the military, or how violence itself isn't something you turn on and off like a light switch. Elected officials dare not dig deep into the ways human beings harm one another, particularly when those who are harmed are women or children. I get the feeling it's not just dangerous reelection territory. It seems too personal, and too real.

I had an infantry corporal once who'd never deployed to a war zone. One day he went apeshit. Tried to chop his wife up with a machete. She, thank god, is fine. He's now in the brig. I often think about him. His is an extreme example, but one that illustrates that violence cannot be contained in neat boxes on the battlefield. And it is naive and irresponsible to think that training folks to kill doesn't affect the way we function in situations where violence is unacceptable. It has taken me over a decade to undo my Marine training, to lose my violent edge. I still ache because of the harm I was willing to do to other people. And I never even saw combat.

If you want to hear the real scoop on DV in the military, talk to

---

* www.c-span.org/video/?442268-1/hearing-focuses-domestic-violence-child-abuse -military.

social workers and psychologists who deal with the impact of intimate partner and family violence on a daily basis. Doc has some dark stories. So do her colleagues. It's time to treat veterans like multidimensional human beings, and not like monolithic heroes. We have a lot of work to do.

Service men's individual and collective shame is often well hidden, but it is palpable, and I know this partly because my otherwise garrulous male veteran friends go silent when the topic of violence against women comes up. We do not talk about rape. We certainly do not talk about the Far East. I've witnessed men speak clearly about the horrors of combat, both in public forums and in private conversations. But I've rarely seen a male veteran speak from the heart about the crimes and indignities forced upon women in and out of the military. Women deserve so much more than this.

Accountability might look like the Marines United equivalent of the 1971 Winter Soldier Investigation, in which US combat veterans publicly confessed to war crimes they committed or observed while serving in Vietnam. Institutions and societies do not move forward unless we confess the ways in which we have harmed others, whether in the past or present. In 2016, veterans joined Native tribes at Standing Rock in protest of the Dakota Access Pipeline that the government was threatening to construct upon sacred lands, potentially contaminating water and soil. Veterans went there explicitly to be human shields for the tribal peoples who had been shot at with rubber bullets and bitten by guard dogs. In a memorable moment, General Wes Clark's son took a knee before the tribal chiefs, begging forgiveness for the crimes white settlers perpetuated against Native peoples. I was deeply moved.

What would it mean for male veterans, then, to acknowledge the way in which women have been harmed by men's military service? Would such a ceremony ever be conceived to ask service women's forgiveness, or the forgiveness of wives and children, or the forgiveness of tens of thousands of women and girls around the globe?

. . .

Young women and their parents often ask me this question: Would you encourage women to join the military? My answer is, vociferously, *yes*. We need more women in the military. And desperately so if anyone cares about the future of the armed forces. I get a rush of pride and optimism when I hear that women and girls want to join. But that rush is always tempered, not just by my own experience but by the continuing facts.

I want every human being to have a shot at health and happiness. While the military affords management experiences that are unparalleled for young people (I cannot call them "leadership" experiences until the military gets to the bottom of its ongoing misogyny), the quality of those experiences is vastly disparate across the armed forces. If success is measured in part by the level of workplace harassment within an institution, women simply have more chance at success in the Army, Navy, and Air Force than they do in the Marines.

This is a call to the Marine Corps as much as it is to prospective service women and concerned parents. Marines love to say they won't fix what's not broken. But the Corps itself is deeply broken. Will the Marines have the honor, courage, and commitment to finally fess up and, like a veteran in need of emotional or mental health support, get some professional help?

I think that the cost to men for participating in military misogyny is often the difficulty—or inability—to gently connect with loved ones and society as a whole.

The cost to women is both obvious and subtle. The cumulative denial of our harassment, a tool we've perfected to survive the trials of being so few, and the infinite ways in which we beat ourselves and one another up—these have long-lasting effects on our health and happiness, too.

It has taken me years to forgive my female peers for their abuse, jealousy, and antagonism. It took years to forgive myself as well, and I admit there are moments when I still get dragged down by voices of self-hatred that quickly morph into voices of hostility toward other women. It takes work, and support from women who deeply realize these dynamics, to realize that this is not our doing, and then to resist the forces that encourage division among us. Every woman who rises up to support another woman will change the face of the military. It is going to require an otherworldly courage and joining forces with guys who are willing to sacrifice some skin to do the right thing.

In the end, no man or institution was going to be able to take the hurt away from me. I had to learn to love myself and really believe that I was worth it. Feeling connected to people who show compassion when I falter and nudge me to find my feet again is where I most find my wings. Each veteran who lets her guard down and shows vulnerability ensures that I can let my guard down as well. It feels so much better without all of that armor.

Epilogue

It's early 2017 and I'm crammed into a tiny professional kitchen with several other student chefs, dressed in a white chef's hat and jacket, apron, checkered pants, and nonskid clogs. I'm covered in sweat, stirring three enormous pots of broth like a witch with a giant ladle. I'm in culinary school, just for joy. My team and I have planned a three-course vegan meal with ramen as the main course. It has enough mushrooms and ginger to kill cancer cells, and has so many layers of flavor that none of our instructors have been able to fully deconstruct it. It is the best damn ramen broth ever.

Alessandra has dug into her Italian roots and volunteered to make whole wheat noodles from scratch. She's covered in flour and patiently winding the handle of the pasta maker, again, and again. Liana and Kristyna, eight months pregnant now, are reaching their arms into enormous vats to massage chiffonaded kale and seaweed for a raw salad. Kevin, the only guy in the group, a fifty-something looking for a second career, has been stuffing vegan dumpling wrappers with roasted kabocha squash and edamame filling. Marcelle, from Brazil, is still fine-tuning the presentation of chocolate cake with mousse made of sake and matcha powder. She's staring down an empty white plate, with a bottle of blueberry coulis in her hand, waiting for design inspiration to strike.

Elyse is a professional vegan chef who I'm convinced looks about fifteen because of her plant-based diet. She and I have volunteered to lead the group in our preparation of a vegan dinner for one hundred people. It has been a slog of recipe testing, late-night editing, and laughing our heads off (Elyse makes Muppet faces when she cooks, which render me helpless). It's my first time working with a group of mostly women—all of us on equal footing—on such an incredibly challenging assignment.

For weeks, my back has been hurting like hell from standing for hours on end with my neck bent over cutting boards, making me wonder what the heck I'm doing throwing myself into such rigorous work all over again. Two women loom large in my life. Chef Hideyo is a former sushi pro whose mission in life is to scare the crap out of new students at the Natural Gourmet Institute. We surround her when she takes her chef's knife out. Her work is a thing of beauty. She could be slicing a rubber tire and it would look like art. Her half-Japanese, half-English scoldings twist many of us into a state of panic, but mostly I smile. When she docks several points on every vegetable in the garden on my knife skills test, it's hard for me to be upset. For the first time in my adult life, I embrace the experience. I am making matchsticks out of carrots, and it is thrilling.

Along with Hideyo, Chef Barb is the other woman straight out of Baughman's rulebook. Barb is an extreme athlete, and I may be the only one who notices her muscles bulging under her chef's jacket. Early on in training she gathers us around and tells us to get our hands out of our pockets. The other students are flummoxed, but I am impressed. I've been trained by the Corps to be able to grab a rifle in milliseconds because my hands will never be caught dead in pockets. Barb is tough and familiar, with a good dose of warmth.

If I didn't know better, I'd think I'd fallen into another version of the Marines. I love the urgency and the attention to detail in this culinary universe. It is absurdly physical, fierce, and loud. Timidity has no place when you're dealing with boiling water, sizzling pans, and sharp knives. It is a completely tactile experience that absorbs all the senses. It's everything I loved in the Corps. It is fast paced and high octane. It feels urgent and satisfying—the flames bursting off the stove top, the risk of scalding and stabbing. The immediacy of delivering the best to customers who couldn't care less about your feelings. The adrenaline is familiar and comforting. And yet something in me has shifted.

The difference here is that there is no need for harm, and no need to one-up the next person. As I work with the women in my school, I quickly realize the potential for women in this world to create something very different from the arrogance and abuse that are infamous in the world of fine dining and cable food shows. Men inexplicably control the world of restaurants, while women continue to nurture hearts and bellies in homes around the globe. It's a world out of order. But I know things can be different. I know because my time in the Corps was also so out of order. We can create, and serve, with love. I'm eager to test this theory in everything I do.

Our final vegan dinner wows me. My entire extended family and several of my friends attend. Every last one of them is a carnivore, but no one misses the meat. People are happy, stuffed, peaceful. No animals have been harmed. And our team of chefs looks fulfilled. It's such a rush.

My dad has been scooping bites off everyone's plates. And Mom has been telling stories to everyone about Dad. They are the grand elders now, still stubborn as hell, but pretty adorable when they're just eating chocolate cake.

Old age has softened them, a bit. Mom and Dad hear about my yoga trainings and silent meditation retreats, first three days, then ten, and then six weeks, and don't get it. Dad's disappointment is palpable, through his scrunched eyebrows and aborted attempts not to say anything to me, but the thing now is, he's trying not to be so mean about it.

It helps me that the Indian prime minister practices yoga daily.

Narendra Modi is directly responsible for getting my father off my
back, at least a little. Dad will never admit it, but he knows I'm hap-
pier listening to myself and ignoring his harsh opinions, a practice
that is eternal and that I am convinced will continue late into my life,
and maybe even after he's gone.

Dad still gets out of control, because he doesn't know how to love
me. I am forever the girl he wants to talk at. He writes hysterical
emails, leaves melodramatic voice mails, reminding me of my mother's fragility, wondering what I am doing with my day, or my life. He
still occasionally calls me stupid. My new thing is to keep my distance
and assert boundaries I was never allowed to have. Not as his daughter. Not as a girl. Not as an Indian woman. I don't need to run to the
Marines. I don't need to run.

He's more fragile than he will ever admit. His ego has never adjusted to not winning that damn Nobel, and I know that and infinite
variations on never feeling good enough eat away at him by the hour.
I remember that Dad has never had the gift of not needing titles or
seeking praise, the gift of learning to love himself from the inside out.
He doesn't know what he's missing. It makes me feel a deep love for
the child he once was.

Mom has aged rapidly because of the trauma she's never come to
terms with, and I think, too, because of mine. It has happened so fast
that our relatives and her colleagues tell me this with rueful voices
and wrinkled expressions, as if aging is strange or unseemly. As if I
can stop her mortality. The control she inflicts upon me, upon herself, is as fierce as ever. She eats like a mouse. She is skin and bones.
"I'm going to get fat," she says, at eighty-six, as if anyone would care
if she had rolls spilling from her midsection. When we meet, she
still only talks about big things far from here: the Russian economy,
that fool Putin. She is retired, but every day goes to her office, a nice
setup the university has arranged because it is what she knows best.
We have rarely ever had a heart-to-heart conversation—about her,
about me, about us. I am coming to accept the silence between us. I

grieve for us both, because it is all I can do now. The best I can do is try to understand.

Listening was forced upon me when I was little. I had no idea that I had a voice, because the only voice that mattered was theirs. Now I realize that all of that listening can be precious. I have, without trying, turned it into empathy. It is exhausting fighting the forces that silence women and girls. It is painful. It is far too often self-harming work in which it is hard to remember what one is trying to change, because we are not being loved in the work that we are doing, and we are not loving ourselves. We have not healed from our own wounds enough to remember what change we want to see in the world or to imagine how we truly want to be in that world.

I dig into my imagination, my experiences, my deep-listening skills. My parents are just human beings, clumsily finding their way. My mother may not have the language or the voice to describe what she went through. She may never understand that shame is not something neither she nor I needs to carry. But not everything requires words. And I can carry some of the speaking, and much more of the hearing, when and how I can. I know the wounds she has borne, intuitively, like I know now what I have borne. The things my mom did to survive and thrive. She's a warrior, to the bone. No warrior sets forth without picking up scars. And I am cut from the same cloth as she is.

Acknowledgments

In 2007, I was fortunate to attend a writing workshop for veterans in lower Manhattan. The poet Yusef Komunyakaa, a recipient of the Pulitzer Prize, read to us from his collection in the lower floor of a West Village brownstone, and seated in a soft leather chair, I felt safe and welcome, despite being surrounded by so many men. This was undoubtedly because of Yusef.

On that day, Yusef was just a man, which is to say, he was more than a veteran. Yusef was reading poems he'd written about Vietnam, but what he'd really written about was the texture of plants and the feel of the heat in Louisiana. About being Black in the United States of America. About fear and longing. He looked at us with warm eyes and told us: "After I came home, it took me fifteen years to write. Take your time."

What a radical thing he'd said. My parents and the world had conditioned me for much more impatience than that. I was trying to piece together a life that would erase and explain my pain. I was rushing in order to save myself.

Like my own healing, this book wanted to be written on its own time. Like braising greens with maximum flavor and depth, there was no rushing this. I could not make sense of my life overnight. Taking one's time is an act of resistance in this world. Stepping back to nurture one's heart is even greater. It is an act of generosity and love, for oneself and others.

Fifteen years after I came home, I have many people to thank for the gift of this book:

Roger Rosenblatt, my first teacher out of the Marine Corps, for believing I could do this.

Robin Morgan, for sisterhood, and more pep talks than I can remember.

Jaclyn Friedman, for your kindness, generosity, and insight.

My agent and secret weapon, Anna Sproul-Latimer. Thank you for nurturing me and this project, again and again.

My editor, Daniella Wexler, for believing in this book and encouraging my vision.

Gregory Jacob, for undying loyalty and friendship. You are one of the few good men. I wish there were a ribbon for that.

Shiva and Uma, for unconditional love and wisdom. May you rest together in fields of strawberries and kale with an endless supply of tennis balls.

Eli Painted Crow, for lifting me up, again and again, in the darkest of times.

Kate Germano, who fought and sacrificed for a better Marine Corps, and still does.

Marsha Four, Rick Weidman, Tom Berger, and John Rowan at Vietnam Veterans of America, for putting women and change before politics.

Master Sergeant Brenda Baughman, USMC, Ret., and Colonel George Bristol, USMC, Ret., for making me a Marine.

Sergeant Major Ray Mackey, USMC, Ret., and Master Sergeant Rodney Cain, USMC, Ret., for teaching, molding, and supporting me.

Sergeants Jennifer Katz and Miranda Hamby, for courage and inspiration, and the Marines of Hotel Company, Marine Combat Training Battalion, for getting it.

Everyone who poured their hearts and souls into SWAN, for transforming the military for generations of young Americans.

Ariela Migdal, Sandra Park, Michael Wishnie, Vania LeVeille, Duffy Campbell, Holly Hemphill, Larry Korb, and Eugene Fidell, for discernment, guidance, and compassion.

Lory Manning, General Pat Foote, Sue Fulton, Donna McAleer, and Allyson Robinson, for encouragement when I really needed it. Also Maricela Guzman, Marti Ribeiro, and Jen Hogg, for having my back.

NoVo Foundation and NY Women's Foundation, for investing so deeply in women's safety and leadership, particularly women of color.

My vipassana and yoga sanghas, and my many teachers, especially Swami Ramananda, Cheri Clampett, Kersten and Monique Mueller, Pascal Auclair, Anushka Fernandopulle, Gina Sharpe, Sally Armstrong, James Baraz, and Catherine McGee: thank you for holding my tender heart.

Integral Yoga Institute, and especially Chandra Jo Sgammato, for giving veterans a safe place to heal, grow, and play.

My dear students, especially Jimmie Farmer, for helping me survive my most difficult years.

The army of healers who helped put me back together again, especially Marcia Stern, Ghislaine Boulanger, Sharon Morrison, Cami Stock, Taylor Hatcher, Britney Falcon, Ellen Chang, Mike Kalajian, and K9s for Warriors.

My friends, for holding me up when writing seemed impossible, especially Eesha, Maurice, Peace, Molly, Parsa, Jaishri, Jules, Barbara, Joe, Nidhi, Emily, and James.

The good people at Coney Island Brighton Beach Open Water Swimmers (CIBBOWS), Trapeze School New York, and Natural Gourmet Institute, for showing me a world of wonder.

Mom and Dad, for your continued patience, trust, and boundless generosity. I couldn't have done this without you.

The women and men who came forward against a sea of opposition to make a better nation. I honor you and offer deep bows of gratitude. If I acted in any way to harm you whether knowingly or unknowingly, I humbly ask your forgiveness.

Sunk By The *BISMARCK*